Capricorn
Rhyming Dictionary
(AID TO RHYME)

by
Bessie G. Redfield

A Perigee Book

How to Use This Book

The reader will notice the carefully arranged groupings of the words, and their endings, which are specifically placed for his convenience. For instance, the endings of each group of words are in the left column, and the references are in the right-hand column in smaller type under *see*, with suffixes which are added to make plurals, or different tenses of verbs. Thus any word with *ly* refers to **E** group of words, and *en* to those ending in **EN**; also that words with the same endings but pronounced differently are starred thus *. When pronounced more than one way, the star is repeated, as, for example, in **OUGH**, which has five different pronunciations.

Perigee Books
are published by
The Berkley Publishing Group
A division of Penguin Putnam Inc.
375 Hudson Street
New York, NY 10014

The Penguin Putnam Inc. World Wide Web site address is
http://www.penguinputnam.com

Library of Congress Cataloging-in-Publication Data

Redfield, Bessie Gordon, date.
    Capricorn rhyming dictionary.

    Reprint. Originally published: 1980.
    1. English language—Rhyme—Dictionaries.   I. Title.
PE1519.R414   1986   423'.1   86-16934
ISBN 0-399-51272-1

Cover design copyright © 1986
          by Jack Ribik

Printed in the United States of America

33   32   31   30   29   28   27   26

GLOSSARY OF POETIC TERMS

accent: a stress of voice on a particular syllable in pronouncing a word. A long mark (´) is used above an accented syllable, while a short mark (˘) is used to indicate an unaccented syllable. Example:

Hăd wé bŭt wórld ĕnoúgh, ănd tíme

alexandrine: an iambic hexameter verse, sometimes having an added syllable. Example:

Thăt, líke | ă woúnd | ĕd snáke, | drăgs íts | slŏw léngth | ălóng.

alliteration: the recurrence of the same consonant sound at the beginning of two or more words. Example:

What a tale of terror, now, their turbulency tells.

amphibrach: a three-syllable foot consisting of a long syllable between two short ones. Example:

Thĕ cláns ăre | ĭmpátiĕnt | ănd chíde thў | dĕláy
(the last foot is not an amphibrach)

amphimacer: a three-syllable foot consisting of a short syllable between two long ones. Example:

Cátch ă stár | fállĭng fást |

anapest: a three-syllable foot consisting of two short syllables preceding one long syllable. Example:

Nĕvĕr héar | thĕ sweĕt mú | sĭc ŏf spéech |

assonance: the recurrence of vowel sounds in a sequence of words, often as a substitute for rhyme. Example:

Shrink his thin essence like a riveled flow'r

ballad: a simple lyrical poem, telling a story or legend and often of a romantic nature and adapted for singing.

ballade: a poem commonly consisting of three stanzas of an identical rhyme scheme, followed by an envoy. The last line of each stanza and the envoy is the same refrain.

ballad stanza: a stanza of four lines in which the first and third lines are in iambic tetrameter. The second and fourth lines are in iambic trimeter and also rhyme. In a common variant, the first and third lines also rhyme. Example:

They followed from the snowy bank
Those footsteps one by one,
Into the middle of the plank—
And further there was none.

blank verse: unrhymed blank verse in iambic pentameter, usually not in formal stanza units.

caesura: the main pause in a line of verse, usually near the middle.

GLOSSARY

Example:
> Know then thyself, | | presume not God to scan

cinquain: a stanza consisting of five lines.

closed couplet: a couplet whose sense is completed within its two lines. Example:
> True wit is nature to advantage dress'd,
> What oft was thought, but ne'er so well express'd.

consonance: the use of and identical pattern of consonants in different words. Example:
> slow, sly, slew, slay

couplet: two consecutive lines that rhyme.

dactyl: a three-syllable foot consisting of one long syllable followed by two short syllables. Example:
> Cánnŏn tŏ | ríght ŏf thĕm |

dimeter: a line of verse having just two feet.

distich: a couplet, often an epigram or maxim.

elegy: a reflective and meditative poem with a solemn or sorrowful theme, often lamenting the dead.

envoy: 1. a short stanza concluding a poem in certain archaic metrical forms. 2. a postscript to a poem, sometimes serving as a dedication.

epic: a long narrative poem celebrating the real or mythical achievements of great personages, heroes or demigods, and written in stately verse conforming to rigid organization and form.

epigram: a brief and pithy remark, often in verse.

feminine ending: when the final syllable in a word is unaccented. Example:
> sóftnĕss

foot: the metrical unit in poetry, consisting of at least one long syllable and one or more short syllables. The foot is usually set off by a vertical line. Example:
> Áll clád | ĭn Lín | cŏln gréen, | wĭth cáps | ŏf réd | ănd blúe |

free verse: verse that does not have a fixed pattern of meter, rhyme, or other poetic conventions.

heptameter: a line of verse consisting of seven feet.

heroic couplet: two consecutive rhyming lines in iambic pentameter, as in a Shakespearian sonnet.

hexameter: a line of verse consisting of six feet.

iamb: a foot consisting of one short syllable followed by one long syllable.

internal rhyme: a rhyme that occurs within the same line. Example:
> My fair, dear Clair

Italian sonnet: a sonnet with a rhyme scheme of abba abba cde dde written in iambic pentameter, though occasionally the rhyme scheme varies in the last six lines. The <u>octave</u> (the first eight lines) usually poses a theme or premise; the <u>sestet</u> (the last six lines) gives the resolution or conclusion.

limerick: a lighthearted poem of five lines with trimeters for the first, second, and fifth lines and dimeters for the third and fourth lines. Example:

> There was an old man of Tobago,
> Who lived on rice, gruel and sago
> Till much to his bliss
> His physician said this,
> To a leg, Sir, of mutton you may go.

lyric: a poem with a particularly songlike quality, which expresses emotions directly and personally.

macaronic verse: a verse in which two or more languages are interlaced.

masculine ending: when the final syllable in a word is accented. Example:

> rĕplý

meter: the basic rhythmic description of a line in terms of its short and long syllables. It describes the sequence and relationship of all syllables in a line of poetry.

monometer: a line of verse consisting of one foot.

nonometer: a line of verse consisting of nine feet.

octave: the first eight lines of an Italian sonnet.

octometer: a line of verse consisting of eight feet.

onomatopoeia: words formed in imitation of the sounds they designate. Example:

> whiz, splash, bang, bow-wow

ottava rima: a stanza of iambic pentameter with a rhyme scheme of <u>abababcc</u>.

pastoral: a poem dealing with simple rural life.

pentameter: a line of verse consisting of five feet.

Petrarchan sonnet: another name for Italian sonnet.

quatrain: a four-line stanza.

refrain: a phrase or line or group of lines that recurs at certain points in a poem, usually at the end of a stanza.

rhyme royal: a stanza written in iambic pentameter with a rhyme scheme of <u>ababbcc</u>.

rhyme scheme: the pattern of rhyme used in a poem.

rondeau: a poem consisting of three stanzas of five, three, and five lines, using only two rhymes throughout, and having a refrain at the end of the second and third stanzas.

rondel: a poem usually consisting of fourteen lines on two rhymes, of which four are made up of the initial couplet repeated in the middle and at the end (although the second line of the couplet is sometimes omitted at the end).

rondelet: a poem consisting of five lines on two rhymes with the first word or words being used after the second and fifth lines as an unrhymed refrain.

run-on line: a line that does not end where there would be a normal pause in speech.

scansion: the process of indicating the pattern of long and short syllables in a line of verse.

septet: a stanza consisting of seven lines.

sestet: a group of six lines, especially those at the end of an Italian sonnet.

sestina: a poem consisting of six stanzas of six lines each, with a final triplet, and using the same terminal words in each stanza but in a different order; originally unrhymed but now having usually two or three rhymes.

Shakespearian sonnet: a sonnet written in iambic pentameter with a rhyme scheme of abab cdcd efef gg. The theme is usually presented in the three quatrains and the poem is concluded by the couplet.

sight rhyme: two or more words which end in identical spelling, but do not rhyme. Example:
though, bough, through

slant rhyme: an approximate rhyme, usually characterized by assonance or consonance.

song: a short and simple poem, usually suitable for setting to music.

sonnet: a poem consisting of fourteen lines in iambic pentameter. The most common forms are the Shakespearian sonnet and the Italian sonnet.

Spenserian stanza: a stanza consisting of eight iambic pentameter lines and a final iambic hexameter line, with a rhyme scheme of ababbcbcc.

spondee: a foot consisting of just two long syllables.

stanza: a fixed pattern of lines or rhyme or both.

tercet: three consecutive lines that rhyme together or relate to an adjacent tercet by rhymes.

terza rima: a poem consisting of eleven-syllable lines arranged in tercets, with the middle line of each tercet rhyming with the first and third lines of the following tercet, and written in iambic pentameter.

tetrameter: a line of verse consisting of four feet.

trimeter: a line of verse consisting of three feet.

triolet: an eight-line stanza in which the first line recurs as the fourth and seventh lines, while the second line recurs as the eighth line.

triplet: a stanza consisting of three lines.

trochee: a two-syllable foot consisting of one long syllable followed by a short syllable.

vers de société: a lighthearted and witty poem, usually brief, dealing with some social fashion or foible.

verse: 1. one line of a poem. 2. a group of lines in a poem. 3. any form in which rhythm is regularized.

villanelle: a poem consisting of (usually) five tercets and a final quatrain, and using only two rhymes throughout.

weak rhyme: a rhyme which falls upon the short syllables.

A NOTE ON SONGWRITING

Just as poems have certain forms or structures, such as a sonnet or limerick, songs also are constructed according to certain patterns. The most popular patterns or song structures are AABA and ABAB. Unlike poetry, these schemes do not refer to rhyme, but to the organization of verses and choruses in a song. Each A is a verse and each B is a chorus. Some songs also have C sections, known as a bridge, which usually comes after a chorus, but may also follow a verse. The bridge adds a new dimension to the dynamics of the song and prevents it from getting monotonous—it is a short melodic and/or rhythmic change. Here are the four most common structures:

1.	A	(verse)
	A	(verse)
	B	(chorus)
	A	(verse)
2.	A	(verse)
	B	(chorus)
	A	(verse)
	B	(chorus)
3.	A	(verse)
	B	(chorus)
	A	(verse)
	C	(bridge)
4.	A	(verse)
	B	(chorus)
	A	(verse)
	B	(chorus)
	C	(bridge)
	B	(chorus)

When writing song lyrics, it's best to keep these musical structures in mind; if you write your lyrics in a pattern that will easily fit into one of these song structures, it will help you (or someone else) when writing the music.

A SOUNDS

Appliqué, attaché, au fait, ballet, **A***
bébé, béret, bouquet, buffet, cabriolet,   *see*
cachet, café, chalet, cliché, consommé,   AY
coryphée, coupé, crochet, croquet, curé,   EIGH
décolleté, déplumé, distrait, épée, ex-   EY*
tempore, fiancée, foyer, glacé, gourmet,   UAY
lettre de cachet, Madame de Sévigné,   UET**
maté, matinée, mauvais, mêlée, métier,   S-AISE
moiré, naïveté, narghile, née, névé,
O.K., padre, papiermâché, passé, per
se, Pompeii, protégée, purée, quai, re-
poussé, requiescat in pace, résumé, re-
troussé, réveillé, risqué, roué, sachet,
sesame, soirée, sujet, toupet, ukulele,
visé

Addenda, Ætna, Agra, Agrippa, **A****
Ahura Mazda, akasha, Alaska, alfalfa,   *see*
Alhambra, Amalthæa, amoeba, am-   ABRA
pulla, anaconda, anathema, Androm-   ACA
eda, apocrypha, aqua, aqua vitæ,   ADA
Aquila, arietta, Atahualpa, Atlanta,   AGA
Attila, Ayesha, Ba, Barbarossa, Beer-   AH
sheba, Bermuda, bertha, beta, biretta,   ALA
Bogota, bonanza, Borsippa, Brahma,   ALPHA
Buddha, Burma, Calcutta, calla, Ca-   AMA

nova, Caracalla, caramba, Casabianca, **A****
Casanova, cascara, Cassandra, catal- ANA
pa, Catawba, Cleopatra, Clytemnestra, ANDA
cobra, comma, contra, copra, Cordova, ANNA
corolla, Cuba, delta, deva, dharma, di- ANZA
gamma, dilemma, dogma, Durga, éclat, ARA
Electra, eureka, Europa, ex cathedra, ATA
extra, farina, fauna, felucca, fra, AVA
Frigga, Gæa, gamma, Ganesa, Garuda, AWAY
geisha, Geneva, Golgotha, grandpa, AY
hacienda, hagiographa, ha-ha, Hecuba, AYA
Hiawatha, Hybla, impedimenta, Inca, EA
Indra, infanta, influenza, infra, jinrick- EBRA
sha, Joppa, Judæa, Ka, Kaaba, kalpa, EDDA
Kamchatka, kappa, Karma, kibla, ELLA
Krishna, Lady Godiva, larva, Laura, EMA
Leda, Lhassa, Libra, Lyra, ma, Ma- ENA
deira, magenta, Magna Charta, Ma- ENNA
hadeva, mahatma, malacca, Malta, ERA
mama, Manila, mantra, marimba, ESTA
Marpessa, Mazeppa, mazurka, mea IA
culpa, Mecca, mesa, miasma, Minerva, ICA
Minnehaha, Mona Lisa, Mount Shasta, IGMA
Mylitta, naphtha, Nova Zembla, IKA
Odessa, okra, Omaha, omega, operetta, ILLA
orchestra, Ouida, ouija, pa, Padua, IMA
pagoda, palestra, Palmyra, pampa, INA
papa, pasha, peseta, piazza, Pietà, IRA
Pisa, polka, puma, pupa, Pyrrha, Ra, ISTA
regatta, Rig-Veda, rotunda, savanna, ITA
Scylla, Seneca, seta, Sheba, Shiva, OA
sierra, Smyrna, soda, sofa, spa, Sparta, ODA
Spinoza, Sumatra, sura, syringa, taf- OGA
feta, Tampa, tapioca, ta-ta, terra OLA
firma, St. Theresa, Topeka, tuba, OMA
tundra, ultra, umbra, Ursa, Valhalla, ONA
Vega, vendetta, Venezuela, veranda, ONDA

vice-versa, viva, vodka, Volga, Voluspa, yucca, Zarathustra

A**
ONNA
ORA
OSA
OTA
ULA
UMBRA
USA
YA
YDRA

Baal, kraal, kursaal, Transvaal

AAL
see
AL

Ab, Ahab, blab, cab, confab, crab, dab, drab, gab, grab, hissing-crab, jab, Moab, nab, Punjab, Queen Mab, Rahab, sand-dab, scab, slab, stab, tab, taxi-cab

AB*
see
ARAB

Squab, swab

AB**
see
OB

Babble, dabble, gabble, grabble, rabble, scrabble, squabble

ABBLE
see
EL
LE

Cabby, drabby, flabby, scabby, tabby

ABBY
see
B**

Astrolabe

ABE
see

Abel, Babel, label

ABEL
see
EL
LE

Able, adorable, affable, allowable, amicable, answerable, arable, assessable, available, breakable, cable, calculable, capable, censurable, commendable, commensurable, comparable, conceivable, consolable, constable, delectable, demonstrable, deplorable, desirable, despicable, detachable, disable, disputable, durable, enable, escapable, estimable, evaporable, execrable, explicable, fable, formidable, friable, gable, get-at-able, hall-table, immeasurable, immutable, impassable, impeccable, impenetrable, imperishable, implacable, impracticable, impregnable, improbable, inalienable, inapplicable, incalculable, incapable, incommensurable, incomparable, inconsolable, incontestable, indefatigable, indefinable, indemonstrable, indescribable, indispensable, indisputable, ineffable, ineradicable, inexcusable, inexorable, inflammable, inscrutable, inseparable, insurmountable, interminable, invaluable, inviolable, invulnerable, irrefragable, irrefutable, irrevocable, jumpable, knowable, laudable, likable, lovable, memorable, monosyllable, mutable, navigable, notable, palatable, palpable, parable, pardonable, passable, peccable, perishable, pleasurable, polysyllable, portable,

ABLE
see
EABLE
EL
ERABLE
IABLE
ITABLE
LE
UABLE
y-ABLY

practicable, pregnable, presentable, **ABLE**
printable, probable, punishable, ques-
tionable, readable, reasonable, recep-
table, redoubtable, refutable, regret-
table, removable, resolvable, retable,
Round Table, revocable, sable, scruta-
ble, seasonable, spankable, stable, sur-
mountable, syllable, table, tarnishable,
taxable, teachable, tenable, terminable,
time-table, tractable, unable, unassail-
able, unavoidable, unbearable, unbe-
lievable, undiminishable, unfathom-
able, unmentionable, unprintable, un-
seasonable, unshakable, unspeakable,
unstable, unstridable, unsurpassable,
unwarrantable, usable, vegetable, voc-
able, vulnerable, warrantable

Ably, adorably, amicably, favorably,   **ABLY**
inevitably, irrevocably, irritably, justi-   *see*
fiably, preferably, presumably, un-   E**
speakably   ABLE-*y*

Baboo, bugaboo, taboo   **ABOO**
see
OO

Abracadabra, candelabra   **ABRA**
see
A**

Danse macabre   **ABRE**
see

Almanac, Armagnac, Balzac, biv-   **AC**
ouac, bric-à-brac, cognac, cul-de-sac,   *see*
ipecac, lac, lilac, Pachamac, Potomac,   ACH*

sandarac, Saranac, shellac, sumac, tabac

AC
ACK
AK
IAC

Alpaca, cloaca, paca, portulaca, Titicaca

ACA
see
A**

Ace, Alsace, anchoring-place, apace, beardless-face, birthplace, brace, chimney-place, commonplace, deface, disgrace, displace, dough-face, dwelling-place, efface, embrace, face, furnace, gold-lace, grace, grimace, hiding-place, Horace, interlace, interspace, lace, mace, macrimé lace, marketplace, menace, misplace, necklace, open-face, pace, palace, place, point lace, pokerface, populace, preface, Queen Anne's lace, race, refuge-place, replace, resting-place, retrace, Samothrace, scapegrace, shame-face, solace, space, surface, tailrace, terrace, trace, trystingplace, unlace, wheyface

ACE
see
ASE*
ed-AIST
   ASTE-*d*
s-IS**
   IZ

Adjacent, complacent

ACENT
see
ENT

Bach, Bel-Merodach, Meshach, Shadrach, stomach, sumach

ACH*
see
AC
ACK

Detach, spinach

ACH**
see
ATCH*

Apache, cache, moustache, pistache **ACHE***
see
ASH*

Ache, head-ache, heart-ache **ACHE****
see
AKE

Drachm **ACHM**
see
AM

Steam-yacht, yacht **ACHT**
see
OT

Audacious, contumacious, curva- **ACIOUS**
cious, edacious, efficacious, fumacious, *see*
gracious, loquacious, mendacious, mor- IOUS
dacious, perspicacious, pertinacious, OUS
predacious, pugnacious, rapacious, sa-
gacious, sequacious, spacious, vera-
cious, vivacious, voracious

Capacity, mendacity, opacity, pers- **ACITY**
picacity, pertinacity, pugnacity, ra- *see*
pacity, sagacity, tenacity, veracity, E**
vivacity, voracity ITY

Aback, Adirondack, alack, apple- **ACK**
jack, attack, back, bareback, black, *see*
bookrack, bookstack, bootblack, boot- AC
jack, canvasback, clack, come-back, ACH*
Cossack, crack, cracker-jack, dirt- AK
track, drawback, flapjack, flashback,
full back, gimcrack, greenback, grip-
sack, gunnysack, hack, hackmatack,

hardtack, hat-rack, haversack, hay-rack, high-low-jack, hi-jack, horseback, hunchback, Jack, knack, knapsack, knick-knack, lack, lampblack, leather-back, lumberjack, pack, paddywhack, pickaback, pitch-black, quack, quarter-back, rack, ransack, razorback, rick-rack, sack, setback, shack, shoe-black, sidetrack, slack, slap jack, smack, smoke-stack, snack, spur-track, squir-rel-track, stack, steeple-jack, switch-back, tack, tamarack, thumb-tack, thwack, toast-rack, track, tricktrack, Union Jack, unpack, whack, wisecrack, wrack, zwieback

ACK

Blacken, bracken, slacken

ACKEN
see
EN

Backer, blacker, cannon-cracker, cracker, Georgia cracker, hi-jacker, nutcracker, slacker

ACKER
see
ER

Blue-jacket, bracket, jacket, mon-key-jacket, packet, pea-jacket, racket, strait-jacket

ACKET
see
ET

Cackle, crackle, grackle, ramshackle, shackle, tackle

ACKLE
see
EL
LE

Barracks

ACKS
see
ACK-*s*

Barnacle, binnacle, debacle, manacle, miracle, obstacle, oracle, pinnacle, receptacle, spectacle, tabernacle, tentacle

ACLE
see
EL
LE

Acre, God's acre, massacre, nacre, simulacre, wiseacre

ACRE
see
ER

Abstract, act, attract, bract, cataract, compact, contract, counteract, detract, distract, enact, exact, extract, fact, impact, inexact, intact, interact, matter-of-fact, pact, protract, react, refract, retract, riot-act, Stamp Act, subtract, tact, tract, transact

ACT
see
ACK-*ed*
ed-EAD*
ED
S-AC-S
ACH*-S
ACK-S
AX

Didactic, lactic, prophylactic, tactic

ACTIC
see
IC

Actor, chiropractor, detractor, extractor, factor, tractor

ACTOR
see
OR

Accuracy, adequacy, advocacy, aristocracy, celibacy, confederacy, contumacy, democracy, diplomacy, effeminacy, fallacy, gynecocracy, illiteracy, intimacy, lacy, legacy, literacy, lunacy, obstinacy, papacy, pharmacy, plutocracy, privacy, racy, supremacy, theocracy

ACY
see
E**
ICACY
IRACY

Accad, ad., bad, Bagdad, ballad, **AD***
brad, cad, Carlsbad, clad, dad, doo- *see*
dad, egad, fad, farad, footpad, forbad, ADE**
gad, Galahad, glad, had, ironclad, AID***
Jehad, lad, lily-pad, mad, mail-clad, IAD
monad, olive-clad, pad, sad, salad, YAD
shad, Sinbad, snowclad, stark-mad,
steel-clad, tetrad, Trinidad, Upanishad,
velvet-clad

Wad **AD****
see
OD

Armada, Canada, cicada, Granada, **ADA**
Haggada, posada, Torquemada *see*
A**

Add **ADD**
see
AD

Addle, paddle, saddle, skedaddle, **ADDLE**
staddle, straddle, swaddle, twaddle, *see*
waddle EL
LE

Abrade, accolade, ambuscade, ar- **ADE***
cade, balustrade, barricade, blade, *see*
blockade, brigade, brocade, cannonade, AID
cascade, cavalcade, centigrade, cha- ENADE
rade, cockade, colonnade, crusade, UADE
deadly nightshade, decade, degrade, S-ADES**
escalade, escapade, esplanade, evade,
everglade, facade, fade, free-trade,
fusillade, glade, harlequinade, home-
made, invade, jade, lade, lampshade,

lemonade, marmalade, masquerade, nightshade, orangeade, palisade, parade, pasquinade, pervade, pomade, readymade, renegade, retrograde, rhodomantade, shade, shoulder-blade, spade, stockade, sunshade, tirade, trade, wade, well-made

ADE*

Comrade, Scheherazade

ADE**
see
AD

Crusader, masquerader, trader

ADER
see
ER

Alcibiades, Cyclades, Hades, Hippotades, Miltiades, Pleiades

ADES*
see
EA*-*s*
EASE

Crusades, palisades

ADES**
see
ADE*-*s*

Badge, cadge, Madge

ADGE
see

Monadic, nomadic, sporadic

ADIC
see
IC

Avocado, bastinado, bravado, Colorado, comerado, crusado, desperado, El Dorado, mikado, prado, renegado, stoccado, tornado

ADO
see
O*

Ambassador, conquistador, depre- **ADOR**
dator, Ecuador, Labrador, matador, *see*
picador, San Salvador, toreador OR

Arcady, lady, landlady, malady, **ADY**
milady, shady *see*
E**

Algæ, antennæ, arbor-vitæ, brae, **Æ**
Danæ, dies iræ, dramatis personæ, *see*
horæ, lapus linguæ, larvæ, lingnum E*
vitæ, minutiæ, Mycenæ, Parcæ, sundæ,
Thermopylæ

Azrael, Ishmael, Israel, Jael, **AEL**
Michael, Raphael *see*
EL
LE

Chafe, safe, unsafe, vouchsafe **AFE***
see
AIF

Carafe **AFE****
see
AFF

Chaff, distaff, draff, Falstaff, flag- **AFF**
staff, gaff, pikestaff, pilgrim staff, riff- *see*
raff, sclaff, shandy gaff, staff, working- AFE**
staff AFFE
ALF
APH

Giraffe **AFFE**
see
AFE**

Abaft, aft, aircraft, anti-aircraft, craft, daft, draft, fore and aft, graft, haft, handicraft, kingcraft, priestcraft, quaft, shaft, statecraft, waft, witch-craft

AFT
see
APH-*ed*
AUGHT**

After, hereafter, rafter, thereafter

AFTER
see
ER

Bag, beanbag, black flag, blueflag, brag, brain-fag, button-bag, carpet-bag, crag, ditty-bag, drag, dufflebag, fag, flag, gag, hag, handbag, jutting-crag, lag, mailbag, money-bag, nag, rag, ragtag, saddlebag, sag, saltbag, sandbag, scallawag, scrag, shag, slag, sleeping-bag, snag, stag, starry flag, tag, wag, water-bag, wig-wag, zigzag

AG
see

Malaga, Naga, rutabaga, saga

AGA
see
A**

Adage, advantage, age, anchorage, appendage, assemblage, baggage, ban-dage, birdcage, bondage, boscage, cabbage, cage, Carthage, cartilage, classic-age, cleavage, coinage, cold-storage, cordage, cottage, courage, cribbage, damage, dangerous age, dis-courage, disparage, dosage, drainage, encourage, enrage, ensilage, equipage, espionage, flowering sage, forage, frontage, fruitage, fuselage, garbage, Golden Age, greengage, Greenwich Vil-lage, herbage, heritage, homage, hos-

AGE*
see
AUGE
EAGE
EDGE
EGE
ERAGE
IAGE
ORAGE
OTAGE
UAGE
S-ES*

tage, image, leafage, leakage, luggage, **AGE***
manage, middle age, mismanage, mort-
gage, mucilage, nonage, orphanage,
ossifrage, outrage, package, page, par-
entage, parsonage, pasturage, patron-
age, percentage, pilgrimage, pillage,
plumage, portage, postage, pottage,
presage, rage, rampage, ravage, rum-
mage, sabotage, sage, salvage, sausage,
savage, saxifrage, scrimmage, scrum-
mage, scutage, seepage, sewage, short-
age, shrinkage, silage, skunkcabbage,
smallage, spoilage, stage, steerage,
stone age, stoppage, storage, suffrage,
tallage, tankage, tillage, title-page,
tutelage, umbrage, upstage, usage,
vantage, vassalage, vicarage, village,
vintage, visage, voyage, wage, wolfish-
rage, wreckage

Appanage, badinage, bon voyage, **AGE****
boscage, camouflage, entourage, es- *see*
pionage, feuillage, garage, massage,
ménage, mirage, persiflage, personage

Agent, press-agent **AGENT**
see
ENT

Dowager, lager, manager, old stager, **AGER**
onager, tanager, wager *see*
ER

Diaphragm **AGM**
see
AM

Champagne, Charlemagne, Bretagne   **AGNE**
see
AIN

Ago, archipelago, dago, farrago, Iago, lumbago, plumbago, sago, solid-ago, virago, years-ago   **AGO**
see
O*

Aragon, Dagon, dragon, flagon, hexagon, octagon, paragon, pentagon, snapdragon, tarragon, tetragon, wagon, waterwagon   **AGON**
see
AN**
ON

Anagram, diagram, pentagram   **AGRAM**
see
AM

Hague, plague, Prague, vague   **AGUE***
see
EG

Colleague, league   **AGUE****
see
UE**

Ague, argue   **AGUE*****
see
U*

Asparagus, sarcophagus, Tagus   **AGUS**
see
US

Abdullah, ah, amah, bah, Beulah, bismillah, blah, cheetah, dahabeeyah, Deborah, fellah, Gomorrah, howdah, hurrah, huzzah, Jehovah, Jonah, jub-   **AH**
see
A**
IAH

bah, Judah, kiblah, maharajah, Ma- **AH**
nassah, Menephtah, Methuselah,
Micah, Mizpah, mullah, Noah, pah,
Pisgah, Ptah, purdah, rajah, Rizpah,
Rosh Hashanah, Selah, shah, Shah-
Namah, Shekinah, Shenandoah, shil-
lelah, sirrah, Terah, Torah, yeah

Adonai, caravanserai, El Shaddai, **AI**
Mordecai, Shanghai, Sinai   *see*
                                                I*

Aramaic, archaic, Hebraic, laic, **AIC**
Lamaic, mosaic, prosaic, Romaic, vol-   *see*
taic   IC

Afraid, aid, air-raid, bondmaid, **AID***
braid, handmaid, inlaid, laid, maid,   *see*
mermaid, milkmaid, overpaid, paid,   ADE*
plaid, poorly-paid, raid, repaid, sea-   AY-*ed*
maid, shepherd's plaid, staid, unpaid,
upbraid, waylaid

Aforesaid, said, Thebaid, unsaid **AID****
                                                see
                                                EAD*

Naif, waif **AIF**
                                                see
                                                AFE*

Arraign, campaign **AIGN**
                                                see
                                                AIN

Straight **AIGHT**
                                                see
                                                ATE

Haik

AIK
see
IKE

Ail, assail, avail, bail, bewail, black-
mail, bobtail, cat-tail, cocktail, curtail,
derail, detail, dinner-pail, dovetail,
draggle-tail, entail, fail, fan-mail, fan-
tail, flail, foxtail, frail, grail, hail, hand-
rail, hangnail, hobnail, jail, mail, main-
sail, mare's tail, monorail, nail, oxtail,
pail, pigtail, pintail, prevail, quail, rail,
remail, retail, ringtail, sail, silver nail,
slaptail, snail, stay-sail, swallow-tail,
taffrail, tail, tattered-sail, thumbnail,
trail, travail, vail, wagtail, wail, wassail

AIL
see
ALE
EIL

Blackmailer, trailer

AILER
see
ER

Acclaim, aim, claim, declaim, dis-
claim, Ephraim, exclaim, maim, Miz-
raim, proclaim, quitclaim, reclaim

AIM
see
AME*

Abstain, again, amain, appertain, at-
tain, bargain, blain, boatswain, brain,
Cain, captain, certain, chain, chamber-
lain, chaplain, chieftain, chilblain,
come-again, complain, constrain, con-
tain, coxswain, cross-grain, curtain,
detain, disdain, domain, drain, drop
curtain, enchain, endless-chain, enter-
tain, explain, fain, foreordain, fountain, gain, grain, ingrain, legerdemain,
main, maintain, Mark Twain, mountain, obtain, ordain, pain, pattering-

AIN
see
AGNE
AIGN
AINE
ANE
EIGN
EIN

rain, plain, plantain, porcelain, pre- **AIN**
ordain, purslain, quatrain, rain, rattle-
brain, refrain, regain, remain, restrain,
retain, sea-captain, simple-swain, soda-
fountain, Spain, Spanish Main, stain,
St. Germain, strain, sustain, suzerain,
swain, tent-curtain, terrain, train,
twain, vain, vervain, villain, weather
stain

Aquitaine, chatelaine, cocaine, Lor- **AINE**
raine, migraine, moraine, ptomaine *see*
AIN

Aint, aquaint, complaint, constraint, **AINT**
faint, liveries-quaint, paint, patron *see*
saint, plaint, quaint, restraint, saint, EINT
self-restraint, taint, warpaint *ly-*E**

Affair, air, armchair, backstair, bath **AIR**
chair, camel's hair, campchair, chair, *see*
Corsair, debonair, éclair, fair, flair, AIRE
hair, horsehair, impair, kinky hair, ARE*
lair, maidenhair, Mayfair, mid air, EAR**
mohair, open-air, pair, repair, rocking- EIR*
chair, sedan-chair, stair, study-chair,
unfair, Vanity Fair, Windsor chair

Brumaire, debonaire, doctrinaire, **AIRE**
Frimaire, legionnaire, millionaire, mul- *see*
timillionaire, questionnaire, savoir AIR
faire, secretaire, solitaire, Vendemaire,
vin ordinaire, Voltaire

Bairn, cairn, Pitcairn **AIRN**
see

Airy, dairy, fairy, hairy | **AIRY**
see
E**

Dais, Sais | **AIS***
see
IS*

Calais, Rabelais | **AIS****
see
A*

Braise, chaise, malaise, Marseillaise, mayonnaise, Père-la-Chaise, polonaise, postchaise, praise, raise, self-praise | **AISE**
see
AISSE
A*-*s*
AIZE
ASE**
AY-*s*
EIGH-*s*

Archaism, Hebraism, Judaism, Lamaism | **AISM**
see
ISM

Bouillabaisse, caisse | **AISSE**
see
AISE

Waist, wasp-waist | **AIST**
see
ASTE

Bait, bull bait, fishbait, gait, plait, portrait, strait, wait, whitebait | **AIT**
see
ATE

Bull baiter, congress gaiter, gaiter, waiter **AITER** *see* ER

Faith, water-wraith, wraith **AITH*** *see*

Saith **AITH**** *see* ETH

Glaive, naive, waive **AIVE** *see* AVE*

Baize, maize **AIZE** *see* AISE

Al Borak, Barak, Irak, Karnak, kodak, yak, yashmak **AK** *see* AC ACH* ACK

Air-brake, bake, betake, brake, cake, canebrake, clambake, coasterbrake, cornflake, drake, earthquake, fake, flake, forsake, gartersnake, give and take, griddlecake, handshake, intake, keepsake, kittiwake, lake, make, mandrake, mercy-sake, mistake, namesake, overtake, pancake, partake, quake, rake, rattlesnake, retake, saffron cake, sake, sea-snake, shake, sheep-bake, sheldrake, shortcake, snake, snowflake, **AKE** *see* ACHE** AQUE** EAK**

spake, stake, sweepstake, take, tipsy- **AKE**
cake, undertake, wide-awake

Awaken, betaken, mistaken, taken, **AKEN**
wind-shaken
see
EN

Baker, breaker, caretaker, dress- **AKER**
maker, haymaker, jail-breaker, law- *see*
breaker, maker, matchmaker, peace- ER
maker, Quaker, sailmaker, Shaker,
shoemaker, spinnaker, tentmaker, un-
dertaker

Abnormal, abysmal, admiral, adum- **AL**
bral, antidotal, antipodal, apocryphal, *see*
arbital, astral, austral, autumnal, AAL
avowal, Bengal, betrayal, betrothal, ANAL
cabal, carnal, cathedral, caudal, cen- EAL
tral, cerebral, cloistral, coastal, colos- EGAL
sal, corral, crystal, demoniacal, de- ENAL
posal, dihedral, disavowal, dismal, dis- ENTAL
missal, dorsal, ducal, enthral, epochal, ERAL
feudal, Fingal, Funchal, gal, gyral, ERIAL
herbal, integral, interval, isothermal, ERNAL
jackal, Jubal, lachrymal, lethal, Luper- ESTAL
cal, madrigal, magistral, mammal, ETAL
marshal, medal, missal, mistral, modal, EVAL
narwhal, nasal, naval, offal, orchestral, IAL
pal, papal, Parsifal, paschal, pedal, IBAL
panal, portrayal, postal, prodigal, pro- ICAL
posal, Provençal, quintal, rascal, rear- IDAL
admiral, rebuttal, rehearsal, renewal, IMAL
reprisal, reversal, rock-crystal, sacer- INAL
dotal, sandal, scandal, seneschal, se- ION-*al*
pulchral, signal, spectral, spiral, spousal, IPAL
storm-signal, survival, synagogal, Taj ITAL

Mahal, teetotal, thermal, total, tribunal, triumphal, universal, upheaval, vandal, vassal, verbal, withdrawal, withal

AL
IVAL
OCAL
ONAL
OPAL
ORAL
ORMAL
ORTAL
OVAL
OYAL
UAL
UGAL
URAL
URNAL
USAL
UTAL
ly-E**
S-ALS

Cabala, gala, Kalevala, Guatemala, Jumala, La Scala, marsala, Sakuntala, Shambhala

ALA
see
A**

Talc

ALC
see

Bald, emerald, herald, piebald, ribald, scald, skald

ALD
see
ALL-*ed*
AUL-*ed*

Heraldry, ribaldry

ALDRY
see
E**

Airedale, ale, bale, chippendale, dale, exhale, farthingale, female, gale, gunwale, hale, impale, inhale, kale,

ALE
see
AIL

male, martingale, musicale, nightingale, pale, percale, regale, rummage-sale, sale, scale, shale, stale, swale, tale, telltale, vale, whale, wholesale, Yale

ALE
EIL

Equivalent, prevalent

ALENT
see
ENT

Aleph

ALEPH
see
IPH

Behalf, calf, half, half and half, sea calf

ALF
see
APH

Ali, Bali, Bengali, Kali, Somali

ALI
see
I**

Australia, bacchanalia, paraphernalia, parentalia, penetralia, regalia, saturnalia, Thalia, Vestalia

ALIA
see
IA

Invalid, squalid, valid

ALID
see
ID

Aurora borealis, chrysalis, Count de Gabalis, cum grano salis, digitalis, oxalis

ALIS
see
IS*

Bilingualism, fatalism, formalism, idealism, imperialism, individualism, nationalism, rationalism, revivalism, royalism, socialism, vandalism

ALISM
see
ISM

Abnormality, actuality, banality, beastiality, carnality, conviviality, duality, equality, eternality, ethereality, fatality, finality, formality, frugality, generality, hospitality, inequality, intellectuality, liberality, locality, mentality, modality, mortality, municipality, neutrality, normality, originality, partiality, personality, plurality, potentiality, principality, prodigality, quality, rascality, reality, speciality, substantiality, technicality, tonality, totality, triviality, vitality

ALITY
see
E**
ITY

Equalize, idealize, immortalize, individualize, legalize, localize, materialize, moralize, mortalize, neutralize, penalize, rationalize, realize, scandalize, signalize, specialize, tantalize, visualize, vocalize

ALIZE
see
IZE

Balk, beanstalk, cakewalk, calk, chalk, cornstalk, intermittent talk, jaywalk, rope-walk, sheep-walk, sidewalk, small-talk, stalk, talk, walk

ALK
see
AWK

All, appall, ball, banquet-hall, baseball, basketball, befall, bird-call, blackball, bookstall, bugle-call, button-ball, call, carry-all, catcall, Chinese Wall, clarion-call, coffee-stall, Cornwall, croquet-ball, dancehall, downfall, enthrall, eyeball, fall, fish-ball, footfall, forestall, fruit-stall, gall, hall, highball, hold-all, install, mall, mudwall, music-hall, musketball, nightfall, overall, pall, pitfall, prison-wall, puffball,

ALL*
see
AUL
AWL
ed-ALD
y-E**
ALLY

rainfall, recall, roll call, sea-wall, small, spit ball, squall, stall, stonewall, tall, tapestried-wall, tea-ball, thrall, wall, waterfall, windfall

ALL*

Shall

ALL**
see
AL

Callow, fallow, hallow, mallow, marsh mallow, sallow, shallow, tallow, wallow

ALLOW
see
OW*

Ally, cynically, dally, diametrically, dilly-dally, eternally, graphically, ideally, mathematically, morally, occasionally, paradoxically, personally, pragmatically, prosaically, rally, rascally, reverentially, rurally, sally, shilly-shally, stoically, tally, technically, totally, typically, tyrannically, vitally

ALLY
see
E****

Balm, becalm, calm, doum palm, embalm, palm, psalm

ALM
see
UALM

Buffalo, halo, water-buffalo

ALO
see
O*

Anomalous, bicephalous, jealous, megacephalous, scandalous

ALOUS
see
OUS

Alp, scalp

ALP
see

Alpha

ALPHA
see
A**

Cavalry, chivalry, rivalry

ALRY
see
E**

Annals, cymbals

ALS
see
AL-S

Alt, asphalt, basalt, cobalt, exalt, halt, malt, rock salt, salt, sea-salt, shalt, smalt, spring-halt

ALT
see
AULT
S-ALTZ

Healthy, stealthy, wealthy

ALTHY
see
E**

Alto, contralto, Rialto

ALTO
see
O*

Casualty, fealty, loyalty, mayoralty, penalty, realty, royalty, salty, vice-royalty

ALTY
see
E**

Waltz

ALTZ
see
ALT-S

Bucephalus, Dædalus, Heliogabalus, Sardanapalus, Tantalus

ALUS
see
US

Bivalve, calve, halve, needle valve, salve, valve

ALVE
see

Abraham, Adam, Adullam, am, amalgam, balsam, bantam, bedlam, beldam, buckram, cablegram, cam, clam, Coulee Dam, cram, dam, dram, Durham, epigram, flotsam, gam, gingham, gram, grand-slam, ham, Hiram, I am, imam, Islam, jam, jetsam, jimjam, lam, macadam, madam, mantram, marconigram, milldam, Omar Khayyam, pam, praam, pram, quandam, ram, Rustam, salaam, scram, sham, Siam, slam, Surinam, swam, sweet-marjoram, telegram, Uncle Sam, wham

AM
see
AGM
AGRAM
AMB
AMME
AMN
ASM
OGRAM

Aceldama, Alabama, Bahama, cyclorama, Dalai Lama, drama, Fujiyama, Gautama, Kama, lama, llama, mama, melodrama, pajama, Panama, panorama, pranayama, Rama, Yama, Yokohama

AMA
see
A**

Dithyramb, iamb, jamb, lamb

AMB
see
AM

Amble, bramble, preamble, scramble, shamble

AMBLE
see
EL
LE

Aflame, blame, came, candle-flame, dame, defame, fame, flame, frame, game, hallowed-flame, hame, inflame,

AME*
see
AIM

lame, name, nickname, oriflame, over- **AME***
came, pen-name, same, selfsame, AIME
shame, stepdame, surname, tame

Madame, Notre Dame **AME****
see
AM

Camel, caramel, enamel **AMEL**
see
EL
LE

Amen, cyclamen, stamen, Tutank- **AMEN**
hamen *see*
EN

Armament, filament, firmament, la- **AMENT**
ment, ligament, lineament, medica- *see*
ment, ornament, parliament, predica- EŃT
ment, sacrament, temperament, testa-
ment, tournament

Gossamer, steamer, streamer, tamer **AMER**
see
ER

Adamic, balsamic, ceramic, dynam- **AMIC**
ic, hydrodynamic, panoramic *see*
IC

Benjamin, gamin **AMIN**
see
IN

Gramme, oriflamme, programme **AMME**
see
AM

Damn   **AMN**
see
AM

Amor, clamor, enamor   **AMOR**
see
OR

Aid-de-camp, champ, clamp, cramp,   **AMP***
damp, decamp, encamp, firedamp,   *see*
glow-worm's lamp, lamp, postage-
stamp, ramp, safety-lamp, scamp,
spirit-lamp, stamp, tamp, tramp, vamp

Dismal Swamp, swamp   **AMP****
see
OMP

Pampa, Tampa   **AMPA**
see
A**

Damper, hamper, pamper, scamper,   **AMPER**
tamper   *see*
ER

Ample, example, sample, trample   **AMPLE**
see
EL
LE

Campus, grampus, hippocampus   **AMPUS**
see
US

Calamus, hippopotamus, ignoramus,   **AMUS**
mandamus, Morituri Salutamus, No-   *see*
stradamus   US

Bigamy, foamy, infamy, monogamy, poetogamy, polygamy, thingamy

AMY
see
E**

Afghan, Ahriman, Alaskan, Alderbaran, alderman, astrakhan, azan, backwoodsman, Balkan, ban, banyan, barrel-organ, began, birdman, bogeyman, Brahman, bran, brogan, bushman, Caliban, can, cancan, capstan, caravan, catamaran, cattleman, caveman, Chinaman, clan, clansman, clergyman, corban, courlan, Cretan, divan, dolman, draftsman, dustpan, Elizabethan, Etruscan, everyman, fan, fantan, fellowman, fireman, fisherman, foreman, Franciscan, freshman, fryingpan, Genghis Khan, gentleman, G-man, Gulistan, hackman, hardpan, harmattan, harridan, helmsman, heman, henchman, Heshvan, highwayman, Hindustan, horseman, hot-watercan, human, husbandman, inhuman, interurban, Iran, Ispahan, Jordan, kaftan, Kashan, khan, Khorassan, Ku-Klux-Klan, Kurdistan, layman, leman, leviathan, Libyan, longshoreman, madman, Magellan, man, marksman, marzipan, medicine-man, merchantman, middleman, midshipman, minute-man, molluscan, Musselman, Naaman, news organ, Nisan, Norman, Norseman, organ, orphan, Oscan, oysterman, pagan, pan, pavan, pecan, Peter Pan, plan, policeman, postman, Pullman, quartan, raglan, ragman, Ramadan, ran, randan, rataplan, rat-

AN*
see
ARIAN
ATAN
EAN**
EDIAN
ERAN
ESAN
IAN
ICAN
ICIAN
IGAN
ISAN
ITAN
OMAN
UAN

tan, redan, Redman, reman, rifleman, **AN***
Roman, rowan, sacristan, sampan,
sandman, sauce-pan, scan, Scotsman,
seaman, sedan, shaman, showman,
silvan, slogan, snowman, Solyman,
Soudan, span, Spartan, spick and span,
spokesman, St. Dunstan, steersman,
stewpan, suburban, suffragan, sultan,
suntan, superhuman, superman,
switchman, sylvan, talisman, tattan,
than, Theban, Tibetan, tincan, Titan,
toboggan, toucan, Trajan, Uhlan,
watchman, Welshman, yeggman, yeoman, Zoan

Swan, wan   **AN****
                                     see
                                     ON
                                     UAN

Ana, Apollonius of Tyanna, arcana,   **ANA**
banana, bandana, Cana, Diana, dulci- *see*
ana, Ecbatana, fata morgana, Guiana, A**
gymkhana, Havana, iguana, lantana,
liana, Louisiana, mañana, Narayana,
Nirvana, quotidiana, Ramayana, sul-
tana, vox humana

Bacchanal, banal, canal   **ANAL**
                                     see
                                     AL

Charabanc, franc   **ANC**
                                     see
                                     ANK

Abeyance, abidance, abundance, ac-
quaintance, admittance, advance, aid-
ance, allowance, ambulance, annoy-
ance, appearance, appurtenance, arro-
gance, askance, assistance, assurance,
attendance, avoidance, balance, barn
dance, bechance, buoyance, chance,
circumstance, clairvoyance, clearance,
concomitance, concordance, conni-
vance, contra-dance, contrivance, con-
veyance, countenance, country dance,
dance, discordance, dissonance, dis-
tance, disturbance, durance, elegance,
encumbrance, endurance, enhance, en-
trance, extravagance, finance, for instance, fragrance, France, freelance,
furtherance, glance, governance, griev-
ance, guidance, hindrance, ignorance,
importance, inelegance, inheritance,
instance, insurance, jubilance, lance,
maintenance, mischance, misfeasance,
monstrance, morrice-dance, noncha-
lance, nuisance, obeisance, observance,
ordinance, ordnance, outdistance,
overbalance, parlance, penance, per-
chance, performance, perseverance,
petulance, pittance, prance, predomi-
nance, protuberance, quittance, reap-
pearance, reconnaisance, redundance,
relevance, reluctance, remembrance,
remittance, remonstrance, renaissance,
repugnance, resemblance, resonance,
riddance, romance, semblance, sever-
ance, shawl-dance, sibilance, signifi-
cance, stance, substance, sun-dance,
superabundance, surveillance, temper-
ance, tolerance, trance, unbalance, ut-

ANCE
see
ANSE
ANT*-s
ENCE
ENSE
ENT-s
IANCE
IENCE
UANCE

terance, valance, vengeance, vigilance, war-dance **ANCE**

Blanch, branch, olive-branch, ranch **ANCH***
see
ANCHE

Stanch **ANCH****
see
AUNCH

Avalanche, carte blanche, Comanche **ANCHE**
see
ANCH*

Blatancy, buoyancy, chiromancy, dactylomancy, discrepancy, expectancy, fancy, flagrancy, flippancy, hesitancy, inconstancy, infancy, necromancy, nonchalancy, occupancy, oneiromancy, pyromancy, radiancy, redundancy, relevancy, sycophancy, tenacy, truancy, vacancy, vagrancy, vibrancy **ANCY**
see
E**
EE

Aforehand, and, band, beforehand, behindhand, Black Hand, bland, borderland, brand, brigand, cab-stand, command, contraband, countermand, demand, disband, eland, elfland, England, expand, fairyland, Ferdinand, firebrand, flower-land, flowerstand, free-hand, garland, gland, grand, grandstand, grassland, Greenland, hand, headland, highland, Holy Land, husband, Iceland, inkstand, inland, island, land, Lapland, Long Island, **AND***
see
IAND

lowland, mainland, misunderstand, moorland, my-land, mythland, New England, Newfoundland, New Zealand, off-hand, Promised Land, quicksand, remand, reprimand, salt-land, Samarkand, sand, saraband, second-hand, Shetland, shorthand, singing-sand, sleight-of-hand, stand, strand, street-band, Switzerland, tableland, Tallyrand, thousand, underhand, understand, unhand, upland, vandal-hand, warlike-band, washstand, waste-land, withstand, witness-stand, woodland, Zululand

AND*

Gourmand, Roland, wand

AND**
see
OND

Ananda, propaganda, Uganda, veranda

ANDA
see
A**

Alexander, bystander, commander, corriander, gander, grander, Highlander, islander, meander, oleander, pander, philander, pomander, salamander, slander

ANDER*
see
ER

Squander, wander

ANDER**
see
ONDER

Candle, chandle, handle, manhandle, panhandle, rush candle, tallow candle

ANDLE
see
EL
LE

Rembrandt	**ANDT** *see* ANT*
Thousandth	**ANDTH** *see*
Apple brandy, bandy, brandy, candy, cherry brandy, handy, Normandy, rock candy, sandy	**ANDY** *see* E**
Aeroplane, bamboo-cane, bane, biplane, cane, cellophane, chicane, counterpane, crane, Dane, dogbane, elecampane, fleabane, henbane, humane, hurricane, hydroplane, inane, insane, lane, mane, marchpane, membrane, monoplane, mundane, pane, plane, profane, purslane, sane, soutane, sugarcane, supermundane, Tamerlane, thane, tisane, triplane, urbane, vane, volplane, wane, wolf's bane, weathervane, windowpane	**ANE** *see* AGNE AIGN AIN EIGN EIN
Castanet, planet	**ANET** *see* ET
Bang, boomerang, chain-gang, clang, fang, gang, hang, hoof-clang, mustang, orang-outang, out-sang, overhang, pang, parasang, Penang, rang, sang, shebang, slang, sprang, tang, twang, whang, whiz-bang, ylang ylang	**ANG** *see* ANGUE INGUE
Arrange, change, derange, estrange, exchange, grange, interchange, mange, range, strange	**ANGE*** *see*

Flange, mélange, orange **ANGE****
see

Anger, danger, endanger, manger, **ANGER**
moneychanger, ranger *see*
ER

Angle, bangle, bespangle, dangle, **ANGLE**
disentangle,, entangle, mangle, new- *see*
fangle, quadrangle, spangle, strangle, EL
tangle, triangle, wangle, wrangle LE

Fandango, mango, tango **ANGO**
see
O*

Cangue, gangue, harangue **ANGUE**
see
ANG

Anglo-mania, decalcomania, dipso- **ANIA**
mania, kleptomania, mania, miscella- *see*
nia, Tasmania, Titania, Transjordania, IA
Transylvania, Urania

Botanic, galvanic, inorganic, inter- **ANIC**
oceanic, mechanic, Messianic, mor- *see*
ganic, oceanic, organic, panic, satanic, IC
titanic, transoceanic, volcanic

Christianity, humanity, inanity, in- **ANITY**
sanity, sanity, urbanity, vanity *see*
E**
ITY

Bank, blank, clank, crank, Cruik- **ANK**
shank, dank, drank, embank, flank, *see*
frank, gangplank, hank, lank, mounte- ANC

bank, plank, point-blank, prank, rank, sank, savings-bank, shank, shrank, spank, stank, swank, tank, thank, yank **ANK** *s*-anx

Ankh **ANKH** *see* ANK

Longshanks, shanks, spindleshanks **ANKS** *see* ANK-*s*

Anna, canna, hosanna, manna, Poly-anna, savanna, Susquehanna **ANNA** *see* A**

Banns **ANNS** *see* AN-*s*

Canny, cranny, Fanny, granny, nanny, tyranny, uncanny **ANNY** *see* E**

Cinzano, guano, llano, Milano, pi-ano, soprano, volcano **ANO** *see* O*

Sans **ANS** *see* AN-*s*

Expanse, manse **ANSE** *see* ANCE

Aberrant, abundant, adamant, air-plant, ant, arrant, arrogant, ascendant, aslant, aspirant, benignant, blatant, bon vivant, buoyant, cant, celebrant, chant, claimant, clairvoyant, cognizant, confidant, consonant, constant, contestant, cormorant, Corybant, courant, covenant, currant, decant, descant, descendant, discordant, dormant, egg-plant, elegant, elephant, emigrant, enchant, equidistant, errant, expectant, extravagant, flagellant, flagrant, flamboyant, flippant, fondant, fragrant, gallant, gallivant, grant, hierophant, hydrant, ignorant, immigrant, implant, important, incessant, inconstant, inelegant, infant, informant, instant, irrelevant, jurant, Levant, lieutenant, malignant, merchant, ministrant, natant, nonchalant, observant, occupant, octant, pant, participant, passant, peasant, pedant, pendant, pennant, petulant, pheasant, pie-plant, plant, pleasant, poignant, postulant, powerplant, predominant, pregnant, protestant, puissant, pursuivant, quadrant, rant, redundant, regnant, relevant, reluctant, remnant, repugnant, resonant, restaurant, resultant, rubberplant, ruminant, search warrant, sextant, slant, stagnant, supplant, supplicant, sycophant, tenant, termagant, tolerant, transplant, trenchant, triumphant, tyrant, ululant, ungallant, unimportant, unpleasant, vacant, vagrant, verdant, vibrant, visitant, warrant

ANT*
see
ANDT
AUNT
EANT
ERANT
IANT
ICANT
ILANT
ITANT
UANT
ed-ED
ly-E**
S-ANCE
ANSE

Au courant, ci-divant, débutant, en passant, nonchalant, piquant, restaurant, soi-disant, want

ANT**
see
AUNT
ONT**

Andante, ante, bacchante, commandante, corybante, Dante, dilettante

ANTE
see
E*

Amaranth

ANTH
see

Antic, Atlantic, frantic, gigantic, pedantic, romantic, transatlantic, unromantic

ANTIC
see
IC

Canto, Campo Santo, coranto, esperanto

ANTO
see
O*

Errantry, gallantry, infantry, pageantry, pantry, peasantry, pedantry, pleasantry

ANTRY
see
E**

Scanty, shanty, warranty

ANTY
see
E**

Laudanum, tympanum

ANUM
see
UM

Manx, phalanx

ANX
see
ANK-*s*

Any, Bethany, botany, Brittany, company, dittany, epiphany, litany, mahogany, many, miscellany, Ro-

ANY
see
E**

many, Tammany, theophany, Tuscany, **ANY**
zany

Bonanza, esperanza, extravaganza, **ANZA**
stanza *see*
A**

Cacao, cocao, curacao, Mindanao **AO**
see
o*

After-clap, burlap, cap, cat-nap, **AP***
chap, clap, claptrap, crap, earlap, *see*
entrap, enwrap, fill-gap, flap, flytrap, APPE
fool's cap, gap, hanap, handicap, hap, *ed*-APT
Jap, kidnap, knap, kneecap, lap, mad-
cap, mayhap, mishap, mobcap, mouse-
trap, nap, nightcap, on-tap, overlap,
pap, Phrygian cap, pointed-cap, rap,
rattle-trap, red cap, sap, satrap, scrap,
shoulder-strap, skull-cap, slap, snap,
stop-gap, strap, tap, thunder-clap,
trap, Turk's cap, unwrap, Venus's-
flytrap, wrap

Swap **AP****
see
OP

Ape, cape, drape, escape, fire-escape, **APE**
gape, grape, landscape, misshape, nape, *see*
rape, red tape, scrape, shape, ship- EPE
shape, tape

Brown paper, diaper, draper, news- **APER**
paper, paper, rice-paper, sandpaper, *see*
skyscraper, wallpaper ER

Jackanapes

APES
see
APE-*s*

Anemograph, anopisthograph, biograph, bolograph, chronograph, cinematograph, epigraph, epitaph, graph, gyrograph, hectograph, heliograph, hierograph, holograph, lithograph, mimeograph, opistograph, pantograph, paragraph, phonograph, photograph, seraph, stenograph, stylograph, telegraph

APH
see
AFE**
ALF
AUGH
UAFF
*ed-*AFT
*y-*APHY

Autobiography, bibliography, biography, cacography, geography, heliography, lexicography, museography, oceanography, orography, orthography, phonography, photography, pyrography, telephotography, topography

APHY
see
E**

Nappe

APPE
see
AP*

Clapper, dapper, flapper, scrapper, snapper, wrapper

APPER
see
ER

Apple, crab apple, dapple, grapple, pineapple, scrapple

APPLE
see
EL
LE

Happy, sappy, scrappy, snappy

APPY
see
E**

Craps, drumtaps, perhaps, snaps, taps

APS
see
AP*-s

Apse, collapse, elapse, lapse, relapse, trapse

APSE
see
AP*-s

Adapt, apt, deep-wrapt, inapt, rapt, slapt, wrapt

APT
see
AP*-*ed*
s-AP*-s

Plaque

AQUE*
see
AC

Opaque

AQUE**
see
AKE

Above par, Adar, afar, Akbar, Alcazar, almemar, altar, antimacassar, astylar, auto-car, avatar, bar, bazaar, beggar, below par, Belshazzar, bipolar, blazing-star, Bolivar, brownsugar, burglar, bursar, Caesar, calabar, calendar, car, caterpillar, cellar, char, cheddar, cigar, cinnabar, coal-tar, cooky-jar, cougar, crockery-jar, crossbar, crowbar, czar, D.A.R., day-star, debar, dog-star, evening-star, Excalibar, exemplar, far, feldspar, gar, Gaspar, Gibraltar, grammar, guitar, Hagar, handle-bar, hangar, horsecar, hussar, interstellar, isobar, Issachar, izar, jack-tar, jaguar, jar, jaunting-car,

AR*
see
ARE**
ARRE
EDAR
IAR
ILAR
OIR**
OLLAR
ULAR
ULGAR
YR
ed-ARD
s-ARS

Julian Calendar, lascar, lazar, Lochin- **AR***
var, lode star, lunar, Macassar, Mada-
gascar, Magyar, Malabar, maple sugar,
mar, medlar, molar, morning-star,
mortar, motor car, nectar, nenuphar,
Ninnar, Omar, par, pedlar, pillar,
Pindar, platform car, polar, Pompey's
Pillar, poplar, Potiphar, realgar, regis-
trar, salt cellar, samovar, sandbar,
scar, scholar, scimitar, Shinar, shoot-
ing-star, side-car, sitar, sleeping-car,
solar, spar, star, stellar, sugar, tar,
tartar, Templar, thus far, Trafalgar,
trolley-car, Vassar, vicar, vinegar,
Zanzibar, Zohar

Civil War, man-of-war, pre-war, war   **AR****
                                       see
                                       ATOR
                                       OR

Cithara, dulcamara, Ishvara, mas-   **ARA**
cara, Para, Sahara, Sara, solfatara,   *see*
Tara, taratantara, tiara   A****

Arab, scarab, street-arab   **ARAB**
                             see
                             AB*

Barb, garb, rhubarb   **ARB**
                       see

Garble, marble, warble   **ARBLE**
                          see
                          EL
                          LE

Arc, Joan of Arc, marc **ARC**
see
ARK

Arch, countermarch, larch, march, **ARCH***
outmarch, overarch, parch, starch *see*

Anarch, hierarch, monarch, oligarch, **ARCH****
patriarch, Petrarch, Plutarch, tetrarch *see*
ARK
s-OX

Anarchy, heptarchy, hierarchy, **ARCHY**
monarchy, oligarchy, tetrarchy *see*
E**

Abelard, afterward, Asgard, award, **ARD**
awkward, backward, backyard, bard, *see*
bastard, blizzard, bombard, boulevard, AR*-*ed*
brickyard, buzzard, calling-card, camel- IARD
opard, Camisard, canard, card, chard, UARD
church-yard, costard, coward, custard, *ly*-E**
dastard, discard, disregard, dockyard,
dullard, eastward, forward, foulard,
froward, gizzard, gold standard, green-
sward, haggard, halyard, hap-hazard,
hard, Harvard, hazard, hog's lard,
homeward, inward, izzard, laggard,
lard, leeward, leopard, lizard, mallard,
mansard, Midgard, mustard, nard,
niggard, northward, onward, orchard,
outward, pard, petard, placard, play-
ing-card, pochard, postcard, poultry-
yard, regard, retard, reward, reynard,
Richard, sard, Savoyard, scabbard,

Scotland Yard, seaward, shard, ship-
yard, shoreward, skyward, sluggard,
southward, standard, steelyard, stew-
ard, stock-yard, straightforward,
sward, tankard, thee-ward, thither-
ward, toward, trump-card, turkey-
buzzard, upward, us-ward, Utgard,
vineyard, ward, wayward, westward,
windward, wizard, yard

ARD

Cowardly, hardly, inwardly, nig-
gardly, outwardly

ARDLY
see
E**

Aware, bare, beware, blare, care,
compare, dare, declare, delftware,
earthenware, ensnare, fanfare, fare,
flare, flatware, glare, hardware, hare,
insnare, mare, nightmare, pare, pebble-
ware, plowshare, prepare, rare, scare,
share, snare, spare, square, stoneware,
tableware, tare, threadbare, thorough-
fare, unaware, ware, warfare, wellfare

ARE*
see
AIR
EIR*
ERE**
IARE

Are, caviare

ARE**
see
AR*

Bearer, cupbearer, shearer, talebearer, wayfarer, wearer

ARER
see
ER

Dwarf, scarf, wharf

ARF
see

Barge, charge, countercharge, dis-
charge, enlarge, large, marge, over-
charge, recharge, surcharge, ultra-large

ARGE
see

Cargo, embargo, largo, supercargo   **ARGO**
see
o*

Aria, Ava Maria, cineraria, malaria,   **ARIA**
Samaria, wistaria   see
IA

Abcedarian, agrarian, antiquarian,   **ARIAN**
barbarian, humanitarian, librarian,   see
nonagenarian, proletarian, sectarian,   AN*
sexagenarian, utilitarian, vegetarian

Ballbearing, clearing, daring, faring,   **ARING**
glaring, hearing, paring, sea-faring   see
ING

Impresario, Lothario, scenario   **ARIO**
see
IO

Apollinaris, Paris, Polaris, Sybaris   **ARIS**
see
IS*

Charity, clarity, disparity, hilarity,   **ARITY**
irregularity, jocularity, parity, par-   see
ticularity, peculiarity, polarity, popu-   E**
larity, rarity, regularity, similarity,
singularity, solidarity, vulgarity

Ark, bark, birth-mark, book-mark,   **ARK**
bulwark, dark, Denmark, disembark,   see
ear-mark, embark, hark, highwater-   ARCH**
mark, landmark, lark, mark, mudlark,
Noah's ark, Ozark, park, Peruvian
bark, pitch dark, pock-mark, post-

mark, quotation-mark, remark, sark, shagbark, shark, shell-bark, skylark, snark, spark, stark, thumb-mark, tit-lark, watermark, wood-lark **ARK**

Carl, gnarl, marl, snarl **ARL**
see

Early, pearly, popularly, scholarly, similarly, singularly **ARLY**
see
E**

Abandoned farm, alarm, arm, baby farm, charm, disarm, false-alarm, farm, forearm, harm, unharm **ARM***
see
ARME
S-ARMS

Lukewarm, swarm, warm **ARM****
see
ORM*

Gendarme **ARME**
see
ARM*

Arms, coat-of-arms, fire-arms, men-at-arms **ARMS**
see
ARM*-s

Warmth **ARMTH**
see

Barn, darn, spun-yarn, tarn, yarn **ARN***
see

Forewarn, warn **ARN****
see
AWN

Carp, harp, jew's harp, scarp, sharp **ARP***
see

Warp **ARP****
see
ORP

Bizarre, Navarre **ARRE**
see
AR*

Arrow, barrow, drill-barrow, harrow, **ARROW**
marrow, narrow, sparrow, wheel-bar- *see*
row, yarrow OW*

Carry, charry, Du Barry, glengarry, **ARRY**
harry, marry, parry, quarry, remarry, *see*
starry, tarry E**

Champs de Mars, Mars **ARS**
see
AR*-s

Marse, parse, sparse **ARSE**
see

Harsh, marsh, salt-marsh **ARSH**
see

Apart, art, black art, braggart, cart, **ART***
chart, counterpart, dart, depart, dog- *see*
cart, Froissart, go-cart, hand-cart, EART
hart, impart, mart, Mozart, ox-cart,
part, pushcart, rampart, smart, start,
tart, upstart, weatherchart

Athwart, stalwart, thwart, wart **ART****
see
ORT

Barter, carter, charter, garter, self-starter, starter

ARTER
see
ER

Swarth

ARTH
see
ORTH*

Carve, starve, wharve

ARVE
see

Adversary, anniversary, apothecary, arbitrary, Barbary, binary, boundary, Calvary, canary, caravansary, cassowary, chary, cinerary, commentary, commissary, constabulary, contemporary, contrary, corollary, customary, dietary, dignitary, disciplinary, dispensary, documentary, dreary, dromedary, Dundreary, eleemosynary, elementary, emissary, fragmentary, functionary, glossary, granary, hoary, honorary, intercalary, involuntary, itinerary, Janizary, lapidary, legendary, library, literary, Mary, mercenary, military, momentary, monetary, notary, ovary, parliamentary, pituitary, planetary, plenary, primary, quandary, quaternary, rosary, rosemary, rotary, rudimentary, salary, sanitary, secondary, secretary, sedentary, solitary, summary, supernumerary, Tartary, temporary, tercentenary, Thackeray, Tipperary, tributary, tutelary, unitary, unwary, vagary, vary, vocabulary, voluntary, votary, wary, Zachary

ARY
see
AIRY
E**
IARY
INARY
ONARY
UARY

Abraxas, alas, Algeciras, arras, Atlas, balsas, Barabbas, Caiaphas, Candlemas, canvas, Carabas, Caracas, Christmas, coal-gas, Cordilleras, Dorcas, embarras, Esdras, fracas, gas, Hatteras, hippocras, Honduras, in vino veritas, Judas, Juventas, Kansas, laughing-gas, Lycidas, madras, Marsyas, Martinmas, Michaelmas, Midas, Mithras, nuda veritas, Pallas, pampas, per fas et nefas, Pocahontas, poison-gas, Puranas, sassafras, St. Nicholas, upas, Ushas, Vedas, Xmas

AS*
see
ASS
EAS
ORAS

As, has, whereas

AS**
see
AZ

Was

AS***
see
AUSE

Airbase, base, bookcase, case, chase, crankcase, debase, erase, lower-case, paper-chase, pillowcase, purchase, show-case, staircase, steeple-chase, suitcase, vanity-case

ASE*
see
ACE
ed-AIST
ASTE

Chrysophrase, metaphrase, paraphrase, phase, phrase

ASE**
see
AISE
AZE

Abash, ash, balderdash, bash, brash, calabash, calash, cash, clash, crash, dash, flash, gash, gnash, goulash, hash, lash, mash, mountain ash, nettle rash,

ASH*
see
ACHE*

potash, plash, rash, sash, Shamash, **ASH***
slapdash, slash, smash, soda-ash, spat-
terdash, splash, succotash, thrash,
trash, Wabash

Backwash, swash, wash, whitewash   **ASH****
see
UASH

Dasher, dishwasher, gate-crasher,   **ASHER**
haberdasher, potato-masher, rasher   *see*
ER

Aphasia, Asia, Aspasia, athanasia,   **ASIA**
Australasia, Eurasia, fantasia, parono-   *see*
masia   IA

Abrasion, evasion, invasion, occa-   **ASION**
sion, persuasion, pervasion   *see*
ION

Amasis, Anabasis, basis, elephan-   **ASIS**
tiasis, emphasis, hypostasis, oasis,   *see*
protasis   IS*

Ask, bask, cask, damask, flask,   **ASK**
gasmask, Iron Mask, mask, task,   *see*
unmask   ASQUE

Basket, casket, gasket, wastebasket   **ASKET**
see
ET

Cataplasm, chasm, ectoplasm, en-   **ASM**
thusiasm, iconoclasm, phantasm, ple-   *see*
onasm, protoplasm, sarcasm, spasm   AM
EM

Diapason, freemason, Jason, mason **ASON**
see
ON

Asp, clasp, gasp, grasp, handclasp, **ASP**
hasp, rasp, unclasp, vulture-grasp, *see*
wasp *ed*-ED

Basque, casque, masque **ASQUE**
see
ASK

Applesass, ass, Balaam's ass, bass, **ASS**
brass, carcass, class, come-to-pass, *see*
compass, crass, crevass, cuirass, cut- AS*
lass, eelgrass, embarrass, encompass, EAS
eye-glass, fieldglass, glass, grass, harass, IAS
hourglass, isinglass, jackass, looking-
glass, marine glass, marsh-grass, mass,
middle-class, morass, opera-glass, out-
class, overpass, pass, pierglass, plate-
glass, repass, sandglass, sea bass,
sherryglass, spun glass, spy-glass,
stained-glass, sunglass, surpass, trass,
trespass, underpass, upperclass, wind-
lass, wineglass

Demi-tasse, en masse, Montparnasse **ASSE**
see
AS*
ASS

Brassy, embassy, glassy, massy, **ASSY**
sassy *see*
E**

Aghast, avast, ballast, blast, bombast, breakfast, broadcast, cast, contrast, downcast, enthusiast, fast, flabbergast, forecast, foremast, gymnast, half-mast, hast, iconoclast, inballast, jiggermast, jury-mast, last, long last, mast, metaphrast, outcast, outlast, overcast, paraphrast, past, peltast, plastercast, repast, sand-blast, seablast, shoemaker's last, steadfast, topmast, vast

AST*
see
ASK-*ed*
ASS-*ed*
ed-ED

Wast

AST**
see
AUST

Baste, chaste, cotton waste, distaste, foretaste, haste, lambaste, paste, post haste, taste, unchaste, waste

ASTE*
see
ACE-*d*
AIST
ASE*-d*
ed-ED

Caste, half-caste

ASTE**
see
AST

Alabaster, aster, burgomaster, caster, courtplaster, disaster, faster, headmaster, master, piaster, pilaster, plaster, quarter-master, schoolmaster taskmaster, Zoroaster

ASTER
see
ER

Bombastic, drastic, ecclesiastic, elastic, fantastic, mastic, monastic, plastic, sarcastic, scholastic, spastic

ASTIC
see
IC

Ghastly, lastly, vastly   **ASTLY**
see
E**

Dynasty, hasty, nasty, pasty, tasty   **ASTY**
see
E**

Embrasure, measure, pleasure, tape measure, treasure   **ASURE**
see
URE

Apostasy, easy, ecstasy, fantasy, free-and-easy, idiosyncrasy, phantasy **ASY**
see
E**

Acrobat, aerostat, Allat, Al Sirat, Ararat, arhat, aristocrat, assignat, at, autocrat, automat, baccarat, bat, blat, bobcat, bodhisat, brat, brick-bat, carat, cat, caveat, chat, chit-chat, civet cat, combat, concordat, cravat, cricket-bat, crush-hat, democrat, diplomat, ducat, fat, format, ghat, gnat, habitat, hat, heliostat, hell-cat, Herat, high-hat, hors de combat, Jack Sprat, Jehosha-phat, jurat, Kit-cat, Maat, Magnificat, Monteserrat, mudflat, muscat, musk-rat, pat, pit-a-pat, plutocrat, pole-cat, rat, rat-a-tat, Rubaiyat, sat, Shebat, slat, spat, tat, that, that's that, theo-crat, thereat, Tiamat, tit-for-tat, tom-cat, top-hat, vat, wax fat, wharf-rat, whereat, wildcat, ziggurat   **AT***
see
IAT

Somewhat, squat, swat, what   **AT****
see
IOT

Nougat	**AT*** *see* A**
Automata, cantata, crux-ansata, data, errata, inamorata, Mahabharata, natura naturata, persona grata, pro rata, sonata, strata, ultimata	**ATA** *see* A**
Fatal, natal, prenatal	**ATAL** *see* AL
Charlatan, Satan, tarlatan, Yucatan	**ATAN** *see* AN*
Batch, boxing-match, catch, cross-patch, dispatch, hatch, latch, lifted-latch, match, melon-patch, nuthatch, overmatch, patch, potlatch, safety-match, scratch, snatch, sulphur match, thatch, unlatch	**ATCH*** *see* ACH**
Dog-watch, night-watch, stop-watch, watch, wrist-watch	**ATCH**** *see* OTCH
Abate, accommodate, adumbrate, agate, annotate, antedate, ate, bifurcate, billingsgate, bookplate, breastplate, caliphate, carbohydrate, carnate, celebrate, celibate, checkmate, chief mate, cognate, compensate, concentrate, confiscate, conflagrate, conflate,	**ATE** *see* AIT AVATE EAT** EATE EBATE

conjugate, co-ordinate, copperplate, correlate, corrugate, coruscate, crate, cremate, date, deflagrate, deflate, demonstrate, desecrate, designate, dictate, dinnerplate, discarnate, distillate, divagate, door-plate, edentate, electroplate, elevate, elongate, elucidate, emigrate, equilibrate, estate, exculpate, exhilarate, expurgate, extirpate, fashionplate, fate, filtrate, first-rate, floodgate, frustrate, gate, Golden Gate, grate, gyrate, hate, helpmate, hibernate, hydrate, illustrate, importunate, impregnate, incarnate, incubate, inculcate, inflate, ingrate, inmate, innate, insenate, instate, insulate, interpenetrate, interrogate, interstate, inundate, late, lucubrate, lustrate, magistrate, magnate, mandate, mate, messmate, methylate, migrate, narrate, negate, Newgate, nictate, nitrate, obfuscate, objurate, orchestrate, ornate, oscillate, ovate, overrate, overstate, palate, pate, penetrate, perpetrate, phosphate, placate, plate, playmate, pomegranate, potentate, promulgate, propagate, prostrate, pulsate, rate, recapitulate, reinstate, remonstrate, roller-skate, rotate, sate, schoolmate, scintillate, second-mate, second-rate, sedate, separate, serrate, skate, slate, sluice-gate, stagnate, stalemate, state, syncopate, tergiversate, tessellate, tinplate, titillate, tollgate, translate, truncate, upto-date, vacate, vacillate, variegate, vegetate, vertebrate, vibrate, Vulgate, wooly-pate

ATE

ECATE
EGATE
EIGHT*
ELATE
ENATE
ERATE
ETE**
IATE
ICATE
IDATE
IGATE
ILATE
IMATE
INATE
IPATE
IRATE
ITATE
IVATE
OATE
OBATE
OCATE
OGATE
OLATE
ONATE
ORATE
OVATE
UATE
ULATE
URATE
S-ATES

Accurately, alternately, desolately, lately, innately, intimately, irately, ornately, passionately, philately, precipitately, sedately, separately, stately

ATELY
see
E**
ELY

Alma-Mater, crater, Dis pater, fireeater, greater, idolater, later, maneater, pater, Stabat Mater, sweater, theater

ATER
see
ER

United States

ATES*
see
ATE-*S*

Fides Achates, Harpocrates, Hippocrates, Mithridates, Socrates

ATES**
see
ES

Aftermath, Ardath, bath, bridlepath, by-path, footbath, footpath, Goliath, hath, lath, math, mudbath, path, Sabbath, sandbath, showerbath, sitz-bath, towpath, Turkish-bath, warpath, wrath

ATH
see
OPATH

Bathe, enswathe, lathe, rathe, scathe, spathe, swathe

ATHE
see

Allopathy, antipathy, apathy, homeopathy, neuropathy, sympathy, telepathy

ATHY
see
E**

Amati, Frascati, Haimavati, Illuminati, literati, Parvati, Sarasvati

ATI
see
I**

Acrobatic, anastigmatic, aquatic, aristocratic, aromatic, Asiatic, autocratic, automatic, axiomatic, chromatic, climatic, diplomatic, dogmatic, dramatic, ecstatic, Eleatic, emblematic, emphatic, epigrammatic, erratic, fanatic, fluviatic, hieratic, hypostatic, idiomatic, lunatic, lymphatic, mathematic, melodramatic, miasmatic, morganatic, operatic, phlegmatic, piratic, plutocratic, pneumatic, polychromatic, pragmatic, prismatic, problematic, rheumatic, sabbatic, semi-aquatic, static, systematic, thematic, theocratic, trichromatic

ATIC
see
IC

Literatim, verbatim

ATIM
see
IM

Gelatin, Latin, matin, satin

ATIN
see
IN

Fascinating, grating, hibernating, lubricating, pulsating, rating

ATING
see
ING

Abdication, acclamation, accusation, administration, admiration, adulation, adumbration, affectation, affirmation, agitation, alteration, amplification, animation, appellation, arborization, attenuation, auto-intoxication, avocation, calculation, cantillation, carnation, causation, cessation, circulation, citation, civilization, collation,

ATION
see
IATION
ION

combination, communication, compen-
sation, concatenation, concentration,
condemnation, condensation, configu-
ration, confirmation, conformation,
conglomeration, congregation, conso-
lation, constellation, consternation,
consultation, consummation, contam-
ination, contemplation, coöperation,
co-ordination, coronation, corporation,
counter-irritation, culmination, dedication, degustation, delegation, depor-
tation, destination, dilapidation, dila-
tion, discrimination, disintegration,
dispensation, dissertation, dissipation,
distillation, donation, duration, eleva-
tion, elimination, elucidation, emana-
tion, embrocation, emigration, emu-
lation, encrustation, enumeration,
equation, eradication, estimation, evo-
cation, exaggeration, exaltation, ex-
hiliration, expectation, expiration, ex-
ploitation, expostulation, extenuation,
exudation, exultation, fixation, flirta-
tion, fluctuation, fornication, fortifica-
tion, fulmination, fumigation, general-
ization, gestation, glorification, grada-
tion, graduation, gravitation, gurgita-
tion, gustation, hallucination, hesita-
tion, identification, illation, illumina-
tion, illustration, imitation, imperson-
ation, incantation, incarnation, incin-
eration, incrustation, individualization,
individuation, inflammation, inflation,
information, innovation, insolation, in-
spiration, installation, insubordination,
insulation, interpenetration, interpola-
tion, interpretation, interrogation, in-

toxication, inundation, investigation, **ATION**
irritation, isolation, iteration, jubila-
tion, laceration, legation, levitation,
libation, liberation, libration, limita-
tion, location, lubrication, lucubration,
lustration, manifestation, manipula-
tion, materialization, mediation, medi-
tation, mensuration, migration, miscal-
culation, miscreation, mitigation, mod-
eration, modulation, mutation, mutila-
tion, natation, nation, negation, nota-
tion, nullification, obfuscation, obla-
tion, obligation, observation, occupa-
tion, oration, organization, orientation,
oscillation, osculation, ossification, os-
tentation, ovation, pagination, partici-
pation, particularization, peculation,
peregrination, perspiration, plantation,
population, potation, precipitation,
predestination, presentation, preserva-
tion, privation, probation, proclama-
tion, prolongation, propagation, provo-
cation, publication, pulsation, punc-
tuation, purification, quotation, radia-
tion, ramification, ration, recantation,
recapitulation, reclamation, recreation,
recrimination, recuperation, reforma-
tion, reforestration, refrigeration, re-
generation, regimentation, regulation,
reincarnation, reiteration, relation,
reparation, repastination, representa-
tion, reputation, reservation, respira-
tion, resuscitation, revelation, rever-
beration, revocation, rotation, ruin-
ation, salutation, salvation, sanitation,
simulation, speculation, stabilization,
stagnation, station, stimulation, sub-

ordination, supererogation, supplica- **ATION**
tion, tabulation, temptation, tergiver-
sation, tintinnabulation, transfigura-
tion, translation, transmigration, trans-
mogrification, transmutation, trans-
portation, trepidation, tribulation, un-
dulation, unification, vacation, vac-
cination, valuation, vaticination, vege-
tation, veneration, ventilation, verifi-
cation, vexation, vibration, violation,
visitation, visualization, vituperation,
vocalization, vocation

Clematis, gratis **ATIS**
see
IS*

Affirmative, alternative, causative, **ATIVE**
communicative, comparative, corrobo- *see*
rative, curative, decorative, derivative, IVE**
evocative, excitative, figurative, form-
ative, germinative, illative, illustrative,
imaginative, imperative, initiative, in-
sinuative, laxative, legislative, lucra-
tive, mediative, meditative, modifica-
tive, narrative, native, negative, nomi-
native, operative, optative, palliative,
predicative, prerogative, preservative,
provocative, purgative, putative, rela-
tive, remunerative, representative, res-
torative, sanative, sedative, superla-
tive, talkative, tentative, terminative,
vocative

Agitato, animato, appogiato, ben **ATO**
trovato, Cato, inamorato, obligato, *see*
pizzicato, Plato, potato, rabato, stac- O*
cato, tomato, vibrato

Accelerator, administrator, agitator, alligator, arbitrator, aviator, curator, dictator, educator, elevator, emigrator, equator, escalator, fornicator, generator, gladiator, imperator, impersonator, incinerator, incorporator, incubator, indicator, instigator, insulator, investigator, liberator, lubricator, mediator, moderator, narrator, navigator, nominator, orator, perambulator, percolator, perpetrator, prestidigitator, prevaricator, procrastinator, procurator, prognosticator, promulgator, radiator, refrigerator, senator, spectator, speculator, testator, translator, ventilator, vibrator

ATOR
see
AR**
OAR
OR

Amatory, anticipatory, conservatory, consignatory, dedicatory, depreciatory, derogatory, dilatory, evocatory, feudatory, fumatory, gyratory, indicatory, inflammatory, laboratory, laudatory, lavatory, mandatory, migratory, objurgatory, obligatory, observatory, oratory, predatory, prefatory, preparatory, propitiatory, purgatory, reformatory, respiratory, sudatory, vibratory

ATORY
see
E**
ORY

Amphitheatre, theatre

ATRE
see
ER

Idolatry, ophiolatry, psychiatry

ATRY
see
E**

Captain Marryatt, kilowatt, watt **ATT**
see
OT

Batter, chatter, clatter, flatter, hat- **ATTER**
ter, matter, patter, platter, scatter, *see*
shatter, smatter, spatter, splatter, ER
subject-matter

Battle, cattle, prattle, rattle, Seattle, **ATTLE**
sham-battle, tattle, tittle-tattle, wattle *see*
EL
LE

Ageratum, Atum, erratum, poma- **ATUM**
tum, stratum, substratum, superstrat- *see*
um, ultimatum UM

Armature, caricature, creature, cur- **ATURE**
vature, denature, entablature, feature, *see*
illnature, immature, judicature, legis- EUR
lature, ligature, literature, mature,
miniature, nature, nomenclature, premature, signature, temperature

Afflatus, apparatus, hiatus, salera- **ATUS**
tus, Pisistratus *see*
US

Esau, Nassau **AU***
see
AW

Esquimau, landau, Pau **AU****
see
O*

Jungfrau, tau	**AU***** *see* OW**
Bedaub, daub	**AUB** *see* AB** OB*
Sauce	**AUCE** *see* OS* OSS
Debauch	**AUCH** *see*
Applaud, defraud, fraud, gaud, laud, maraud, Maud	**AUD** *see* AW-*ed* *ed*-ED
Quohaug	**AUG** *see* OG
Gauge	**AUGE** *see* AGE
Laugh	**AUGH*** *see* AFE
Faugh	**AUGH**** *see* AW

Aught, caught, distraught, dread-
naught, fearnaught, fraught, naught,
onslaught, self-taught, taught, un-
taught, well-taught

AUGHT*
see
AUT*
OUGHT

Draught

AUGHT**
see
AFT

Haughty, naughty

AUGHTY
see
E**

Caterwaul, caul, Gaul, haul, maul,
overhaul, Paul, Saul

AUL
see
AWL
ed-ALD

Assault, catapault, default, fault,
somersault, treasure-vault, vault

AULT
see
ALT
S-ALTZ

Capernaum, meerschaum

AUM
see
UM

Faun, Marble Faun

AUN
see
AWN

Craunch, haunch, launch, paunch,
staunch

AUNCH
see
ANCH**

Aunt, daunt, flaunt, gaunt, haunt,
jaunt, taunt, vaunt

AUNT
see
ANT**
ed-ED
S-ONSE

Bucentaur, centaur, dinosaur, mino-
taur, plesiosaur

AUR
see
OR

Epidaurus, ichthyosaurus, plesio-
saurus, Taurus, thesaurus

AURUS
see
URUS
US

Santa Claus

AUS
see
AUSE

Applause, because, cause, clause,
pause

AUSE
see
AUS
AW-*s*

Exhaust, Faust, holocaust

AUST
see
OST*

Gauze

AUZE
see
AUSE

Aeronaut, Argonaut, juggernaut,
taut

AUT*
see
AUGHT*

Sauerkraut

AUT*
see
OUT

Nautch

AUTCH
see

Mauve ·········· **AUVE**
see
OVE*

Slav ·········· **AV**
see
AVE**

Ava, Balaklava, Bhairava, cassava, **AVA**
guava, Java, lava *see*
A**

Aggravate, excavate **AVATE**
see
ATE

Architrave, behave, brainwave, **AVE***
brave, cave, close shave, concave, *see*
conclave, crave, deprave, engrave, AIVE
enslave, forgave, galley-slave, grave,
hairwave, heatwave, Hertzian wave,
knave, lave, marcel wave, margrave,
misbehave, nave, octave, pilgrim-stave,
quarry-slave, rave, save, sea-wave,
shave, shortwave, slave, stave, tidal
wave

Have **AVE****
see
AV

Caravel, gavel, gravel, navel, ravel, **AVEL**
travel, unravel *see*
EL
LE

Craven, engraven, haven, heaven, **AVEN**
leaven, raven, smooth-shaven *see*
EN

Cadaver, claver, engraver, graver, **AVER**
palaver, quaver, shaver, waver   *see*
                                        ER

Gravy, navy, wavy   **AVY**
                                        see
                                        E**

Blue law, bucksaw, cat's-paw, caw,   **AW**
Choctaw, claw, coleslaw, draw, flaw,   *see*
forepaw, foresaw, gew-gaw, guffaw,   AWE
handsaw, haw, hee-haw, in-law, jack-   UAW
daw, jackstraw, jaw, jig-saw, kickshaw, *ed*-AUD
law, lockjaw, macaw, mackinaw, maw,   S-AUSE
outlaw, paw, pawpaw, pshaw, raw,   OR-*s*
rickshaw, Saginaw, Salic Law, scroll-
saw, see-saw, straw, taw, thaw, under-
jaw, Warsaw, withdraw

Away, caraway, castaway, fade-   **AWAY**
away, far-away, fly-away, rockaway,   *see*
runaway, stayaway, stowaway,   A**
straightaway, while away

Bawdry, tawdry   **AWDRY**
                                        see
                                        E**

Awe, overawe   **AWE**
                                        see
                                        AW

Awk, fish-hawk, gawk, henhawk,   **AWK**
Mohawk, moulting-hawk, news hawk,   *see*
sparrowhawk, squawk, tomahawk   ALK
                                        y-E**

Awl, bawl, brawl, cawl, crawl, drawl, **AWL**
goat-shawl, scrawl, shawl, sprawl, *see*
trawl, yawl   UALL
                                     ed-ALD

Brawn, dawn, day-dawn, deep- **AWN**
drawn, drawn, false-dawn, fawn, lawn, *see*
long-drawn, overdrawn, pawn, prawn, ARN**
rosy-fingered dawn, sawn, spawn, with- ONE**
drawn, yawn   ORN

Ajax, anthrax, anti-climax, battle- **AX***
ax, bees-wax, borax, climax, flax, Hali- *see*
fax, head-tax, income tax, lax, opopa- AC-*s*
nax, overtax, Pax, pickax, poll-tax, ACHS
relax, sealing-wax, smilax, surtax, syn- ACK-*s*
tax, tax, thorax, toad-flax, wax, zax ACT-*s*

Coax, hoax   **AX****
                                   see
                                  OKE-*s*

Affray, airway, allay, All Fool's Day, **AY**
All Soul's Day, alpha-ray, alway, any- *see*
way, Appian Way, arbor day, archway, A*
array, assay, astray, ay, bay, Bay of AWAY
Biscay, belay, beta-ray, betray, blue- EIGH
jay, Bombay, Botany, Bay, bray, EY
breakfast tray, by-play, byway, Ca- UAY
thay, causeway, Charlotte Corday, UET**
clay, cutaway, dapple-gray, daresay, *ed*-ADE*
day, decay, defray, delay, disarray, AID*
dismay, display, doomsday, doorway, *s*-A*-*s*
dray, everyday, essay, fast day, fay, AISE
field day, flay, foray, fray, Friday, AIZE
gainsay, gamma-ray, gangway, gay, ASE**
gray, half-pay, halfway, hatchway, AYS

hay, headway, heyday, highway, holi- **AY**
day, horseplay, hurray, inlay, jay,
Judgment-day, lamp-ray, Labor-day,
lay, leeway, mainstay, Malay, Manda-
lay, man Friday, market-day, mascu-
line-array, may, midday, midway,
Milky-Way, miracle-play, mislay,
Monday, Mother's day, natal-day,
nay, noonday, Norway, nosegay, now-
aday, N-ray, Ojibway, outlay, out-of-
the-way, outstay, passageway, Passion
Play, pathway, pay, photo-play, play,
popinjay, portray, pray, prepay, pri-
vate-way, railway, ray, redletter day,
relay, repay, roundelay, runaway, run-
way, Saint's-Day, Saturday, say, shay,
silver-gray, slay, sluice-way, soothsay,
speedway, spillway, splay, spray, stay,
sting ray, stray, subway, Sunday,
sway, tag-day, Thursday, today, To-
kay, Tuesday, ultra violet ray, under-
pay, underway, war-array, water-way,
waylay, Wednesday, welladay, Whit-
sunday, workaday, X-ray, yesterday

Himalaya, Maya   **AYA**
see
A**

Assayer, layer, payer, piano-player,   **AYER**
prayer, slayer, soothsayer, sprayer,   *see*
taxpayer   ER

Bygone-days, fable-days, now-a-   **AYS**
days, salad days, side-ways   *see*
AY-*s*

Alcatraz, Boaz, Shiraz, topaz   **AZ**
see
AS**
AZZ

Ormazd   **AZD**
see

Ablaze, amaze, blaze, craze, daze,   **AZE**
emblaze, faze, gaze, glaze, haze, maze,   *see*
raze, stargaze   AISE
AY-*s*
y-AZY

Bombazine, magazine   **AZINE**
see
INE**

Amazon, blazon, emblazon   **AZON**
see
ON

Jazz   **AZZ**
see
AZ

Crazy, glazy, hazy, lazy   **AZY**
see
E**

E SOUNDS

Acme, adobe, agape, Ananke, ane- **E***
mone, Aphrodite, Ariadne, Astarte,   *see*
Ate, be, bene, campanile, Chile, Chloe,   A*
Circe, Comanche, Cybele, Danae,
Daphne, dele, Don Quixote, epitome,
Euterpe, evoe, festina lente, finale,
fricasse, Ganymede, Ge, Gethsemane,
Goethe, he, Hebe, Il Trovatore, King
Rene, Lao-Tse, Lethe, macrame, may-
be, me, m.d., Melpomene, Miserere,
Mitylene, Nepenthe, netsuke, Nike,
Niobe, nota bene, padre, phoebe,
Phryne, Proserpine, Psyche, recipe,
sake, salame, Selene, Semele, sesame,
she, sotto voce, stele, tele, the, tse-tse,
ukulele, Ultima Thule, viva-voce, we,
would-be, Yangtse, ye, Zantippe

Abruptly, accordingly, adroitly, **E****
Allegheny, amply, anchovy, angry,   *see*
anomaly, army, aunty, avowedly,   ABBY
baby, badly, bankruptcy, bel-esprit,   ABLY
belfry, belly, biddy, bigotry, blackly,   ACITY
blameworthy, Blavatsky, blindly,   ACY
bloodthirsty, booby, bossy, brawny,   ADY
briskly, buddy, buggy, bunchy, Bur-   AE
gundy, bushy, busy, caddy, calumny,   AIN-*ly*
canopy, certainly, certainty, cheeky,   AINT-*ly*
chiefly, choosy, chunky, clingingly,   AIRY

clumsy, cocky, colonelcy, conspiracy,
controversy, copy, corruptly, country,
county, coyly, cozy, crafty, cuppy,
curtly, daily, daisy, darkly, deftly,
deucedly, dicky, dingy, dirty, doughty,
downy, dowry, dreary, drowsy, dumpy,
early, easy, eighty, elegy, empty, en-
treaty, envy, epilepsy, eurythmy,
faulty, fifty-fifty, filthy, finicky, fishy,
flaky, flatly, fleshy, flimsy, flinty,
flossy, flunky, fool-hardy, forestry,
forty, frailty, frenzy, freshly, friendly,
frisky, frosty, frowsy, fusty, fuzzy,
galaxy, garden-party, gaudy, gawky,
gayly, ghostly, glossy, godly, goodly,
goofy, gossipy, gramercy, greatly,
grimy, grisly, grouchy, grumpy, guilty,
half-empty, haply, happy-go-lucky,
harpy, hazy, heady, healthy, heathen-
ishly, heavy, hoity-toity, honestly,
hooky, horny, huffy, husbandry, hy-
pocrisy, idiocy, imperiously, industry,
inly, Italy, ivy, jaunty, jelly, jeopardy,
Jewry, jiffy, jointly, jolly, jumpy,
kilty, kindly, kingly, lanky, larceny,
leafy, lethargy, liberty, Lombardy,
lousy, lucky, lumpy, lycanthropy,
mammy, meaty, mercy, mimicry, min-
strelsy, miry, missy, misty, monopoly,
mostly, mouldy, muchly, muddy,
mumsy, Muscovy, namby-pamby, narrowly, natty, nearly, neatly, neigh-
borly, nervy, newly, newsy, nifty,
nightly, nimbly, nippy, noisy, note-
worthy, novelty, oily, oozy, orgy, out-
lawry, overstudy, paddy, palfry, palsy,
paltry, panicky, panoply, pansy, partly,

E**

AL-*y*
ALDRY
ALITY
ALLY
ALRY
ALTHY
ALTY
AMY
ANCY
ANDY
ANITY
ANNY
ANT*-*ly*
ANTE
ANTRY
ANTY
ANY
APHY
APPY
ARCHY
ARDLY
ARITY
ARLY
ARRY
ARY
ASSY
ASTLY
ASTY
ASY
ATELY
ATHY
ATORY
ATRY
AUGHTY
AVY
AZY

party, pastry, patty, pebbly, perfidy, perilously, perky, pesky, philanthropy, pigmy, pithy, pixy, plucky, podgy, poky, polyandry, poppy, porphyry, pot-belly, poultry, praiseworthy, priestly, priory, privy, progeny, pudgy, Punch and Judy, puppy, pussy, rainy, raspy, ready, regularly, remedy, revelry, risky, rocky, roughly, ruby, ruddy, Rugby, rusty, rutty, sacristy, saintly, saucy, scaly, scraggy, scratchy, scrawny, scurvy, seaworthy, secretly, sentry, shabby, sharply, sharpy, shifty, shindy, shoddy, sightly, sissy, sketchy, slangy, slightingly, slimy, smithy, smugly, snoozy, snugly, softly, softy, solemnly, sooty, sovereignty, sparingly, speak-easy, spiffy, spongy, sporty, sprightly, spunky, squally, steady, stealthy, stingy, stocky, strategy, study, subsidy, sultry, superbly, surly, suzerainty, swanky, swarthy, tansy, tantivy, tapestry, tawdry, tawny, taxidermy, tetchy, theory, therapy, Thessaly, thinly, third-party, thirty, thorny, thoroughly, thrifty, throaty, tidy, timothy, toady, toby, toddy, tootsy-wootsy, topsy-turvy, trebly, tricky, twenty, ugly, understudy, unearthly, uneasy, unerringly, unfriendly, ungainly, unknowingly, unlucky, unsteady, unwieldy, veery, vestry, villainy, wanly, waxy, wealthy, weary, weekly, wheezy, whimsy, willingly, windy, wintry, wishy-washy, wooly, wordy, wormy, worry, worthy, wrongly, yearly

E**
EA*
EALTH-*y*
ECTLY
ECY
EDY
EE
EEDY
ELRY
ELY
EMY
ENARY
ENCY
ENLY
ENNY
ENTLY
ENTRY
ENTY
ERGY
ERITY
ERLY
ERRY
ERY
ESTY
ESY
ETRY
ETTY
ETY
EVY
EWY
EY**
I**
IARY
IBLY
ICACY
ICITY
ICKLE

E**

ICY
IDITY
IDLY
IE*
IETY
IGHTY
IGY
ILITY
ILLY
ILY
INARY
ING-*ly*
INKY
INNY
INTLY
INY
IPSY
IRACY
IRY
ISH-*ly*
ISKY
ISTRY
ITTY
ITY
IVERY
IVITY
OBBY
OCHE
ODY
OGGY
OGY
OLLY
OLY
OMY
ONLY
ONRY

E**

ONY
OODY
OPHY
OPPY
OQUY
ORITY
ORRY
ORY
OSITY
OSY
OSYNE
OTRY
OUSLY
OWDY
OWLY
OWY
UAL-*y*
UALLY
UARY
UBBY
UGGY
UITY
ULKY
ULLY
ULTY
ULY*
UMMY
UNDRY
UNDY
UNNY
UNY
UPTCY
URDY
URGY
URITY
URLY

E**
URRY
URTLY
URY
USTY
USY
UTTY
UTY
YE**
S-EASE*
IE*-*S*

Beeftea, blue-sea, cambric tea, chart-less sea, choppy sea, Dead Sea, flea, guinea, high-sea, lea, over sea, pea, plea, Red Sea, sea, sweet-pea, tea, undersea, unsailed-sea

EA*
see
E**
S-ADES*
EASE*

Adrastea, area, azalea, Boadicea, Bona Dea, cetacea, Chaldea, Crimea, Ea, Gaea, Galatea, hydrangea, Idumea, kea, Korea, Laodicea, Leucothea, Medea, nausea, panacea, Penthesilea, Rhea, spiræa, trachea

EA**
see
A**

Yea

EA***
see
A*

Changeable, impermeable, ineffaceable, malleable, peaceable, permeable, serviceable, sizeable, traceable, unchangeable

EABLE
see
EL
LE

Peace

EACE
see
EASE**

Beach, bleach, cleach, each, im-
peach, over-reach, peach, preach,
reach, teach

EACH
see
EECH
es-EZ

Beacon, deacon

EACON
see
ON

Arrow-head, balm of Gilead, bed-
spread, bedstead, behead, big-head,
block-head, Book of the Dead, bread,
brownbread, bulkhead, bullhead, cab-
bage-head, copperhead, dead, dead-
head, dread, drowsi-head, dunderhead,
figurehead, forehead, gingerbread, gor-
gon-head, hammer-head, head, hogs-
head, homestead, instead, lead, logger-
head, masthead, Oread, overhead,
overspread, pilot-bread, pinhead, read,
roadstead, Roundhead, saphead, shew-
bread, shortbread, sleepy-head, sore-
head, spearhead, spread, squarehead,
stead, sweetbread, thread, towhead,
tread, turtlehead, unread

EAD*
see
ACT-*ed*

Bead, knead, lead, mead, plead,
read, reread

EAD**
see
EDE

Breadth

EADTH
see
EDTH

Bay-leaf, clover-leaf, fallen-leaf, fig-
leaf, flyleaf, goldleaf, leaf, palm-leaf,
rose-leaf, sheaf

EAF*
see
EEF
IEF
S-EAVE-*s*

Deaf

EAF**
see
EF

Acreage, lineage, mileage

EAGE
see
AGE*

Beagle, eagle, gold-eagle, spread-eagle

EAGLE
see
EL
LE

Beak, bespeak, bleak, creak, freak, grosbeak, leak, outspeak, peak, sneak, speak, spring-aleak, squeak, streak, teak, tweak, weak, wreak

EAK*
see
EAKE
EEK
IQUE

Beefsteak, break, daybreak, heart-break, outbreak, steak

EAK**
see
AKE

Anneal, appeal, armorial seal, cochi-neal, commonweal, conceal, congeal, deal, heal, leal, meal, misdeal, New Deal, oatmeal, peal, piecemeal, repeal, reveal, seal, self-heal, solomon's seal, squeal, steal, teal, veal, weal, zeal

EAL*
see
EEL
ILE**
ed-IELD

Realm

EALM
see
ELM

Dealt

EALT
see
ELT

Commonwealth, health, stealth, wealth

EALTH
see
ly-E**

Beam, bream, coldcream, Coldstream, cream, crossbeam, day-dream, Devonshire cream, dream, gleam, gulfstream, hornbeam, ice-cream, midstream, moonbeam, ream, scream, seam, steam, stream, sunbeam, team

EAM
see
EEM
IME**

Bean, bemean, clean, dean, demean, dry-clean, glean, jean, lean, mean, string-bean, unclean, wean, yean

EAN*
see
EEN
INE**

Atlantean, Caribbean, cerulean, cetacean, crustacean, Epicurean, Herculean, hyperborean, Korean, Mediterranean, mid-ocean, nectarean, ocean, pæan, Promethean, protean, pygmean, subterranean, superterranean, terpsichorean, terranean, unknown-ocean

EAN**
see
AN*
EN
IEN*

Miscreant, pageant, recreant, sergeant

EANT
see
ANT*

Ash-heap, cheap, heap, leap, neap, reap, sand-heap

EAP
see
EEP

Appear, blear, clear, crystal-clear, dear, disappear, dog-ear, drear, ear, endear, fear, gear, hear, King Lear, lean-year, leap-year, linear, lunar year, ·my dear, near, overhear, reappear, rear, sear, smear, solar year, spear, steering-gear, tear, year, yesteryear

EAR*
see
EER
ERE
IER
ed-EARD**

Bear, bugbear, forebear, Great Bear, koala bear, northern-bear, pear, polar-bear, prickly pear, swear, tear, teddy-bear, underwear, wear
EAR**
see
AIR
ARE*

Research, search
EARCH
see
ERCH
IRCH
URCH

Heard, overheard, unheard
EARD*
see
ERD
URD

Beard, Bluebeard, Old Man's beard, shaggy-beard
EARD**
see
EAR*-*ed*

Shakespeare
EARE
see
EER

Earl, mother-of-pearl, pearl, seed-pearl
EARL
see
IRL
URL

Earn, learn, unlearn, yearn
EARN
see
ERN
URN

Hearse, rehearse
EARSE
see
ERCE
ERSE
URSE

Bleeding-heart, broken-heart, faint- **EART**
heart, heart, inmost-heart, sweetheart   *see*
ART*

Dearth, earth, fuller's earth, hearth, **EARTH**
unearth   *see*
ERTH

Æneas, Boreas, pancreas   **EAS***
see
AS*

Seven Seas   **EAS****
see
ESE

Appease, disease, displease, ease, **EASE***
heartease, please   *see*
ADES*
E*-*s*
EESE*

Axle-grease, cease, crease, decease, **EASE****
decrease, elbow-grease, increase, lease,   *see*
release, surcease   EECE
ed-IEST**

Leash   **EASH**
see
EESH

High treason, rainy season, reason, **EASON**
season, treason   *see*
ASON
ON

Beast, east, Far East, feast, least, love-feast, Near East, northeast, southeast, yeast

EAST*
see
IEST**
ISTE
YST**

Abreast, breast, redbreast

EAST**
see
EST

Aisle-seat, backseat, bearded-wheat, beat, bleat, box-seat, browbeat, buckwheat, cheat, cleat, countryseat, crabmeat, deadbeat, defeat, drumbeat, eat, entreat, feat, forcemeat, heartbeat, heat, maltreat, meat, mince-meat, mistreat, neat, overeat, peat, repeat, reseat, rustic-seat, seat, sweetmeat, treat, unseat, wheat

EAT*
see
EET
EIT*
ed-ED

Great

EAT**
see
EATE

Sweat, threat

EAT***
see
ET

Aureate, baccalaureate, create, laureate, miscreate, nauseate, permeate, procreate, recreate, roseate

EATE
see
ATE
EAT**

Beneath, bequeath, heath, 'neath, sheath, smoke-wreath, underneath, wreath

EATH*
see
EATHE
EETH

Breath, death **EATH****
see
AITH**
ETH

Breathe, sheathe, unsheathe, wreathe **EATHE**
see
EATH*

Cordovan leather, feather, heather, **EATHER**
leather, pinfeather, sole leather, weath- *see*
er, white feather ER

Bandeau, beau, bureau, chateau, **EAU**
manteau, plateau, portmanteau, ron- *see*
deau, Rousseau, tableau, tonneau, O*
trousseau, weather bureau

Bereave, cleave, eave, heave, inter- **EAVE**
weave, leave, sheave, sick-leave, weave *see*
EEVE
EVE
S-EAF*-S

Beaver, weaver **EAVER**
see
ER

Bab el Mandeb, cobweb, cubeb, deb, **EB**
Horeb, neb, pleb, Seb, spider-web, web *see*
EBB

Debate, rebate **EBATE**
see
ATE

Ebb **EBB**
see
EB

Glebe, grebe, plebe

EBE
see

Algebra, zebra

EBRA
see
A**

Debt

EBT
see
ET

Aztec, Quebec, sec, spec, Toltec, xebec

EC
see
ECK

Deprecate, Hecate, hypothecate, imprecate

ECATE
see
ATE

Decent, indecent, recent

ECENT
see
ENT

Beck, bedeck, breakneck, by heck, check, crookneck, deck, fleck, flyspeck, gooseneck, henpeck, kopeck, leatherneck, longneck, low-neck, mizzen-deck, neck, peck, pinchbeck, quarter-deck, rebeck, recheck, reck, roughneck, rubberneck, shipwreck, smart-aleck, speck, stiff-neck, swan-neck, upperdeck, wreck

ECK
see
EK
EQUE
ed-ECT
s-EX

Freckle, heckle, speckle

ECKLE
see
EL
LE

Abject, affect, architect, bisect, circumspect, collect, confect, connect, correct, defect, deflect, deject, detect, dialect, direct, disinfect, disrespect, dissect, effect, eject, elect, erect, expect, genuflect, imperfect, incorrect, indirect, infect, inflect, inject, insect, inspect, intellect, intersect, introspect, neglect, object, perfect, pluperfect, prefect, prelect, project, prospect, protect, recollect, reflect, reject, respect, resurrect, retrospect, sect, select, self-respect, stage-effect, stick insect, subject, suspect

ECT
see
ECK-*ed*
S-ECK-S
EX

Correctly, directly, objectly, perfectly

ECTLY
see
E**

Collector, deflector, detector, director, elector, erector, Hector, inspector, projector, prospector, protector, rector, reflector, sector, stamp-collector, tax-collector

ECTOR
see
OR

Fleecy, prophecy, secrecy

ECY
see
E**

Accented, accosted, accredited, addle-pated, affrighted, aged, agitated, anointed, antiquated, barricaded, bed, beloved, benighted, bigoted, biped, bird-witted, bled, blended, blessed, bloodshed, bobsled, booted, bow-legged, branded, bred, brooded,

ED*
see
AID**
EAD
ID
IED**
UID

bruited, buffeted, carted, catfooted,
close-fisted, coasted, cold-blooded,
comforted, conceited, confounded, cor-
roded, crabbed, crowned, cursed, dark-
red, defeated, deflected, disquieted,
double-bed, dumbfounded, elated,
elected, ended, evil-minded, fair-
minded, false-hearted, feather-bed, fed,
fled, fretted, garden-bed, half-hearted,
high-minded, hoisted, home-bred, hon-
eyed, hot-bed, hot-headed, hundred,
ill-bred, imbed, inbred, indebted, infra-
red, invented, jagged, jewel-studded,
kilted, kindred, knotted, lamented,
learned, led, left-handed, light-footed,
long-winded, lowbred, Manfred, milk-
fed, misled, Mohammed, naked, nar-
row-minded, newly-wed, nodded, one-
sided, over-fed, oyster-bed, pixilated,
precipated, prompted, quadruped, rail-
roaded, recommended, red, red-handed,
reported, resounded, restricted, resusci-
tated, sacred, Samoyed, shed, shredded,
single-bed, single-handed, slab-sided,
sled, snowshed, sober-minded, sped,
spirited, spoon-fed, spotted, stark-
naked, stilted, stout-hearted, sure-
footed, talented, Tancred, thorough-
bred, translated, trundle-bed, un-
abated, unaccented, uncomforted, un-
derbred, underfed, unpolluted, un-
spotted, unsuited, untested, untrans-
lated, unwarranted, unwed, unwonted,
variegated, vested, wafted, watershed,
well-fed, whole-hearted, wicked,
wooded, woodshed, worsted, wretched,
zed

ED*

ACT-*ed*
ANT*-*ed*
ASP-*ed*
AST-*ed*
ASTE-*d*
AUD-*ed*
AUNT-*ed*
EAD*-*ed*
EAT*-*ed*
EDE-*d*
END-*ed*
ET-*ed*
ICT-*ed*
IDE-*d*
IED**
IELD-*ed*
IFT-*ed*
IGHT-*ed*
ILT-*ed*
IT-*ed*
OAST-*ed*
OINT-*ed*
ORD*-*ed*
OST*-*ed*
ULT-*ed*
UTE-*d*

Accursed, airconditioned, Argus-
eyed, backed, barelegged, beloved,
bereaved, bleached, brazen-faced,
breathed, caracoled, cloyed, cowled,
cured, curtained, dark-eyed, dead-eyed,
delved, deranged, drenched, drowsed,
electrotyped, endorsed, enveloped,
etched, far-fetched, fettered, flagged,
fringed, frog-eyed, full-fledged, gnarled,
gypped, hallowed, hardboiled, hen-
pecked, horned, Janus-faced, keyed,
landlocked, low-necked, mottled, mul-
lioned, newly-wed, pampered, par-
celled, peopled, petered, pillowed,
refurbished, reserved, riprapped, rock-
ribbed, scowled, sequestered, shame-
faced, skewered, slant-eyed, smacked,
snarled, so-called, star-spangled,
stitched, strait-laced, stuccoed, sway-
backed, tattered, tempered, three-
cornered, two-faced, unlettered, un-
peopled, unreined, unremembered, un-
scathed, untrammeled, wed, well-
groomed, winced, winged, withered

ED**
see

Edda

EDDA
see
A**

Accede, antecede, cede, centipede,
concede, expede, impede, intercede,
precede, recede, rede, retrocede, se-
cede, stampede, supersede, Swede,
velocipede, Venerable Bede

EDE*
see
EED
ed-ED

Suede

EDE**
see
ADE

Dredge, edge, fledge, foreknowledge, kedge, keen-edge, knowledge, ledge, mountain-edge, on edge, pledge, sedge, selvedge, sledge, waters-edge, wedge

EDGE
see
AGE*
EAGE
EGE
IDGE

Comedian, median, tragedian

EDIAN
see
AN*
IAN

Accredit, credit, edit, discredit

EDIT
see
IT

Credo, teredo, Toledo, torpedo, tuxedo

EDO
see
O*

Hundredth

EDTH
see
EADTH

Aqueduct, deduct

EDUCT
see
UCT

Comedy, higgledy-piggledy, remedy, tragedy

EDY
see
E**

Absentee, agree, alee, apogee, ash-tree, banshee, bee, bootee, Bo-tree, bumblebee, calipee, carefree, Chaldee, Cherokee, chick-a-dee, chimpanzee, coatee, coffee, committee, conferee, Cree, debauchee, devotee, disagree,

EE
see
E**
IGREE
S-IES**
IEZE

divorcee, dungaree, elderberry-tree, **EE**
employee, fancy-free, fee, fiddle-dee-
dee, fig-tree, flee, foresee, free, fricassee,
fringe-tree, Galilee, garnishee, gee,
ghoulish-glee, glee, goatee, grandee,
guarantee, hard-alee, hat-tree, honey-
bee, indorsee, jamboree, jubilee, Judas-
tree, knee, lee, legatee, lessee, levee,
marquee, mulberry-tree, nominee, ogee,
oversee, parent-tree, Parsee, patentee,
Pawnee, payee, Pharisee, pledgee,
pongee, presentee, prithee, puttee,
quilting-bee, rappee, referee, refugee,
repartee, rupee, Sadducee, scot-free,
scree, see, set-free, settee, Shawnee,
shoe-tree, snicker-snee, soiree, spelling-
bee, spondee, spree, squeegee, suttee,
talkee-talkee, tee, te-hee, tepee, thee,
third degree, three, toffee, tree, trustee,
vendee, warrantee, wee, whoopee,
Yankee, Zuyder Zee

Fleece, golden-fleece, Greece   **EECE**
see
EESE**

Beech, beseech, breech, leech, **EECH**
screech, speech, village-leech   *see*
EACH
es-EZ

Agreed, aniseed, apostle's creed, **EED**
bindweed, birdseed, bleed, breed, *see*
chickweed, cotton-seed, creed, cross- EAD**
breed, decreed, deed, exceed, feed, flax- EDE
seed, freed, full speed, gleed, Godspeed, YD
greed, half-breed, hayseed, heed, in- *ed*-ED
deed, Indian weed, ironweed, jewel- *y*-EEDY

weed, knock-kneed, knotweed, linseed, **EED**
meed, misdeed, need, overfeed, pig-
weed, pokeweed, poppy-seed, proceed,
reed, screed, seaweed, seed, sneeze-
weed, speed, steed, stinkweed, succeed,
title-deed, tobacco-weed, treed, tweed,
weak-kneed, weed, whispering-reed

Darning needle, pine needle, needle, **EEDLE**
wheedle   *see*
        EL
        LE

Greedy, needy, reedy, seedy, speedy, **EEDY**
weedy   *see*
        E**

Beef, coral-reef, reef, shereef   **EEF**
        see
        IEF

Cheek, cleek, creek, Greek, hide-   **EEK**
and-seek, leek, meek, next-week, peek,   *see*
reek, seek, sleek, week   EAK*
        IEK
        IQUE

Balance-wheel, cartwheel, chain-   **EEL**
wheel, cogwheel, creel, despot's heel,   *see*
eel, emery wheel, feel, Ferris-wheel,   EAL*
flywheel, genteel, heel, high-heel, Jez-   ILE**
reel, keel, kneel, millwheel, newsreel,   *ed-*IELD
paddle-wheel, peel, potter's wheel,
prayer wheel, reel, shabby-genteel,
spinning-wheel, steel, Virginia reel,
water-wheel, wheel

Beseem, deem, esteem, redeem, seem, self-esteem, teem

EEM
see
EME

Aberdeen, a-tween, baleen, between, bowling green, canteen, careen, Colleen, e'en, eighteen, fellaheen, fifteen, fourteen, go-between, green, Hallowe'en, has-been, keen, lateen, Maureen, might-have-been, nankeen, nineteen, ocean-green, overween, Paris-green, peen, preen, putting green, queen, sateen, screen, sea-green, seen, seventeen, sheen, sixteen, smoke-screen, spleen, thirteen, tureen, 'tween, umpteen, unseen, velveteen, village-green, ween, wintergreen

EEN
see
EAN*
ENE
IEN**
IENE
S-EENS

Greens, smithereens, teens

EENS
see
EEN-S

Asleep, Bo-peep, cheep, chimney-sweep, clean sweep, creep, deep, donjon-keep, keep, knee-deep, oversleep, peep, sheep, skin-deep, sleep, steep, sweep, upkeep, weep, well-sweep, Uriah Heep

EEP
see
EAP

Carpet-sweeper, creeper, deeper, gamekeeper, housekeeper, keeper, lighthouse-keeper, office seeker, peeper, seeker, sky-sleeper, steeper, sweeper

EEPER
see
ER

Auctioneer, beer, buccaneer, cameleer, carabineer, career, chanticleer, charioteer, cheer, compeer, decreer,

EER
see
EIR**

deer, domineer, engineer, fallow-deer, **EER**
freer, gazetteer, ginger-beer, jeer, leer, ERE*
mountaineer, muleteer, musk-deer, IER**
musketeer, mutineer, nearbeer, over- *ed*-EARD**
seer, peer, pioneer, privateer, profiteer,
queer, racketeer, reindeer, rootbeer,
seer, sheer, sight-seer, sneer, spruce
beer, steer, veer, veneer, volunteer

　　Lees, Maccabees, Pyrenees　　　**EES**
　　　　　　　　　　　　　　　　see
　　　　　　　　　　　　　　　　E**-*s*
　　　　　　　　　　　　　　　　EE-*s*
　　　　　　　　　　　　　　　　ES*

　　Cheese, creese, Edam cheese, head-　**EESE***
cheese, Swiss cheese　　　　　　　　　*see*
　　　　　　　　　　　　　　　　EASE*
　　　　　　　　　　　　　　　　EEZE

　　Geese　　　　　　　　　　　　**EESE****
　　　　　　　　　　　　　　　　see
　　　　　　　　　　　　　　　　EASE**
　　　　　　　　　　　　　　　　EECE
　　　　　　　　　　　　　　　　ESE
　　　　　　　　　　　　　　　　IS***

　　Baksheesh, hasheesh　　　　　　**EESH**
　　　　　　　　　　　　　　　　see
　　　　　　　　　　　　　　　　EASH

　　Afreet, balance-sheet, beet, bitter-　**EET**
sweet, Blackfeet, crow's-feet, discreet,　*see*
feet, fleet, greet, indiscreet, meadow-　EIPT
sweet, meet, parakeet, peet, proof-　EIT*
sheet, sheet, skeet, sleet, stern-sheet,　ETE*
stocking-feet, street, sweet, tweet,
Wall Street, winding-sheet

Dragon's teeth, false teeth, teeth — **EETH**
see
EATH*

Seethe, teethe — **EETHE**
see
EATHE

Beeve, peeve, reeve, sleeve — **EEVE**
see
EIVE

Breeze, faintest-breeze, freeze, land-breeze, sneeze, squeeze, sweetscented-breeze, wheeze — **EEZE**
see
EASE*
EIZE
IEZE
IE*-*s*

Chef, clef — **EF**
see
EAF

Bereft, cleft, deft, heft, left, reft, theft, weft — **EFT**
see

Defy, liquefy, putrefy, stupefy — **EFY**
see
I*

Bandy-leg, beg, cribbage-peg, dreg, keg, leg, mumbletypeg, nutmeg, peg — **EG**
see
AGUE*
EGG

Illegal, legal, regal, vice-regal — **EGAL**
see
AL

Aggravate, congregate, delegate, legate, relegate, segregate

EGATE
see
ATE

Allege, college, cortège, privilege, sacrilege

EGE
see
EDGE
IDGE

China-egg, egg, nest-egg, ostrich-egg, yegg

EGG
see
EG

Legion, region

EGION
see
ION

Apothegm, phlegm

EGM
see
EM

Abednego, alter ego, ego, forego

EGO
see
O*

Daddylonglegs, dregs, sea-legs

EGS
see
EG-*s*

Eh, El Gezireh, Gizeh, Nineveh, Tecumseh

EH
see
A*

Lorelei

EI*
see
I*

Lei, rei **EI****
see
AY

Cassiopeia, hygeia, pharmacopæia **EIA**
see
IA

Nereid, Perseid **EID**
see
ID

Beige **EIGE**
see
EGE

Inveigh, neigh, outweigh, Raleigh, **EIGH**
sleigh, weigh *see*
EY*
ed-AID*

Eight, feather weight, freight, heavy- **EIGHT***
weight, hundred-weight, paperweight, *see*
pennyweight, weight ATE

Height, mountain-height, sleight **EIGHT****
see
IGHT

Deign, feign, foreign, reign, sover- **EIGN**
eign *see*
AIN

Nonpareil, unveil, veil **EIL***
see
AIL
ALE

Ceil   **EIL****
                                        see
                                        EEL

Hussein, mullein, protein, Shin Fein,   **EIN***
skein, vein   *see*
                                        AIN

Frankenstein, Holstein, Rubenstein,   **EIN****
stein   *see*
                                        INE

Seine, vicereine   **EINE**
                                        see
                                        AIN

Being, fleeing, freeing, seeing   **EING**
                                        see
                                        ING

Feint   **EINT**
                                        see
                                        AINT

Receipt   **EIPT**
                                        see
                                        EAT*

Heir, their   **EIR***
                                        see
                                        ERE**

Weir   **EIR****
                                        see
                                        EAR

Weird	**EIRD**
	see
	EARD**
	EAR-*ed*
Edelweiss, gneiss	**EISS**
	see
	ICE*
Conceit, deceit	**EIT***
	see
	ETE
Albeit, counterfeit, forfeit	**EIT****
	see
	IT
Deity, homogeneity, ipseity, seity, spontaneity	**EITY**
	see
	E**
	ITY
Apperceive, conceive, deceive, perceive, preconceive, receive	**EIVE**
	see
	IEVE*
Seize	**EIZE**
	see
	EEZE
	ES*
Baalbek, Melchizedek, Sebek, topek, trek, Vathek	**EK**
	see
	ECK
Eke	**EKE**
	see
	EEK

Angel, apparel, archangel, asphodel, **EL**
barrel, befel, Beth-el, brothel, calomel,   *see*
cancel, cantonflannel, chancel, channel,   ABEL
charnel, chattel, chisel, citadel, compel,   AEL
corbel, counsel, cudgel, damozel, dam-   AMEL
sel, dispel, easel, El, evangel, excel,   AVEL
expel, fardel, flannel, flour-barrel, gam-   ELL
brel, gimel, hazel, hostel, hydromel,   ENNEL
impel, infidel, Israfel, jewel, Jezebel,   EREL
kernel, kummel, lapel, laurel, libel,   ERYL
lintel, marvel, minstrel, missel, model,   EVEL
mongrel, morsel, Mount Carmel, mus-   IEL
catel, mussel, nickel, Noel, panel,   IVEL
parallel, parcel, pastel, personnel, pet-   OVEL
rel, pimpernel, pommel, pretzel, propel,   OWEL
quarrel, rebel, remodel, repel, rondel,   UEL
satchel, scalpel, scoundrel, scrannel,   UNNEL
sentinel, shekel, shrapnel, sorrel, span-   USEL
drel, stormy petrel, tael, tassel, tim-   YL
brel, tinsel, trammel, vessel, wastrel,   *ed*-ELD
weasel, Whitechapel, witch-hazel,   *y*-E**
woodsorrel, yodel, yokel   ELY

Addle, air-castle, amble, ample, **LE**
ankle, Aristotle, astraddle, axle, baffle,   *see*
bamboozle, battle, beagle, beetle,   ABBLE
boodle, bridle, bubble, bugle, bundle,   ABLE
bungle, burble, burgle, carbuncle,   ACKLE
castle, cat's-cradle, cattle, chortle,   ACLE
church-steeple, clientele, cockle, cod-   ADDLE
dle, Constantinople, couple, cradle,   AMBLE
crossword-puzzle, crumple, cuttle,   AMPLE
dawdle, dazzle, decuple, dingle, dis-   ANDLE
mantle, double, embezzle, empurple,   ANGLE
entitle, fettle, foible, fondle, foozle,   APPLE
forecastle, frazzle, gargle, gentle, gur-   ARBLE
gle, haggle, idle, inveigle, jungle,   ATTLE

kindle, kirtle, ladle, mantle, maple, meddle, mollycoddle, monocle, mottle, muffle, muscle, myrtle, new-fangle, noodle, nozzle, octuple, ogle, oodle, pebble, peddle, peduncle, people, piffle, pinochle, poodle, purple, quadruple, quintuple, raffle, rankle, razzle-dazzle, reshuffle, Roman candle, rubble, schnozzle, scuffle, septuple, shuffle, shuttle, snaffle, snuffle, socle, spangle, sparkle, stag-beetle, staple, startle, stubble, subtle, supple, temple, tickle, tinkle, tipple, title, toddle, tousle, treacle, treadle, treble, trouble, truffle, trundle, tussle, tweedle, uncle, un-ruffle, waffle, waggle

LE

EABLE
EAGLE
ECKLE
EEDLE
ELLE
EMBLE
ESTLE
ETTLE
IABLE
IBBLE
IBLE
ICKLE
ICLE
IDDLE
IDLE
IFLE
IGGLE
IMBLE
IMPLE
INDLE
INGLE
INKLE
IPLE
IPPLE
IRCLE
ISTLE
ITTLE
IZZLE
OBBLE
OBLE
OGGLE
OPLE
OSTLE
UBLE
UCKLE
UDDLE

LE
UGGLE
UMBLE
URDLE
URTLE
USTLE
UZZLE
YCLE

Belate, elate, prelate, relate   **ELATE**
see
ATE

Belch, squelch   **ELCH**
see

Beheld, eld, geld, held, meld, upheld, **ELD**
weld, withheld   *see*
EL-*ed*

Veldt   **ELDT**
see
ELT

Careless, defenceless, gestureless, **ELESS**
guileless, homeless, lifeless, measure-   *see*
less, nevertheless, noiseless, priceless,   ES**
purposeless, senseless, shameless, shoe-   ESCE
less, spaceless, tasteless, timeless, use-   ESS
less, vagueless, valueless, verdureless,
wireless

Bandelet, bracelet, corselet, ocelet, **ELET**
omelet, wavelet   *see*
ET

Delf, elf, herself, himself, itself, my-   **ELF**
self, oneself, pantry-shelf, pelf, self,   *see*
shelf, thing-in-itself, thyself, yourself

Twelfth

ELFTH
see

Elia, Cordelia, lobelia, Ophelia, parahelia

ELIA
see
IA

Goblin, javelin, zeppelin

ELIN
see
IN

Elk

ELK
see

Alarum-bell, ankle-bell, artesian well, befell, bell, blue-bell, bombshell, buy-and-sell, cell, churchbell, cockle-shell, convent bell, cowbell, curfewbell, dell, diving-bell, doorbell, dumb-bell, dwell, eggshell, ell, fare-thee-well, fare-well, fell, foretell, ground swell, hare-bell, heather-bell, hell, jell, knell, mis-spell, nutshell, Oliver Cromwell, over-sell, pell-mell, quell, resell, retell, school-bell, seashell, sell, shell, sleigh-bell, smell, spell, swell, tell, tortoise-shell, vesper-bell, well, whitewashed-cell, William Tell, yell

ELL
see
EL
ELLE

Capella, citronella, fenestrella, Isa-bella, nigella, pimpinella, predella, prunella, stella, tarantella, umbrella, villanella

ELLA
see
A**

Bagatelle, coutelle, damozelle, fon-tanelle, Gabrielle, gazelle, immortelle, La Pucelle, mademoiselle, Moselle, nacelle, spirituelle, villanelle

ELLE
see
ELL

Dardanelles	**ELLES** *see* ELL-*S*
Bookseller, screw propeller, speller, story-teller, teller	**ELLER** *see* ER
Cello, hello, martello, Othello, punchinello, violoncello	**ELLO** *see* O*
Bed-fellow, fellow. Longfellow, mellow, yellow	**ELLOW** *see* O* OW*
Elm, helm, overwhelm, slippery-elm, St. Anselm, whelm	**ELM** *see* EALM
Felon, Fenelon, melon, watermelon	**ELON** *see* ON
Help, kelp, whelp, yelp	**ELP** *see*
Hostelry, jewelry, revelry	**ELRY** *see* E**
Else	**ELSE** *see*
Belt, delt, dwelt, felt, heartfelt, knelt, lifebelt, melt, pelt, smelt, spelt, welt	**ELT** *see* EALT

Svelte **ELTE**
see
ELT

Helter-skelter, shelter, swelter, welter **ELTER**
see
ER

Delve, helve, shelve, twelve **ELVE**
see
S-ELVES

Elves, ourselves, selves, shelves, **ELVES**
themselves, yourselves *see*
ELVE-*s*

Antiquely, blithely, chastely, coarse- **ELY**
ly, comely, completely, concretely, *see*
contumely, conversely, crudely, di- ATELY
vinely, entirely, exquisitely, freely, E**
homely, inanely, infinitely, intuitively, EL-*y*
lately, leisurely, lithely, loosely, lovely,
merely, naïvely, namely, obliquely,
obtrusively, precisely, princely, pro-
fusely, purely, rarely, relatively, rely,
safely, savagely, scarcely, shapely,
sincerely, solely, sorely, strangely, sub-
limely, supremely, surely, tamely,
tensely, timely, unlovely, untimely,
vaguely, wifely

Ad valorem, anadem, anthem, be- **EM**
gem, cave canem, diadem, emblem, *see*
gem, harem, hem, ibidem, idem, item, AM
Jerusalem, Moslem, poem, postmor- ASM
tem, problem, proem, pro tem, sachem, EGM
Shem, solar system, stem, stratagem, EMN
system, tandem, them, theorem, totem, IAM
Zemzem IEM

Alma Tadema, anathema, cinema, eczema, ulema

EMA
see
A*

December, dismember, ember, member, November, remember, September

EMBER
see
ER

Assemble, dissemble, reassemble, resemble, tremble, tout ensemble

EMBLE
see
EL
LE

Bireme, blaspheme, Carême, extreme, La Bohème, quinquereme, scheme, supreme, theme, trireme

EME
see
EAM
IME**

Accoutrement, achievement, acquirement, amusement, assuagement, at-one-ment, attunement, bereavement, casement, cement, cerement, chastisement, clement, denouement, displacement, divulgement, element, embezzlement, encouragement, enlargement, escapement, excitement, impalement, implement, improvement, inclement, infringement, management, measurement, movement, pavement, postponement, pronouncement, refinement, reimbursement, reinforcement, requirement, retirement, settlement, sub-basement, supplement, tenement, vehement

EMENT
see
ENT

Bessemer, blasphemer, schemer

EMER
see
ER

Condemn, contemn, solemn   **EMN**
see
EM

Demon, lemon   **EMON**
see
ON

Hemp   **EMP**
see

Attempt, contempt, exempt, pre-   **EMPT**
empt, tempt, unkempt   see

Academy, alchemy, blasphemy,   **EMY**
Domremy, enemy, Ptolemy   see
E**

Aden, ashen, Aten, auf wiedersehen,   **EN**
barren, batten, begotten, beholden,   see
bitten, boughten, brazen, brethren,   AMEN
brighten, burden, chicken, chosen,   AKEN
cozen, crestfallen, dampen, darken,   ASTE-*n*
delicatessen, den, dew-beladen, Dolly   AVEN
Varden, dolmen, down-trodden, dozen,   EAN**
Dryden, Eden, embolden, enliven,   EMEN
fatten, fen, flaxen, forbidden, forgot-   ENNE
ten, foughten, frighten, frozen, Galen,   EVEN
garden, gentlemen, glen, glisten, glu-   IEN*
ten, goose-pen, Goshen, gotten, guinea-   IMEN
hen, harden, hasten, heathen, heavy-   IZEN
laden, hen, herb-garden, hidden, hoy-   OGEN
den, Hymen, hyphen, idle-pen, ill-   OKE-*n*
gotten, ken, kindergarten, kinsmen,   OKEN
kitchen, kitten, laden, lengthen, lenten,   OMEN
lessen, lichen, lighten, liken, linden,   OVEN
linen, listen, madden, mad-men, Mag-   UMEN

dalen, maiden, marshy-fen, men, men-haden, mitten, mizzen, moisten, molten, mullen, Munchausen, new-fallen, oaken, oaten, often, olden, open, Origen, overladen, paten, pen, pig-pen, pollen, poverty-stricken, quicken, quill-pen, redden, re-open, risen, roof-garden, rotten, sadden, Saracen, schoolmen, silken, siren, smarten, soften, storm-driven, strength-en, stricken, sudden, sullen, swollen, table-linen, ten, terror-stricken, then, thicken, tungsten, unforsaken, un-loosen, untrodden, vestry-men, vixen, warden, warren, waxen, weather-beat-en, wen, when, whiten, wooden, worm-eaten, wren, written, Yemen, yen

EN
YGEN
ly-E**
s-ENS

Arena, Athena, duena, hyena, no-vena, phenomena, philopena, Porsena, prolegomena, subpœna, verbena

ENA
see
A**

Grenade, hand-grenade, promenade, serenade

ENADE
see
ADE*

Arsenal, Juvenal, phenomenal, venal

ENAL
see
AL

Centenary, mercenary, septenary

ENARY
see
ARY

Hyphenate, oxygenate, rejuvenate, senate

ENATE
see
ATE

Absence, abstinence, acquiescence, adolescence, appetence, back fence, belligerence, cadence, circumference, coincidence, commence, condolence, conference, confidence, continence, corpulence, correspondence, credence, decadence, defence, difference, diffidence, diligence, divergence, divulgence, effulgence, eminence, essence, evidence, excellence, excrescence, fence, Florence, florescence, fraudulence, hence, immanence, impertinence, impotence, impudence, inadvertence, incandescence, incidence, incompetence, inconsequence, independence, indigence, indolence, indulgence, inference, influence, innocence, insistence, intelligence, interference, intumescence, iridescence, irreverence, jurisprudence, lapidescence, magnificence, negligence, non-occurrence, occurrence, offence, omnipotence, omnipresence, opulence, par-excellence, pence, penitence, persistence, Peter-pence, petrescence, phosphorescence, pre-eminence, preference, presence, prevalence, prominence, Provence, providence, prudence, quintessence, recurrence, redolence, reference, reminiscence, renascence, residence, resplendence, resurgence, reticence, reverence, self-defence, senescence, silence, sixpence, snake fence, subsistence, sufference, thence, tower-of-silence, transference, turbulence, violence, virulence, whence

ENCE
see
ANCE
ANT*-s
ENSE
ENT-s
IENCE
UENCE

Bench, blench, clench, drench, French, intrench, monkey-wrench,

ENCH
see

oak-bench, quench, retrench, stench, **ENCH**
stone-bench, trench, unclench, wench,
workbench, wrench

Agency, appetency, clemency, co- **ENCY**
gency, cognency, competency, con- *see*
sistency, constituency, contingency, E**
currency, decency, deficiency, delin-
quency, despondency, efficiency,
emergency, exigency, fervency, fre-
quency, impotency, inadvertency, in-
cipiency, inclemency, inconsistency,
incumbency, independency, indigency,
infrequency, leniency, nascency, pat-
ency, permanency, persistency, perti-
nency, potency, pungency, regency,
tendency, transparency

Amend, append, ascend, attend, **END**
befriend, bend, blend, candle-end, *see*
commend, comprehend, condescend, UEND
contend, defend, depend, descend, dis- *ed*-ED
tend, dividend, emend, end, expend, *ly*-E**
extend, fend, forfend, friend, Godsend,
impend, intend, interblend, legend,
lend, mend, offend, pend, perpend,
portend, pretend, recommend, rend,
reprehend, reverend, send, spend,
superintend, suspend, tail-end, tend,
transcend, trend, unbend, vend, vili-
pend, wend, Zend

Addenda, agenda, hacienda **ENDA**
see
A**

Bartender, defender, double-ender, **ENDER**
engender, expender, fender, gender, *see*
lavender, legal-tender, mender, offend- ER

er, pretender, provender, sea-lavender, **ENDER**
spender, surrender, suspender, tender

Crescendo, diminuendo, innuendo **ENDO**
see
O*

Calends, odds-and-ends **ENDS**
see
END-*s*

Acetylene, contravene, convene, **ENE**
damascene, epicene, ethylene, gan- *see*
grene, hygiene, intervene, kerosene, EEN
Magdalene, Nazarene, Nicene, ob- IEN**
scene, pliocene, pyrene, scene, serene, INE**
supervene

Eye-opener, gardener, listener, scriv- **ENER**
ener *see*
ER

Genet, Plantagenet, tenet **ENET**
see
ET

Ginseng **ENG**
see
ING

Avenge, challenge, lozenge, revenge, **ENGE**
scavenge, Stonehenge *see*

Length, strength, wave-length, **ENGTH**
whole-length *see*

Armenia, gardenia, Iphigenia, millenia, neomania

ENIA
see
IA

Arsenic, eugenic, hygienic, Saracenic, scenic

ENIC
see
IC

Amenity, serenity

ENITY
see
ITY

Evenly, heavenly, keenly, openly, queenly, slovenly, suddenly

ENLY
see
EN-*ly*

Antenna, Avicenna, gehenna, henna, Porsenna, senna, Sienna, Vienna

ENNA
see
ENA

Cayenne, comedienne, Parisienne, tragedienne

ENNE
see
EN

Fennel, kennel

ENNEL
see
EL

Catch-penny, fenny, fippenny, ha'-penny, penny, spinning-jenny

ENNY
see
E**

Amiens, Athens, Camoëns, Dickens, dozens, homo sapiens, lens, nolens volens, wooded glens

ENS
see
EN-*s*

Condense, dense, dispense, expense, frankincense, horse sense, immense, incense, intense, license, nonsense, offense, pretense, recompense, sense, suspense, tense

ENSE
see
ENCE
ENT-*s*

Censer, condenser, denser

ENSER
see
ER

Abhorrent, accent, acknowledgment, adjournment, adolescent, adornment, advent, albescent, alignment, amendment, annulment, antecedent, apartment, arborescent, ardent, argent, arpent, ascent, astonishment, astringent, bent, bewilderment, bombardment, brazen serpent, cent, cerement, circumfluent, circumvent, cogent, comment, competent, consent, consignment, consistent, content, convergent, co-respondent, correspondent, crescent, current, decadent, descent, deterrent, diligent, disalignment, discernment, discontent, dissent, divergent, embankment, emulgent, encampment, endearment, enjoyment, enrollment, enthralment, environment, equipment, escarpment, establishment, evanescent, event, excellent, existent, extent, ferment, fervent, foment, fragment, fulfilment, gent, Ghent, horrent, illcontent, impellent, impotent, inadvertent, incandescent, incoherent, incompetent, inconsistent, incumbent, indent, independent, indictment, indigent, innocent, insolvent, insurgent,

ENT
see
ACENT
AGENT
ALENT
AMENT
ECENT
EMENT
ERENT
ICENT
IDENT
IENT
IMENT
INENT
OLENT
ONENT
UENT
ULENT
ULGENT
UMENT
ly-ENTLY
s-ENCE

ENT

intelligent, intent, interlucent, intermittent, intumescent, invent, iridescent, judgment, lambent, latent, latescent, lent, lucent, magnificent, maladjustment, malcontent, nascent, nonexistent, non-payment, oddment, ointment, omnipotent, omnipresent, opalescent, parchment, parent, patent, payment, pendent, penitent, pent, percent, permanent, persistent, phosphorescent, pigment, potent, precedent, present, prevent, prudent, pschent, pungent, punishment, putrescent, quiescent, ravishment, recent, red cent, redolent, refreshment, refringent, refulgent, regent, relent, relucent, reminiscent, rent, repellent, repent, resent, resentment, resplendent, respondent, resurgent, retrenchment, rodent, scent, segment, senescent, sent, serpent, shipment, silent, solvent, spent, stringent, student, superincumbent, superintendent, talent, tangent, tent, torment, torrent, transcendent, translucent, transparent, treatment, tumescent, Turkish crescent, unbent, under-current, underwent, unravelment, urgent, vent, vestment, vice-regent, well-content, went

ENTAL
see
AL

Accidental, continental, detrimental, elemental, experimental, fundamental, incidental, instrumental, mental, monumental, occidental, Oriental, ornamental, parental, regimental, rental, sacramental, temperamental, transcontinental

Carpenter, center, enter, re-enter, renter, self-center

ENTER
see
ER

Eleventh, n-th, seventh, tenth

ENTH
see

Amentia, dementia

ENTIA
see
IA

Eloquently, eminently, frequently, gently, innocently, intently, patiently, penitently, permanently, presently, prominently, prudently

ENTLY
see
E**
ENT-*ly*

Memento, pimento

ENTO
see
O*

Entry, gentry, sentry

ENTRY
see
E**

Plenty, twenty, seventy

ENTY
see
E**

Borneo, Camdeo, cameo, Galileo, Laus Deo, Leo, Montevideo, nil sine Deo, rodeo, Romeo, vireo

EO
see
O*

Sheol

EOL
see
OL

Anacreon, bludgeon, burgeon, cameleon, clay pigeon, curmudgeon, dudgeon, dungeon, eon, escutcheon, gal-

EON
see
ON

leon, Gideon, luncheon, melodeon, **EON**
Napoleon, neon, Odeon, pantheon,
peon, pigeon, stoolpigeon, sturgeon,
surgeon, truncheon, widgeon

Alliaceous, aqueous, argillaceous, **EOUS**
beauteous, cinereous, consanguineous, *see*
contemporaneous, courageous, courte-   AMUS
ous, erroneous, fabaceous, ferreous,   EUS*
gallinaceous, gaseous, gorgeous, hetero- IOUS
geneous, hideous, homogeneous, igne-   OUS
ous, instantaneous, ligneous, malva-   UOUS
ceous, miscellaneous, osseous, out-   US
rageous, papaveraceous, piteous, right- *ly*-OUSLY
eous, saponaceous, simultaneous, spon-
taneous, subaqueous, subterraneous,
succedaneous, terraqueous, vitreous

Amenhotep, doorstep, footstep, **EP**
goose step, instep, lockstep, mint-   *see*
julep, misstep, overstep, pep, prep,   S-EPS
quick step, rep, side-step, step, two-
step

Crêpe   **EPE**
                                       see
                                       APE

Steppe   **EPPE**
                                       see
                                       EP

Biceps, corbiesteps, forceps   **EPS**
                                       see
                                       EP-S

Accept, adept, concept, crept, except, inept, intercept, kept, percept, precept, slept, stept, swept, transept, unkept, well-kept, wept, wind-swept, yclept

EPT
see

Pepys

EPYS
see
EEP-*s*

Cheque

EQUE
see
ECK

Adder, adorer, alter, amber, angel water, antler, archer, artificer, assayer, astrologer, babbler, backwater, badger, Baedeker, banker, banner, banter, barber, bather, bellwether, berserker, billposter, blather, blue-singer, boiler, bolster, boner, booster, bootlegger, bouncer, breakwater, broiler, bungstarter, bunker, butler, buyer, buzzer, caliber, camper, Cancer, canter, Casper, chamber, chandler, chapter, charger, Chaucer, checker, chiseler, choler, chooser, chorister, cipher, clabber, clapper, clinker, cloister, cobbler, conceiver, condoler, confer, conger, consumer, costumer, cowcatcher, coworker, creeper, cricketer, crosser, cruiser, dabster, dagger, dapper, daughter, decanter, deceiver, decipher, differ, dissenter, dodder, draper, drawer, dredger, dresser, dulcimer, duller, duster, eager, Easter, either, elder, embroider, encounter, err,

ER
see
ACKER
ACRE
ADER
AFTER
AGER
AILER
AITER
AKER
AMER
AMPER
ANDER
ANGER
APER
APPER
ARER
ARTER
ARTYR
ASHER
ASTER
ATER
ATRE

Esther, etcher, ether, exploiter, falter,
farmer, farther, faster, father, feeler,
fibber, fiber, filter, fire-eater, flivver,
fodder, follower, forefather, forefinger,
forerunner, former, foster, four poster,
frankfurter, free-thinker, free trader,
fuller, further, gambler, gangster, gar-
ner, gather, geyser, Gheber, gibber,
golfer, grandfather, greater, green-
grocer, grosser, gutter, halter, hammer,
hanger, hanker, harder, hawker, haw-
ser, headquarter, heather, heckler,
heifer, helicopter, her, hill-climber,
holster, hostler, huckster, hunger, idler,
importer, improper, infer, inter, jabber,
Jacob's ladder, jammer, jasper, jaw-
breaker, jaywalker, juggler, kilter,
kosher, laborer, ladder, lamplighter,
lancer, larder, larger, lather, laughter,
launder, lawyer, leader, ledger, leper,
lesser, lifer, lighter, linen duster, lob-
ster, loiter, longer, loud speaker,
lounger, Luther, madder, man-eater,
maneuver, manner, manslaughter,
marker, masher, meager, merger,
Mesmer, milder, mineral water, minister, minster, miter, monger, monster,
mossbunker, mouser, muffler, mummer, murder, necromancer, ne'er,
neither, neuter, news-monger, nowhither, officer, oldster, onlooker,
ostler, outer, oyster, pacer; panther,
partner, passenger, paternoster, pau-
per, peddler, pepper, performer, pew-
ter, pilfer, pitcher, planter, platter,
player, plumber, plunder, plunger,
poacher, Poet's Corner, pointer, porker,

ER

ATTER
ATYR
AUR
AVER
AYER
EATHER
EEPER
ELLER
ELTER
EMBER
EMER
ENDER
ENER
ENSER
ENTER
EPHYR
ERER
ERR
ESTER
ETER
ETHER
ETRE
ETTER
EUR
EVER
EWER
IAR
IBRE
ICKER
IDER
IDITY
IER
IFER
IGGER
ILDER
ILER

potato-masher, pouter, preacher, pre-
fer, presbyter, primer, producer,
prompter, proof-reader, propeller,
proper, prosper, psalter, Ptolemy Soter,
pucker, punster, purser, quarter, quicksilver, quitter, racer, rather, rath-
skeller, rattler, reconnoiter, redeemer,
red pepper, reefer, refer, reflector,
reformer, rejoiner, respecter, rhymster,
ringleader, roadster, rooster, rope-
ladder, rose water, roster, rougher,
saber, saucer, saunter, scalper, scandal-
monger, scavenger, scepter, scooter,
scraper, scribbler, scriber, scupper,
seeker, seersucker, seltzer, Sepher,
sepulcher, Shalmaneser, sharpshooter,
sherry cobbler, shockabsorber, shop-
lifter, shopper, shyer, shyster, silver,
simper, slaughter, sleep-walker, slipper,
smarter, smuggler, snubber, snuffer,
soccer, sock-dologer, soda-water, som-
ber, sooner, sou'wester, spanker, spec-
ter, spinster, sprinkler, stage-whisper,
stagger, Star Chamber, star-gazer,
steamboiler, stenographer, stepladder,
stiffer, stomacher, stopper, stretcher,
stroller, sucker, super, sundowner,
supper, sutler, swagger, swashbuckler,
sweater, sweeter, swindler, talebearer,
tallow-chandler, Tam-o'-Shanter, tank-
er, tauter, teacher, teetotaler, temper,
tempter, tether, thaler, Tiber, timer,
tipster, together, toper, tougher, trader,
transfer, transformer, traveler, trick-
ster, trooper, trotter, tumbler, ulster,
upholster, upper, user, usher, vacuum
cleaner, Vancouver, verger, vesper,

ER

ILLER
IMBER
IMMER
INDER
INER
INGER
INKER
INNER
INTER
IPER
IPPER
IR
IRE
ISER
ISHER
ISTER
ITER
ITTER
IVER
IZER
OBBER
OBER
OCKER
OCRE
OER
OFFER
OGRE
OKER
OLDER
OLVER
OMBER
OMER
ONDER
ONER
OOMER
OONER

Vichy water, vintner, voucher, Wagner, waiter, warbler, warder, water, waver, way-farer, Webster, well-wisher, whaler, whimper, whisker, whisper, whiter, whither, wilder, wind-jammer, wine-bibber, wither, woodpecker, wrapper, wrecker, youngster

ER
OPHER
OPPER
ORDER
ORTER
OTHER
OULDER
OUNDER
OUR
OVER
OW*-*er*
OWDER
OWER
UBBER
UCRE
UDDER
UER
UIRE
UMBER
UMNER
UNDER
UR
URER
USTER
UTTER
UVRE
ing-ING
ly-E**

Camera, chimera, cholera, diptera, era, genera, Hera, lepidoptera, opera, Pera, Riviera, Sisera

ERA
see
A**

Conquerable, considerable, discoverable, imponderable, insuperable, intolerable, invulnerable, miserable, prefer-

ERABLE
see
ABLE

able, tolerable, unconquerable, venerable, vulnerable

ERABLE

Amperage, average, beverage, brokerage, leverage, peerage, steerage

ERAGE
see
AGE*

Collateral, consul-general, ephemeral, equilateral, fal-de-ral, federal, feral, funeral, general, lateral, liberal, literal, mackeral, mineral, numeral, quadrilateral, several, trilateral

ERAL
see
AL

Lateran, Lutheran, Teheran, veteran

ERAN
see
AN*

Exuberant, intolerant, itinerant, protuberant, tolerant

ERANT
see
ANT*

Adulterate, aerate, berate, commiserate, confederate, conglomerate, considerate, degenerate, desperate, enumerate, exaggerate, exasperate, exhilarate, exonerate, exuberate, federate, generate, illiterate, immoderate, incarcerate, incinerate, inconsiderate, intemperate, inveterate, iterate, lacerate, liberate, literate, macerate, moderate, numerate, obliterate, operate, preponderate, recuperate, refrigerate, reiterate, remunerate, reverberate, temperate, tolerate, transliterate, vituperate, vociferate

ERATE
see
ATE

Acerb, adverb, herb, kerb, potherb, proverb, reverb, Serb, superb, verb

ERB
see
URB

Coerce, commerce, terce, sesterce

ERCE
see
EARSE
ERSE
URSE

Perch

ERCH
see
IRCH

Cowherd, halberd, herd, potsherd, shepherd, swineherd

ERD
see
EARD
IRD
ORD**
URD

Adhere, ampere, Apollo Belvedere, atmosphere, austere, bathysphere, cashmere, cassimere, cohere, Guinevere, hemisphere, here, inhere, insincere, interfere, mere, Paul Revere, persevere, revere, sere, severe, sincere, sphere, stratosphere

ERE*
see
EER
IER

Anywhere, confrere, elsewhere, ere, everywhere, Folies Bergère, gruyère, nowhere, porte-cochère, somewhere, there, where

ERE**
see
AIR
ARE*
IARE
IERE

Were

ERE***
see
IR

Doggerel, mackerel, pickerel **EREL**
see
EL

Adherent, belligerent, coherent, dif- **ERENT**
ferent, incoherent, indifferent, inher- *see*
ent, irreverent, reverent ENT

Interferer, loiterer, philanderer, roy- **ERER**
sterer, sorcerer, wanderer *see*
ER

Entereth, fluttereth, hindereth, ling- **ERETH**
ereth, tendereth *see*
ETH

Serf **ERF**
see
URF

Berg, erg, iceberg, Heidelberg, kilerg, **ERG**
Nuremberg, Venusberg *see*
URG

Absterge, converge, deterge, diverge, **ERGE**
emerge, merge, serge, submerge, verge *see*
IRGE
URGE

Clergy, energy **ERGY**
see
E**

Algeria, bacteria, cafeteria, diph- **ERIA**
theria, Egeria, hysteria, Iberia, Siberia *see*
IA

Aerial, immaterial, imperial, material, serial

ERIAL
see
AL
IAL

Atmospheric, choleric, climacteric, congeneric, esoteric, etheric, exoteric, generic, Homeric, mesmeric, neoteric, tumeric, spheric

ERIC
see
IC

Bijouterie, Conciergerie, eerie, Erie, Jacquerie, Janesserie, lingerie, menagerie, reverie

ERIE
see
IE*

Imperil, peril

ERIL
see
IL

Culverin, Erin, glycerin

ERIN
see
IN

Algerine, glycerine, pelerine, tangerine

ERINE
see
INE**

Bickering, burnt-offering, careering, covering, drink-offering, gathering, glistering, glittering, ingathering, loitering, long suffering, muttering, offering, sin-offering, smoldering, tapering, thank-offering, votive offering, wandering, whispering, wool-gathering, westering

ERING
see
ER-*ing*
ING

Ephemeris, Eris, sui generis

ERIS
see
IS*

Cherish, feverish, gibberish, impov- **ERISH**
erish, pantherish, perish, queerish   *see*
ISH

Demerit, inherit, merit   **ERIT**
see
IT

Asperity, austerity, celerity, dex- **ERITY**
terity, insincerity, posterity, prosper- *see*
ity, severity, sincerity, temerity, verity ITY

Clerk, beserk, hauberk, jerk, perk **ERK**
see
IRK
URK

Merle   **ERLE**
see
EARL

Cleverly, easterly, elderly, formerly, **ERLY**
latterly, meagerly, motherly, northerly, *see*
orderly, overly, properly, quarterly, E**
slenderly, soberly, southerly, tenderly, ER-*ly*
Waverly, westerly

Berm, germ, isotherm, pachyderm, **ERM**
sperm, term, therm   *see*
IRM

Altern, bittern, cavern, cistern, **ERN**
cithern, concern, discern, eastern, ern, *see*
fern, govern, Hohenzollern, intern, EARN
jack-o'lantern, kern, lantern, leathern, ERNE
lectern, magic lantern, misgovern, OURN*
modern, northern, pattern, postern, URN

silvern, slattern, southern, stern, sub-
altern, tavern, tern, tree fern, western,
zithern

ERN

Eternal, external, fraternal, infernal,
internal, maternal, paternal, sempiter-
nal, supernal, vernal

ERNAL
see
AL

Interne, Jules Verne, sauterne

ERNE
see
ERN

Bolero, cavalero, Cicero, hero, Nero,
numero, pampero, Prospero, Rio de
Janeiro, sombrero, Trocadero, zero

ERO
see
O*

Acheron, chaperon, Decameron,
hanger-on, heron, Oberon, Percheron

ERON
see
ON

Adulterous, boisterous, cadaverous,
cantankerous, dangerous, dexterous,
generous, lecherous, numerous, ob-
streperous, oderiferous, onerous, pes-
tiferous, ponderous, preposterous, pros-
perous, slanderous, somniferous, splen-
diferous, thunderous, viperous

EROUS
see
OUS

Excerpt

ERPT
see
URP-*ed*

Err

ERR
see
ER

Croix de guerre, nom de guerre, parterre, pied-à-terre

ERRE
see
AIR
ARE*

Berry, blackberry, blueberry, cherry, cranberry, elderberry, equerry, ferry, gooseberry, loganberry, merry, mulberry, raspberry, sherry, spiceberry, strawberry, Tom-and-Jerry

ERRY
see
ERY

Algiers, divers, headquarters, Ghebers, Seven Sleepers, Sicilian Vespers

ERS
see
ER-*s*

Adverse, asperse, converse, disperse, diverse, Erse, immerse, intersperse, inverse, obverse, perverse, reverse, terse, transverse, traverse, universe, verse

ERSE
see
EARSE
ERCE
URSE
ed-IRST
ORST

Erst

ERST
see
IRST

Advert, alert, assert, avert, concert, contravert, convert, covert, desert, dessert, disconcert, divert, Egbert, exert, expert, extravert, filbert, inert, insert, introvert, invert, malapert, overt, pert, pervert, re-assert, revert, sherbert, vert

ERT
see
IRT
UIRT
URT

Berth

ERTH
see
IRTH

Liberty, poverty, property

ERTY
see
E**

Cerberus, Hesperus

ERUS
see
US

Conserve, deserve, nerve, observe, preserve, reserve, serve, swerve, unnerve, unreserve, verve

ERVE
see
URVE

Adultery, anti-slavery, archery, artery, artillery, bakery, battery, blustery, brewery, bribery, buffoonery, cajolery, celery, cemetery, chancery, chandlery, chicanery, creamery, crockery, cutlery, deanery, debauchery, discovery, distillery, drapery, drudgery, effrontery, embroidery, emery, fakery, feathery, fernery, fiery, finery, fippery, fishery, flattery, flummery, foolery, forgery, frippery, gallery, grapery, greenery, grocery, gunnery, haberdashery, hatchery, hosiery, housewifery, imagery, ironmongery, jewellery, jittery, jugglery, knavery, lamasery, lathery, leathery, lottery, lubbery, machinery, mastery, millinery, misery, mockery, monastery, mummery, mystery, napery, nunnery, nursery, onery, pearl-fishery, peppery, perfumery, periphery, phylactery, pottery, presbytery, powdery, prudery, psaltery, quackery, query, raillery, recovery, refinery, revery, rockery, roguery, rogues gallery, rookery, scenery, self-

ERY
see
E**
ERRY
IVERY
ORY
OWERY
URY

mastery, shivery, showery, shrubbery, **ERY**
skulduggery, slavery, silvery, slippery,
soldiery, sorcery, spidery, surgery,
thievery, thuggery, tomfoolery, tot-
tery, tracery, treachery, trickery,
trumpery, upholstery, venery, very,
waggery, watery, whispering-gallery,
witchery

   Beryl   **ERYL**
                                        see
                                        IL

   Aborigines, Achilles, Albigenses,   **ES***
Anchises, Andes, Antilles, antipodes,   *see*
Apelles, Archimedes, Ares, Aristides,   ADES*
Aristophanes, Artaxerxes, auspices,   ATES**
Averroës, Azores, Bacchantes, Benares,   EASE
bay-leaves, Bes, Bootes, Buenos Ayres,   EES
Celebes, Ceres, Cervantes, Corybantes,   EIZE
crevasses, Damocles, Dark Ages, de-   ESE
grees, Demosthenes, Dives, doges,   IDES*
Dolores, Druses, Empedocles, Epi-
phanes, Erinyes, Euphrates, Ganges,
Graces, Hades, Heracles, Hercules,
Hermes, herpes, Holofernes, lares,
Lemures, Los Angeles, Manes, Me-
phistopheles, Mercedes, Middle Ages,
molasses, Moses, Oannes, oases, omnes,
open spaces, Orestes, penates, Pericles,
Pisces, Praxiteles, Procrustes, Sevres,
similes, Thales, Themistocles, Thersi-
tes, tresses, Ulysses, vortices, Xerxes,
Ximenes

   Ducks-and-drakes, Fates, gules, Guy   **ES****
Fawkes, Holmes, Medes, Naples,   *see*

Rhodes, skittles, small clothes, stars and stripes, steppes, Ten Lost Tribes, Thebes, Wales, wolves

ES**

Yes

ES***
see
ESCE
ESS

Courtesan, diocesan, parmesan

ESAN
see
AN*

Acquiesce, coalesce, convalesce, effervesce, effloresce, evanesce, intumesce, opalesce

ESCE
see
ES***
ESS

Burmese, Cantonese, Chinese, diocese, Japanese, maltese, manganese, obese, Pekinese, Portuguese, Siamese, Singhalese, Sudanese, these, Viennese, Veronese

ESE
see
EAS**
IECE
IEZE
IS***
ISE***

Beset, boneset, reset

ESET
see
ET

Afresh, enmesh, flesh, fresh, grossflesh, horseflesh, mesh, refresh, thresh

ESH
see

Amnesia, anæsthesia, freesia, magnesia, Polynesia, Rhodesia, silesia

ESIA
see
IA

Anamnesis, antithesis, exegesis, Genesis, hypothesis, Lachesis, Nemesis, palingenesis, parenthesis, parthenogenesis, synthesis, telekinesis, thesis

ESIS
see
IS*

Desk, kneeling-desk, office desk

ESK
see
ESQUE

Arabesque, burlesque, grotesque, Moresque, Normanesque, picturesque, romanesque, statuesque

ESQUE
see
ESK

Abbess, abruptness, access, address, agelessness, aggressiveness, aloofness, antiqueness, artfulness, artless, awareness, bashfulness, bitterness, bless, bloodless, bootless, bottomless, boundlessness, brainless, burgess, buttress, calmness, caress, cheerfulness, chess, childishness, childless, closeness, clothespress, cloudless, compress, confess, congress, correctness, countless, cress, cypress, darkness, dauntless, deaconess, diffuseness, digress, dispossess, distress, dress, duchess, dulness, duress, eagerness, earnestness, effortless, egress, empress, enchantress, endless, ess, excess, exhaustless, expertness, express, eye-witness, fathomless, fastness, faultless, fearless, foolishness, footless, forgetfulness, forgiveness, formless, foulness, fruitless, fullness, goddess, godlessness, golden-tress, governess, groundless, guess, hairless, hardness, harness, heiress, helpless, hornless, hostess, huntress, idleness,

ESS
see
ELESS
ES**
ESCE
ESSE
ILESS
INESS
ed-EST

impress, ingress, jazzless, laundress, **ESS**
less, licentiousness, lightness, limitless,
lioness, listless, luckless, matchless,
mattress, meekness, mellowness, mess,
mistress, motionless, mulishness, nak-
edness, nameless, nearness, needless,
negress, ness, nothingness, numberless,
obligingness, obsess, odorless, ogress,
oneness, oppress, overdress, passive-
ness, pathless, peacefulness, peeress,
peerless, perfectness, piggishness, Pilgrim's Progress, poetess, pointless,
possess, powerless, preparedness, pre-
possess, press, priestess, princess, prior-
ess, process, profess, progress, prowess,
pythoness, Queen Bess, quenchless,
questionless, questless, quickness,
quietness, rankness, rashness, rayless,
readdress, recess, reckless, redness,
redress, regardless, regress, repress,
resistless, restless, retrogress, righte-
ousness, rudeness, ruthless, seamless,
seamstress, shadowless, shepherdess,
shiftless, shoreless, shrewdness, shy-
ness, sinless, sleepless, slothfulness,
slyness, sorceress, spaceless, spaceless-
ness, speechless, spotless, stainless,
stewardess, stillness, success, sugarless,
sullenness, sunless, supineness, sup-
press, sweetness, tactless, tenantless,
tenderness, thankless, thickness,
thoughtfulness, thoughtless, thriftless,
thusness, tigress, timeless, timeless-
ness, toothless, traitress, transgress,
treeless, undress, unless, uprightness,
upsidedownness, vagueness, voluptu-
ousness, waitress, wantonness, water-

cress, weakness, weightless, wickedness, wilderness, winepress, witless, witness, worthless, youthfulness

ESS

Finesse, largesse, noblesse

ESSE
see
ESS

Accession, cession, concession, confession, depression, digression, expression, impression, intercession, obsession, precession, procession, profession, progression, recession, regression, repression, retrocession, retrogression, session, succession, suppression, transgression

ESSION
see
ION

Acid test, addrest, alkahest, almagest, arrest, basest, behest, beholdest, bendest, best, bitterest, blendest, blessedest, blest, Budapest, cheapest, chest, chiefest, coarsest, congest, contest, coolest, crest, deprest, describest, despisest, detest, digest, dishonest, dispossest, divest, divinest, drest, driftest, earnest, enterest, Everest, exactest, forest, forlornest, frailest, fullest, genteelest, harvest, honest, horridest, id est, immodest, implorest, infest, inquirest, intensest, interest, invest, jest, keenest, laborest, lest, limberest, longest, manifest, mare's-nest, mayest, middle-west, minutest, modest, molest, nest, obscurest, opprest, palimpsest, pest, possest, prest, protest, purest, quietest, reforest, remotest, rest, returnest, rinderpest, robbest, second-

EST
see
EAST**
ESS-*ed*
IEST*
UEST

best, shreddest, sincerest, slickest, still- **EST**
est, stretchest, suggest, swiftest, temp-
est, test, thirstest, unblest, unmolest,
unrest, urgest, vaguest, vest, west,
widest, wildest, wottest, wrest, zest

Fiesta, podesta, siesta, Vesta, Zend **ESTA**
Avesta   *see*
                                        A**

Festal, pedestal, vestal   **ESTAL**
                                        see
                                        AL

Ester, fester, forester, jester, nor'- **ESTER**
wester, quester, rhymester, semester,   *see*
sequester, yester   ER

Nestle, pestle, trestle, wrestle   **ESTLE**
                                          see
                                        EL
                                          LE

Manifesto, presto   **ESTO**
                                          see
                                          O*

Amnesty, dishonesty, honesty, im- **ESTY**
modesty, lese-majesty, majesty, mod-   *see*
esty, travesty, testy   E**

Cheesy, courtesy, heresy, poesy, **ESY**
prophesy   *see*
                                          E**

Abet, aigret, alphabet, anchoret, **ET**
asset, beget, bet, blanket, bonnet,   *see*
booklet, bouncing-Bet, brevet, Bridget,   ACKET
brisket, brooklet, bucket, budget, buf-   ANET

fet, bullet, cabaret, cadet, calumet, chaplet, circlet, claret, cloudlet, comet, cornet, corset, cosset, couplet, court-poet, covet, cresset, crotchet, curb-market, curvet, cygnet, deep-set, dragnet, dulcet, eaglet, egret, Emerald Tablet, emmet, epithet, facet, faucet, ferret, fish-net, flageolet, flibbertigib-bet, floweret, forget, freshet, fret, frisket, gadget, garnet, garret, gas-jet, gauntlet, get, gibbet, giblet, gimlet, goblet, gorget, gusset, hamlet, hatchet, helmet, hic jacet, hornet, inlet, inset, interpret, jennet, jet, junket, kismet, lancet, landaulet, latchet, leaflet, let, leveret, linnet, magnet, mallet, market, met, millet, minaret, moppet, mullet, musket, net, offset, onset, outlet, owlet, pallet, pamphlet, panne velvet, para-pet, pellet, pet, plummet, poet, poke bonnet, posset, privet, prophet, pullet, puppet, quartet, quintet, quodlibet, ratchet, regret, reset, ret, ricochet, ringlet, rivet, russet, scarlet, secret, set, sextet, sherbet, signet, singlet, sonnet, spinet, stet, stockinet, stockmarket, streamlet, sub-let, sunbonnet, sunset, tablet, tabouret, target, tea-set, Tebet, Thibet, thickset, tippet, toilet, To Let, Tophet, trinket, troutlet, turret, ultra-violet, upset, valet, varlet, velvet, videlicet, violet, wallet, wet, whet, wristlet, yet

ET
ASKET
EAT***
EBT
ELET
ENET
ESET
ETTE
ICKET
IDGET
IET
INET
IVET
OCKET
OMET
ONET
OSET
UET*
UGGET
ULET
UMPET
ed-ED

Centripetal, decretal, gun-metal, metal, petal

ETAL
see
AL

Etch, fetch, homestretch, ketch, outstretch, sketch, stretch, vetch, wretch

ETCH
see

Athlete, compete, complete, concrete, Crete, delete, deplete, effete, esthete, incomplete, mete, obsolete, Paraclete, replete, secrete

ETE*
see
EAT*
EET
UITE*

Tête à tête, fête, machete

ETE**
see
ATE

Altimeter, anemometer, barometer, cyclometer, Demeter, deter, diameter, gas-meter, heliometer, hydrometer, kilometer, meter, orometer, pedometer, perimeter, peter, pyrometer, saltpeter, speedometer, thermometer, trumpeter, variometer

ETER
see
ER

Abideth, affordeth, alloweth, Ashtoreth, beginneth, bestoweth, breaketh, chanceth, changeth, compriseth, dwelleth, Elizabeth, encompasseth, fleeth, flieth, gaveth, guideth, howleth, keepeth, lodgeth, loveth, Macbeth, maketh, Nazareth, observeth, seeth, Seth, shibboleth, sleepeth, slideth, taketh, useth, wakeneth, waneth, weepeth

ETH
see
AITH**
EATH**
ERETH
ILETH

Bell-wether, nether, tether, together, wether, whether

ETHER
see
EATHER
ER

Æsthetic, apathetic, arithmetic, ascetic, athletic, cosmetic, emetic, energetic, frenetic, genetic, geodetic, hermetic, homiletic, magnetic, noetic, onomatopoetic, parenthetic, pathetic, peripatetic, phonetic, phrenetic, poetic, polysynthetic, prophetic, sympathetic, synthetic

ETIC
see
IC

Leto, magneto, veto

ETO
see
O*

Breton, Eton, phaeton, simpleton, skeleton

ETON
see
ON

Kilometre, metre, saltpetre

ETRE
see
ETER

Chronometry, coquetry, geometry, marquetry, musketry, parquetry, poetry, psychometry, symmetry, trigonometry

ETRY
see
E**

Aigrette, anisette, barette, blanquette, briquette, brochette, brunette, chemisette, cigarette, collarette, coquette, corvette, cravenette, croquette, curette, dinette, epaulette, etiquette, flannelette, fourchette, gazette, grisette, historiette, kitchenette, Lafayette, layette, leatherette, lorgnette, lunette, maisonnette, Marie Antoinette, midinette, mignonette, moquette,

ETTE
see
ET

novelette, oubliette, palette, parquette, **ETTE**
pipette, planchette, poussette, quar-
tette, quintette, rosette, roulette, satin-
ette, serviette, silhouette, soubrette,
statuette, suffragette, toilette, vedette,
vignette, vinaigrette, voiturette, wag-
onette

Begetter, better, dead letter, fetter, **ETTER**
getter, letter, red-letter, Roman letter, *see*
setter, typesetter, uncial letter, un- ER
fetter, wetter, whetter

Confetti, Rossetti, spaghetti **ETTI**
see
I**

Fettle, kettle, mettle, nettle, settle, **ETTLE**
tea-kettle *see*
EL
.LE

Allegretto, amoretto, falsetto, **ETTO**
ghetto, libretto, palmetto, Rigoletto, *see*
stiletto, terzetto, Tintoretto O*

Betty, jetty, petty, pretty **ETTY**
see
E**

Crotchety, fidgety, nicety, ninety, **ETY**
pernickety, rackety, rickety, safety, *see*
subtlety, surety, velvety E**

Epictetus, impetus, quietus **ETUS**
see
US

Feud **EUD**
see
UDE

Pseudo **EUDO**
see
O*

Athenaeum, Colosseum, Herculane- **EUM**
um, linoleum, lyceum, mausoleum, *see*
museum, odeum, petroleum, rheum, IUM
Te Deum OM

Amateur, bonheur, chauffeur, coif- **EUR**
feur, connoisseur, enterpreneur, fleur, *see*
grandeur, liqueur, masseur, monsieur, IR
raconteur, seigneur, sœur, voyageur OUR**
UR

Alpheus, Asmodeus, Briareus, cadu- **EUS**
ceus, coleus, hic liber est meus, Mor- *see*
pheus, nucleus, Orpheus, Peleus, Per- UCE
seus, Prometheus, Proteus, scarabæus, US
Smintheus, Theseus, Zeus

Berceuse, Betelgeuse, chartreuse, **EUSE**
danseuse, masseuse *see*
ERS
URS

Sleuth **EUTH**
see
UTH

Kislev **EV**
see

Coeval, medieval, primeval

EVAL
see
AL

Eve, Midsummer eve

EVE
see
EAVE
IEVE

Bevel, dishevel, level, revel, sea-level, spirit-level

EVEL
see
EL

Eleven, even, seven

EVEN
see
EN

Cantilever, dissever, ever, fever, for-ever, lever, never, retriever, sever, soever, whatever, whensoever, who-ever, whomsoever, whosoever

EVER
see
ER

Dare-devil, devil, evil, printer's devil, she-devil

EVIL
see
IL

Brevity, levity, longevity

EVITY
see
ITY

Bevy, chevy, levy

EVY
see
E**

Anew, askew, bedew, beefstew, be-shrew, bestrew, blew, brand-new, brew, corkscrew, crew, curfew, curlew, dew, drew, eschew, feverfew, few, Hebrew,

EW
see
AGUE***
IEW

hew, honey-dew, immew, Jew, knew, merry-andrew, mew, mildew, nephew, new, pew, phew, renew, screw, sew, shrew, sinew, skeleton crew, skew, slew, smew, spew, St. Andrew, St. Bartholomew, stew, strew, threw, thumbscrew, unscrew, Wandering Jew, whew, withdrew, yew

EW
o**
ou*
u
ue*
ed-EWD
s-OSE**
USE*

Lewd, shrewd

EWD
see
UDE

Bejewel, crewel, jewel, newel

EWEL
see
EL

Ewer, fewer, hewer, reviewer, sewer, skewer

EWER
see
ER

Hewn, rock-hewn, rough-hewn, sewn, strewn, unhewn

EWN
see
OON

King's Mews, news

EWS
see
EW-*s*

Newt

EWT
see
OOT**

Chewy, dewy, mildewy, screwy, sinewy, skewy

EWY
see
E**

Annex, apex, biconvex, circumflex, codex, complex, convex, duplex, flex, haruspex, ibex, ilex, index, inflex, multiplex, murex, perplex, pollex, pontifex, reflex, rex, sex, silex, simplex, vertex, vex, vortex

EX
see
ECK-*s*
ECT-*s*
EQUE-*s*
ed-EXT

Next, pretext, text, vex't, what-next

EXT
see
EX-*ed*

Abbey, Alderney, alley, attorney, barley, bey, blarney, bluey, bogey, bowling-alley, burley, chimney, choosey, chop-suey, chutney, clayey, cockney, convey, covey, courtsey, darkey, dingey, disobey, Dombey, donkey, dopey, fluey, flunkey, galley, gin rickey, gluey, grey, Guernsey, gulley, hackney, Hennessey, hey, jersey, jitney, jockey, journey, key, Killarney, lackey, lamprey, linsey-woolsey, malmsey, master-key, medley, monkey, Monterey, motley, obey, Odyssey, okey, Orkney, osprey, palfrey, parley, parsley, pass-key, phoney, phooey, Pompey, posey, pulley, purvey, Shelley, shimmey, Sidney, skeleton-key, surrey, survey, they, tourney, trey, trolley, turkey, turnkey, valley, volley, watchkey, Westminster Abbey, whey, whimsey, whiskey, Wolsey

EY
see
A*
AY
E**
s-IES**

All-seeing Eye, buckeye, bull's eye, cock-eye, evil-eye, eye, needle's eye, ox-eye, sheep's eye, wall-eye

EYE
see
I*
IE**

Cortez, fez, oyez, Suez, Velasquez

EZ
see
EACH-*es*
OICE-*s*

Trapeze

EZE
see
EEZE
ESE

Intermezzo, mezzo

EZZO
see
O*

I SOUNDS

Alibi, alkali, alumni, Delphi, demi, Eli, fungi, genii, I, Magi, Malachi, modus operandi, pi, rabbi, semi, Shang-ti, vox populi

I*
see
AI
EFY
EYE
IE**
IFY
IGH
ISFY
ULY**

Agni, Amalfi, Amenti, Ani, Assisi, bacardi, banditti, Bartholdi, beri-beri, bhakti, Buonarotti, Cabiri, cadi, Capri, chianti, Chili, conoscenti, Cotopaxi, daiquiri, Disraeli, do-re-mi, droshki, effendi, ennui, Fascisti, Fiji, Firdausi, Fo-hi, frangipani, Gandi, Garibaldi, Gehazi, Gobi, Hadji, hari-kari, Hawaii, Hopi, houri, Jami, khaki, kiwi, Lakshmi, lapis lazuli, Leonardo da Vinci, Loki, Machiavelli, Mahdi, Maori, Medici, Miami, Midi, mufti, Nagasaki, Nazami, Nazi, obi, okapi, Parvati, patchouli, peccavi, Pehlevi, peri, piccalilli, Pompeii, potpourri, quasi, Rishi, Saadi, salmagundi, sans-souci, saki, sakti, sbirri, scudi, ski, soldi, spermaceti, sri, Sufi, Tauri, taxi, Tiki, Tishri, Trimurti, tutti-frutti, Uffizi, Valmiki,

I**
see
ALI
ATI
E*
EE
ETTI
IE*
IGREE
INI
IORI
ITI
OLI
ONI

Vasari, Verdi, vermicelli, visconti, **I****
voici, Yogi

Abyssinia, acacia, Aglaia, Alexan- **IA**
dria, ambrosia, Andalusia, aphrodisia, *see*
apologia, Arabia, Arcadia, artemisia, A**
Assyria, Bessarabia, Bœotia, Bohemia, ALIA
Bolivia, braggadocia, Britannia, Cala- ANIA
bria, California, Cambodia, camellia, ARIA
Cappadocia, cassia, Circassia, claustro- ASIA
phobia, Columbia, cyclopedia, Cyn- EIA
thia, Czecho-Slovakia, dahlia, deutzia, ELIA
Dionysia, Discordia, dyspepsia, ency- ENIA
clopedia, Etruria, emphorbia, fuchsia, ENTIA
gilia, godetia, Hibernia, hydrophobia, ERIA
Hypatia, hypochrondia, India, in- ESIA
ertia, insignia, insomnia, intelligentsia, OLIA
Ischia, Ismailia, kleptomania, Lemuria, ONIA
loggia, Lucrezia Borgia, Malaysia, OPIA
Manchuria, memorabilia, Mesopota- ORIA
mia, militia, minutia, misericordia,
Moravia, neuralgia, nostalgia, Nubia,
Olympia, onomatopœia, paranoia, Pa-
tricia, Persia, Perugia, petunia, phantasmagoria, phobia, Phoenicia, Phry-
gia, pointsettia, Portia, Prussia, Py-
thia, raffia, rudbeckia, Russia, salvia,
Scandinavia, Scythia, sedilia, sepia,
sequoia, stadia, stevia, St. Sofia, sym-
posia, Syria, Thalia, tibia, Transcau-
casia, Trinosophia, via, via media,
Zenobia

Amiable, inexpiable, insatiable, in- **IABLE**
variable, justifiable, liable, pitiable, *see*
pliable, reliable, satiable, sociable, un- ABLE
deniable, variable EL
LE

Ammoniac, aphrodisiac, cardiac, ce-
leriac, demoniac, elegiac, hypochon-
driac, kleptomaniac, maniac, pericar-
diac, symposiac, Syriac, theriac, Zodiac

IAC
see
AC

Iliad, jeremiad, myriad, naiad,
Olympiad, Pleiad, triad

IAD
see
AD

Carriage, foliage, gun carriage, horse-
less carriage, marriage, verbiage

IAGE
see
AGE*

Jeremiah, Messiah, Mount Moriah,
pariah, Zedekiah

IAH
see
AH

Actuarial, alluvial, ambrosial, anti-
monial, antisocial, Belial, bestial, bi-
ennial, burial, celestial, centennial,
ceremonial, circumferential, circum-
stantial, colonial, coloquial, commer-
cial, congenial, connubial, consequen-
tial, convivial, cordial, courtmartial,
credential, crucial, decennial, deferen-
tial, denial, dial, differential, diluvial,
entente cordial, equatorial, equinoctial,
Escurial, essential, evidential, facial,
filial, financial, finial, fluvial, glacial,
impartial, imperial, inconsequential,
industrial, inessential, inferential, in-
fluential, initial, jovial, labial, mano-
rial, martial, matrimonial, memorial,
menial, mercurial, non-essential, nup-
tial, official, palatial, parochial, par-
tial, patrimonial, penitential, perennial,
pestilential, phial, pluvial, post-pran-

IAL
see
AL
ERIAL
ICIAL
ORIAL

dial, potential, Prairial, prandial, pre-
glacial, presidential, primordial, pro-
verbial, providential, provincial, pru-
dential, racial, radial, residential, re-
trial, reverential, secretarial, self-
denial, social, spatial, special, substan-
tial, sundial, terrestrial, testimonial,
torrential, trial, triennial, trivial, uncial, uncongenial, unsocial, venial, vial

IAL

In memoriam, Miriam, Priam, Siam,
sweet-William

IAM
see
AM
EM

Amphibian, Andalusian, antedilu-
vian, antinomian, Arcadian, artesian,
Assyrian, Bacchanalian, bathycolpian,
beautician, Bodleian, Bohemian, Brob-
dingnagian, Carthusian, Castilian,
Christian, Cimmerian, Circassian, Cis-
tercian, Confucian, Corinthian, custo-
dian, Cyprian, Dickensian, diluvian,
Draconian, durian, Eleusinian, Ely-
sian, Ephesian, equestrian, Essenian,
Ethiopian, fringed-gentian, fustian,
guardian, Hanoverian, Hertzian, Hi-
bernian, Indian, Ionian, isthmian,
Itrurian, Justinian, Lilliputian, Luca-
dian, Lydian, Machiavellian, magian,
Manchurian, Merovingian, metaphysi-
cian, Midian, Midlothian, Norwegian,
Nubian, Olympian, Ossian, Parisian,
Parthian, pedestrian, Peloponnesian,
Persian, Perugian, Peruvian, Pierian,
plebian, Pomeranian, Pythian, Ra-
belaisian, reptilian, riparian, ruffian,

IAN
see
AN*
ARIAN
EDIAN
ICAN
ICIAN
IDIAN
ORIAN

salarian, Saturnalian, saurian, Shake-   **IAN**
sperian, Siberian, simian, Spenserian,
St. Sebastian, Stygian, Sumerian, Swa-
bian, Tasmanian, tertian, theologian,
Thespian, Titian, tragedian, Umbrian,
Uranian, Utopian, valerian, Venetian,
Wagnerian, Zoroastrian

Affiance, allegiance, alliance, appli-   **IANCE**
ance, brilliance, compliance, dalliance,   *see*
defiance, insouciance, invariance, lux-   ANCE
uriance, radiance, reliance, variance

Chateaubriand, viand   **IAND**
      see
      AND*

Brilliant, compliant, defiant, giant,   **IANT**
luxuriant, mediant, pliant, principiant,   *see*
radiant, reliant, suppliant, valiant,   ANT*
variant

Briar, familiar, friar, liar, peculiar,   **IAR**
sweetbriar, unfamiliar, Whitefriar   *see*
      AR*
      ER
      IRE

Tiara   **IARA**
      see
      A**

Billiard, galliard, poniard, Spaniard   **IARD**
      see
      ARD

Apiary, auxiliary, aviary, benefi-
ciary, breviary, diary, incendiary, in-
termediary, judiciary, pecuniary, peni-
tentiary, plenipotentiary, subsidiary,
tertiary

IARY
see
AIRY
E**
IE*
UARY

Alias, Ananias, bias, Deo gratias,
Elias, paterfamilias, Phidias, Tiresias,
Zacharias

IAS
see
AS*

Commissariat, fiat, lariat, proletar-
iat

IAT
see
AT*

Abbreviate, affiliate, alleviate, ap-
preciate, appropriate, associate, colle-
giate, conciliate, denunciate, depreci-
ate, deviate, dissociate, excruciate, ex-
patiate, expatriate, expediate, expiate,
expropriate, filiate, foliate, humiliate,
immediate, inappropriate, infuriate,
ingratiate, insatiate, intercollegiate,
intermediate, luxuriate, mediate, mis-
appropriate, negotiate, noviciate, ob-
viate, officiate, opiate, palliate, prin-
cipiate, propitiate, radiate, repatriate,
repudiate, retaliate, satiate, striate,
substantiate, transubstantiate, trifoli-
ate, vitiate

IATE
see
ATE
ITATE

Abbreviation, appreciation, aviation,
denunciation, expatriation, initiation,
negotiation, principiation, pronuncia-
tion, renunciation

IATION
see
ATION
ION

Ad lib., bib, Carib, corn-crib, crib, dib, drib, fib, glib, jib, nib, Ninib, rib, sahib, Sennacherib, sparerib, turbid, umbrella-rib

IB
see
UIB

Cannibal, Hannibal, intertribal, tribal

IBAL
see
AL

Dribble, fribble, nibble, quibble, scribble

IBBLE
see
EL
LE

Ascribe, bribe, circumscribe, describe, imbibe, inscribe, jibe, oversubscribe, prescribe, proscribe, scribe, subscribe, transcribe, tribe

IBE
see

Exhibit, inhibit, prohibit

IBIT
see
IT

Accessible, audible, Bible, collapsible, combustible, comprehensible, compressible, contemptible, convertible, corrigible, corruptible, credible, crucible, dirigible, discernible, divisible, edible, eligible, exhaustible, fallible, feasible, flexible, forcible, frangible, fusible, gullible, horrible, illegible, impassible, imperceptible, impossible, inaccessible, inaudible, incombustible, incompatible, incomprehensible, incontrovertible, inconvertible, incorrigible, incorruptible, incredible, indefensible, indestructible, inedible,

IBLE
see
EL
LE

inexhaustible, infallible, inflexible, in- **IBLE**
sensible, intangible, intelligible, invin-
cible, invisible, irascible, irresistible,
irresponsible, legible, mandible, neg-
ligible, ostensible, partible, passible,
perceptible, permissible, plausible, pos-
sible, reducible, refrangible, repress-
ible, resistible, responsible, reversible,
risible, sensible, susceptible, tangible,
terrible, thurible, vendible, visible

Audibly, forcibly, glibly, indelibly, **IBLY**
invisibly, possibly, terribly, visibly *see*
E**

Calibre, fibre **IBRE**
see
ER

Attribute, contribute, distribute, **IBUTE**
tribute *see*
UTE

Accoustic, acrostic, agnostic, agres- **IC**
tic, akashic, alembic, allopathic, an- *see*
electric, anopisthographic, angelic, ACTIC
Antarctic, anthropographic, antiseptic, AIC
anti-toxic, Arabic, Arctic, asbestic, AMIC
aspic, attic, authentic, azoic, baldric, ANIC
barbaric, basic, benefic, bishopric, ANTIC
black magic, cambric, cataclysmic, ASTIC
cathartic, caustic, Celtic, cherubic, ATIC
chic, chivalric, civic, classic, concen- ENIC
tric, Coptic, cosmic, cryptic, cubic, ERIC
cynic, decasyllabic, Delphic, diagnos- ETIC
tic, diametric, domestic, eccentric, ec- ICK
lectic, ecliptic, egocentric, elliptic, em- IFIC
piric, endemic, eolithic, epic, epidemic, INIC

ethic, eupeptic, eurythemic, evangelic,
fabric, forensic, formic, frozen music,
Gaelic, Gallic, garlic, geocentric, geo-
desic, geometric, gnostic, Gothic, graph-
ic, gum arabic, hectic, heliocentric,
hermeneutic, heroic, hieroglyphic,
hierographic, homopathic, hydraulic,
hydroelectric, iambic, Icelandic, idyl-
lic, intrinsic, Ionic, Islamic, italic,
karmic, lethargic, lyric, magic, majes-
tic, malic, metallic, metamorphic,
metric, mimic, monolithic, monosylla-
bic, mystic, mythic, natureopathic,
neolithic, Nordic, obstetric, Olympic,
optic, Orphic, orthopedic, orthorhom-
bic, oxalic, palæstric, paleolithic, pane-
gyric, patronymic, phallic, physic, pic-
nic, picric, Pindaric, polytechnic, poly-
theistic, pragmatic, prognostic, prussic,
psychiatric, psychic, psychoanalytic,
public, Punic, pyrotechnic, relic, re-
public, rhombic, rubric, runic, rustic,
salic, salicylic, sapphic, satiric, seismic,
seraphic, Slavic, sic, skeptic, spic,
stenographic, stoic, strategic, sulphuric,
styptic, syllabic, symmetric, syndic,
technic, telepathic, telestic, thalassic,
therapeutic, thermometric, theurgic,
tombic, toreutic, toxic, traffic, tunic,
tyrannic, unauthentic, Vedic

IC
ISTIC
ITIC
ODIC
OGIC
OLIC
OMIC
ONIC
OPIC
ORIC
OTIC
ed-ICT
s-IX

Africa, America, angelica, arnica,
Attica, basilica, Britannica, Corsica,
harmonica, hepatica, Jamaica, japon-
ica, majolica, materia medica, mica,
nux vomica, pica, replica, sciatica,
silica, veronica

ICA
see
A**

Delicacy, efficacy, indelicacy, intricacy

ICACY
see
ACY
E**

Aeronautical, allegorical, anthropological, artistical, biblical, biographical, biological, canonical, chemical, chronological, clerical, comical, conical, cosmical, cosmogonical, critical, cylindrical, cynical, diabolical, ecclesiastical, emblematical, empirical, encyclical, ethnological, etiological, etymological, evangelical, farcial, finical, genetical, geographical, grammatical, heretical, hermeneutical, hierarchical, historical, horological, hypercritical, hypocritical, hypothetical, hysterical, identical, illogical, inimical, ironical, lackadaisical, logical, lyrical, magical, majestical, medical, meteorological, methodical, metrical, mimical, morphological, musical, mystical, mythological, nautical, nonsensical, numerical, ontological, optical, paradoxical, pathological, periodical, philosophical, physical, piratical, poetical, pontifical, practical, pragmatical, psychical, quizzical, radical, rhetorical, sabbatical, satirical, semi-tropical, skeptical, sophistical, spherical, stoical, surgical, symbolical, symmetrical, technical, technological, theatrical, theoretical, tragical, tropical, typical, tyrannical, unsophistical, vertical, vortical, whimsical

ICAL
see
AL

African, American, angelican, Mexican, pan-american, pelican, publican, republican, Vatican

ICAN
see
IAN

Applicant, communicant, insignificant, lubricant, mendicant, significant, supplicant

ICANT
see
ANT*

Abdicate, certificate, communicate, complicate, dedicate, delicate, domesticate, duplicate, eradicate, excommunicate, extricate, fabricate, fornicate, imbricate, implicate, indelicate, indicate, intoxicate, intricate, lubricate, masticate, pontificate, predicate, prevaricate, prognosticate, reduplicate, rusticate, sophisticate, supplicate, syndicate, vindicate

ICATE
see
ATE

Advice, allspice, beggar-lice, bice, device, dice, entice, field-mice, high-price, ice, interslice, low-price, mice, nice, not-nice, price, rice, sacrifice, slice, spice, splice, suffice, thrice, trice, twice, vice

ICE*
see
ISE**

Accomplice, apprentice, armistice, artifice, auspice, avarice, Beatrice, benefice, box-office, cantatrice, caprice, chalice, cicatrice, cornice, cowardice, crevice, dentifrice, hospice, injustice, justice, lattice, licorice, malice, malpractice, mounted-police, notice, novice, office, police, poultice, practice, precipice, prejudice, pumice, summer solstice, service, surplice, winter solstice

ICE**
see
IFICE
IS*
ISE****
ISS
ed-IST
s-IES**

Magnificent, munificent, reticent	**ICENT** *see* ENT
Enrich, Greenwich, Ipswich, ostrich, rich, sandwich, which	**ICH** *see* ICHE ITCH
Niche	**ICHE** *see* ICH
Artificial, beneficial, judicial, official, prejudicial, sacrificial, superficial, unofficial	**ICIAL** *see* IAL
Geometrician, magician, musician, optician, patrician, Phœnician, physician, politician, statistician, technician	**ICIAN** *see* IAN
Fratricide, germicide, infanticide, matricide, parricide, regicide, suicide, vermicide	**ICIDE** *see* IDE
Agnosticism, Catholicism, criticism, didacticism, empiricism, eroticism, fanaticism, gnosticism, mysticism, romanticism, witticism	**ICISM** *see* ISM
Deficit, explicit, illicit, implicit, licit, solicit	**ICIT** *see* IT
Authenticity, causticity, domesticity, duplicity, eccentricity, electricity, ellipticity, felicity, lubricity, periodicity, publicity, rusticity, sphericity, simplicity	**ICITY** *see* E** ITY

Bailiwick, beggar-tick, Benedick, **ICK**
brick, broomstick, candlestick, chick, *see*
chopstick, click, cowlick, crick, derrick, IK
dirty trick, double-quick, drop-kick, *ed*-ICT
drumstick, fiddle-stick, flick, glass- *ly*-E**
brick, goldbrick, hayrick, Herrick, s-IX
homesick, joss-stick, kick, lick, limerick, lipstick, maulstick, maverick,
Moby Dick, niblick, nick, pick, Pick-
wick, pinprick, polostick, prick, quick,
rick, rollick, seasick, sick, slapstick,
slick, St. Patrick, swizzle-stick, thick,
tick, toothpick, trick, walkingstick,
wick, yardstick, Yorick

Bicker, dicker, flicker, pricker, rag- **ICKER**
picker, slicker, snicker, sticker, thicker, *see*
wicker ER

Cricket, picket, thicket, ticket, **ICKET**
wicket *see*
ET

Fickle, mickle, pickle, prickle, sickle, **ICKLE**
tickle, trickle *see*
EL
LE

Finicky, panicky **ICKY**
see
E**

Auricle, canticle, chicle, chronicle, **ICLE**
conventicle, cubicle, cuticle, icicle, *see*
particle, pendicle, radicle, vehicle, EL
ventricle, versicle LE
YCLE

Calico, medico, Mexico, Pimlico, portico, Porto Rico, pro bono publico

ICO
see
o*

Harmonicon, Helicon, icon, irenicon, lexicon, Rubicon, silicon

ICON
see
ON

Academics, analytics, classics, dogmatics, dynamics, eclectics, empirics, ethics, genetics, kinetics, mathematics, metaphysics, metrics, physics, politics, psychics, statistics, tactics, thermodynamics, topics

ICS
see
IC-*s*

Addict, afflict, benedict, conflict, constrict, contradict, convict, depict, derelict, district, edit, evict, inflict, interdict, predict, relict, restrict, strict, verdict

ICT
see
IC-*ed*
ICK-*ed*
ed-ED

Benediction, diction, fiction, friction, interdiction, jurisdiction, malediction, prediction

ICTION
see
ION

Epicure, manicure, pedicure

ICURE
see
URE

Icy, impolicy, policy, spicy

ICY
see
E**

Acid, acrid, amid, Andromedid, aphid, avid, bi-cuspid, bid, candid, Cid, coverlid, David, did, Euclid, fervid, fetid, flaccid, florid, forbid, frigid, gelid, gravid, Haroun al-Rashid, hid,

ID
see
ALID
ED
EID

horrid, hybrid, ibid, id, insipid, in-   **ID**
trepid, invalid, katydid, kid, Leonid,   IED**
lid, limpid, livid, lucid, lurid, Madrid,   UID
masjid, mid, morbid, non-skid, orchid,   UMID
outbid, outdid, Ovid, pallid, pellucid,   UPID
placid, prussic acid, putrid, pyramid,   YD
rabid, rancid, rapid, rid, rigid, sayid,
skid, slid, solid, sordid, splendid, stolid,
taurid, timid, torpid, torrid, turbid,
turgid, underbid, undid, valid, Valla-
dolid, vapid, viscid, vivid

Bridal, cotidal, tidal, suicidal   **IDAL**
                                          see
                                          AL

Candidate, delapidate, elucidate, in-   **IDATE**
timidate, invalidate, lapidate, liquid-   *see*
ate, validate   ATE

Diddle, fiddle, griddle, middle, rid-   **IDDLE**
dle, twiddle, unriddle   *see*
                                           EL

Abide, alongside, aside, astride,   **IDE**
autumn-tide, backslide, bedside, be-   *see*
side, betide, bona fide, bride, broad-   EYE-*d*
side, bromide, carbide, chide, coincide,   ICIDE
collide, confide, countryside, cyanide,   IED*
decide, deride, dioxide, divide, ebb-   UIDE
tide, eventide, fireside, floodtide, gar-   *ed*-ED
den-side, glide, hayride, hide, hillside,   *s*-IDES**
homicide, imbibe, ingleside, inside,
landslide, lopside, neap tide, noontide,
ocean-tide, outride, outside, over-ride,
oxhide, oxide, peroxide, preside, pride,
provide, rawhide, reside, ride, ringside,

roadside, seaside, set-aside, Shrovetide, side, slide, stand aside, stride, subside, sulphide, summertide, tide, wayside, Whitsuntide, wide, worldwide, yuletide

IDE

Accident, coincident, confident, incident, occident, over-confident, president, provident, resident, strident, trident

IDENT
see
ENT

Backslider, cider, circusrider, glider, outrider, outsider, provider, rider, roughrider, spider, wider

IDER
see
ER

Aristides, cantharides, caryatides, Eumenides, Eumolpides, Hebrides, Hesperides, Maimonides, Oceanides, Thucydides

IDES*
see
ES*

Besides, bestrides, coincides, Ides, Old Ironsides

IDES**
see
IDE-*s*

Abridge, auction bridge, bridge, cartridge, Coleridge, covered bridge, drawbridge, footbridge, low bridge, partridge, pepperidge, porridge, ridge, tollbridge

IDGE
see
AGE
EGE

Bridget, fidget, midget

IDGET
see
ET

Antemeridian, meridian, nullifidian, Numidian, ophidian, quotidian

IDIAN
see
IAN

Acidity, aridity, avidity, cupidity, **IDITY**
fluidity, humidity, insipidity, intimity,   *see*
intrepidity, lucidity, placidity, rapid-   E**
ity, sapidity, solidity, stupidity   ITY

Bridle, idle, sidle, unbridle   **IDLE**
     see
     EL
     LE

Frigidly, idly, languidly, rigidly, **IDLY**
timidly, vividly   *see*
     E**

Corridor, cuspidor, Fructidor, humi- **IDOR**
dor, Messidor, Thermidor   *see*
     OR

Didst, midst   **IDST**
     see

Width   **IDTH**
     see

Bowie, brie, brownie, calorie, cap-à- **IE***
pie, collie, coolie, coterie, dearie,   *see*
Dixie, dominie, fantasie, gillie, girlie,   E**
kelpie, kiltie, lassie, lorrie, mashie,   ERIE
Mme. Curie, movie, nixie, organdie,   I**
parapluie, porgie, prairie, prima facie,   S-EASE
rookie, sharpie, sortie, specie, talkie,   E*-S
Valkyrie   IES**

Belie, die, hie, huckleberry-pie, **IE****
humble-pie, lie, magpie, mince-pie,   *see*
necktie, pie, potpie, tie, untie, vie   EYE°
     I*

IE**
ed-IED*
s-ISE*

Altar-piece, fowling-piece, frontis-piece, itty-bitty piece, mantelpiece, masterpiece, mouthpiece, niece, piece, tailpiece

IECE
see
EASE**
ISE***

Allied, amplified, atrophied, certi-fied, citified, complied, countryfied, cried, crucified, defied, deified, denied, died, dried, espied, fortified, fried, glorified, gratified, hog-tied, implied, intensified, justified, lied, liquefied, magnified, mortified, multiplied, mum-mified, occupied, ossified, petrified, pied, pre-occupied, pried, purified, qualified, relied, replied, sanctified, satisfied, shied, spied, stupefied, sun-dried, supplied, tongue-tied, tried, un-occupied, unsatisfied, unversified, ver-sified

IED*
see
EYE-*d*
IDE
IE**-*d*

Ablebodied, astonied, buried, candid, dallied,. ivied, levied, mutinied, pal-sied, parodied, serried, Siegfried, studied, taxied, travestied, varied, wearied

IED**
see
ED
ID

Bas-relief, belief, brief, chief, dis-belief, grief, handkerchief, kerchief, mischief, relief, thief, unbelief

IEF
see
EAF*
EEF
s-EAVE-*s*

Besiege, liege, siege

IEGE
see
IGE

Shriek

IEK
see
EAK*
EEK

Abdiel, Ariel, cocker-spaniel, Daniel, Gamaliel, oriel, spaniel, spiel, Uriel

IEL
see
EL

Afield, cornfield, field, infield, out-field, paddyfield, shield, stubblefield, wield, windshield, yield

IELD
see
ed-ED
EAL*-*ed*
EEL-*ed*

Carpe diem, per diem, requiem

IEM
see
EM

Alien, St. Julien, T'ien

IEN*
see
EAN**

Lien, mien

IEN**
see
EEN

Audience, clairaudience, conscience, convenience, experience, faience, in-convenience, inexperience, nescience, obedience, omniscience, patience, pre-science, resilience, sapience, science, subservience

IENCE
see
ENCE

Ambient, ancient, client, convenient, deficient, desipient, ebullient, efficient, emollient, esurient, expedient, gradi-

IENT
see
ENT

ent, incipient, inconvenient, inexpedi-
ent, ingredient, insufficient, lenient,
nescient, obedient, omniscient, Orient,
patient, percipient, proficient, pruri-
ent, recipient, reorient, resilient, sal-
ient, sapient, sentient, subservient,
sufficient

IENT

Angrier, atelier, barrier, bier, brazier,
brigadier, carrier, cashier, cavalier,
chandelier, chiffonier, chillier, collier,
courier, courtier, croupier, crozier,
dossier, duskier, easier, fancier, farrier,
financier, fox terrier, frontier, glacier,
glazier, grenadier, heavier, hoosier,
lordlier, manlier, merrier, mightier,
Montpellier, moodier, osier, pannier,
pier, prettier, premier, rapier, ruddier,
soldier, sorrier, terrier, tier, toy soldier,
town crier, vizier, Whittier, Xavier

IER*
see
ER
EAR*
ERE*

Amplifier, brier, flier, magnifier,
plier, purifier, sweet-brier

IER**
see
IRE
S-IRES

Fierce, pierce, tierce

IERCE
see

Arrière, boutonière, jardinière, por-
tière

IERE
see
ERE**

Apple pies, cries, dragon-flies, fire-
flies, flies, fortifies, lies, pies, plies,
ratifies, skies, squash pies, supplies,
tries, wailing-cries

IES*
see
IE**-S
ISE*
Y-S

Absurdities, argosies, Aries, arteries, **IES****
Caesar's Commentaries, cavities, cen- *see*
turies, charities, cities, comedies, con- E****-**s
geries, courtesies, curiosities, darbies, EEZE
dictionaries, doweries, duties, Early BY****-**s
Nineties, East Indies, economies, ICE****-**s
eddies, effigies, Eleusinian Mysteries, IE***-**s
exigencies, fairies, fallacies, fantasies, IS******
fillies, fisheries, flag-lilies, frailties,
Furies, gullies, harpies, idolatries, mis-
eries, monies, Notes and Queries,
obsequies, oddities, orgies, pansies,
peonies, pickaninnies, pigmies, pixies,
ponies, quanderies, rareties, remedies,
reveries, roaring forties, rubies, scur-
ries, series, species, strawberries, super-
ficies, superfluities, theories, trophies,
Tuileries

Airiest, driest, earliest, flabbiest, **IEST***
funniest, leakiest, lowliest, prettiest, *see*
ricketiest, rustiest, scantiest, sorriest, EST
stateliest, swankiest, tidiest, trickiest, UEST
wittiest, worthiest

High-priest, priest **IEST****
see
EASE****-**d
EAST*****
ISTE

Diet, disquiet, quiet, Soviet **IET**
see
ET

Anxiety, contrariety, gaiety, im- **IETY**
piety, moiety, noteriety, piety, pro- *see*
priety, satiety, sobriety, society, va- E******
riety

Adieu, lieu, prie-dieu, purlieu, Riche- **IEU**
lieu   *see*
     U

Achieve, believe, disbelieve, grieve, **IEVE***
make-believe, relieve, reprieve, re-   *see*
trieve, St. Genevieve, thieve   EAVE
     EIVE
     S-IEVES

Sieve   **IEVE****
     see
     IVE**

Forty Thieves, retrieves, thieves **IEVES**
     see
     IEVE*-S

Interview, mountain-view, pre-view, **IEW**
purview, review, view   *see*
     EW
     O**

Frieze   **IEZE**
     see
     EASE*
     EE-S
     ESE

Alif, aperitif, calif, Chateau d'If, if, **IF**
khalif, motif   *see*
     IFE
     YPH

Alewife, bowie-knife, fife, housewife, **IFE**
inner-life, jack-knife, life, loosestrife,   *see*
midwife, pocket-knife, rife, strife, wife,   S-IVE*-S
wild-life

Fifer, lifer, Lucifer, thurifer   **IFER**
see
ER

Bailiff, biff, caitiff, Cardiff, cliff, hip-   **IFF**
pogriff, jiff, mastiff, midriff, miff, Peck-   *see*
sniff, plaintiff, pontiff, sheriff, skiff,   IF
sniff, stiff, tariff, tiff, whiff   IPH
YPH

Teneriffe   **IFFE**
see
IFF

Horrific, omnific, pacific, prolific,   **IFIC**
scientific, soporific, specific, sudorific,   *see*
terrific, transpacific, unprolific   IC

Edifice, orifice, sacrifice   **IFICE**
see
ICE**

Rifle, stifle, trifle   **IFLE**
see
EL
LE

Anguilliform, cruciform, cuneiform,   **IFORM**
oviform, triform, uniform, vermiform   *see*
ORM

Adrift, chimney-swift, drift, gift,   **IFT**
lift, makeshift, rift, shift, shoplift, sift, *see*
snowdrift, spendthrift, swift, thrift,   *ed*-ED
uplift

Beautiful, bountiful, dutiful, fanci-
ful, merciful, pitiful, plentiful, over-
dutiful

IFUL
see
UL

Aerify, amplify, beautify, calcify,
certify, clarify, classify, codify, crucify,
deify, disqualify, diversify, dulcify,
edify, electrify, falsify, fortify, fructify,
gratify, horrify, identify, ignify, in-
demnify, intensify, justify, lapidify,
lignify, liquify, magnify, modify, mol-
lify, mortify, mummify, mystify, no-
tify, nullify, ossify, pacify, personify,
petrify, purify, qualify, ramify, ratify,
rectify, requalify, revivify, salsify,
sanctify, solidify, specify, speechify,
stultify, terrify, testify, transmogrify,
unify, verify, versify, vilify, vivify

IFY
see
I*
EFY
IGH
Y

Big, bigwig, brig, cat-rig, cig, dig,
earwig, fig, gig, guinea-pig, jig, lady-
pig, nig, periwig, phennig, pig, prig,
rig, scratch-wig, swig, thimblerig,
thingumajig, trig, twig, whig, whirli-
gig, wig

IG
see

Cardigan, hooligan, ptarmigan

IGAN
see
AN*

Frigate, fumigate, fustigate, insti-
gate, investigate, irrigate, litigate,
mitigate, navigate, obligate, profligate

IGATE
see
ATE

Prestige, vestige

IGE*
see
IEGE

Oblige   **IGE***
                                                see

Bigger, digger, gold-digger, jigger,   **IGGER**
nigger, outrigger, rigger, square-rigger,   *see*
trigger   ER

Higgle, jiggle, niggle, wiggle, wriggle   **IGGLE**
                                                  see
                                                  EL
                                                  LE

Anigh, high, knee-high, nigh, sigh,   **IGH**
thigh, wellnigh   *see*
                                                  I*

Affright, after-sight, airtight, alight,   **IGHT**
all-right, arc-light, aright, beacon-   *see*
light, bedight, benight, bight, birth-   EIGHT**
right, blight, bright, bull-fight, candle-   ITE*
light, copyright, daylight, delight,   YTE
dimlight, downright, drop-light, eye-   *ed*-ED
bright, eyesight, fight, flashlight, flight,
floodlight, fly-by-night, footlight, fore-
sight, fortnight, fright, frosty-night,
gaslight, goodnight, headlight, hind-
sight, honor-bright, insight, Isle of
Wight, knight, light, limelight, lusty-
knight, midnight, might, moonlight,
night, outright, overnight, oversight,
pilot-light, playwright, plight, prize-
fight, purple-night, rapid-flight, red-
light, right, rush-light, sea-fight,
searchlight, second-sight, shining light,
sidelight, sight, sit-tight, skylight,
slight, spotlight, stagefright, starlight,
sticktight, summer's night, sunlight,

tail-light, taper-light, tight, tonight, **IGHT**
traffic-light, Twelfth-night, twilight,
upright, watertight, wheelwright,
wight, wright, yesternight

Almighty, blighty, flighty, high and **IGHTY**
mighty, highty-tighty, mighty, nighty   *see*
                                        E**

Enigma, sigma, stigma   **IGMA**
                                        see
                                        A**

Align, assign, benign, condign, con-   **IGN**
sign, design, ensign, malign, resign,   *see*
sign, traffic-sign   INE*
                                        ed-IND*

Amigo, indigo, vertigo   **IGO**
                                        see
                                        O*

Bigot, spigot   **IGOT**
                                        see
                                        OT

Filigree, pedigree, perigee   **IGREE**
                                        see
                                        EE

Effigy, prodigy   **IGY**
                                        see
                                        E**

Batik, Bolshevik, mujik, sheik   **IK**
                                        see
                                        EAK
                                        IK

Paprika, swastika **IKA**
see
A**

Alike, aspen-like, belike, bike, child- **IKE**
like, dike, dislike, fanlike, ghostlike, *see*
gnomelike, gooselike, hitch-hike, AIK
homelike, hunger-strike, ladylike,
marline-spike, mike, pike, proboscis-
like, saintlike, sphinxlike, spike, sports-
manlike, statue-like, strike, suchlike,
swanlike, tike, trance-like, turnpike,
unlike, viselike, wandlike, war-like

Anvil, April, argil, Azrafil, basil, **IL**
Boabdil, boll weevil, Brazil, cavil, *see*
cheveril, civil, codicil, council, coutil, ERIL
daffodil, distil, fibril, fossil, fulfil, fusil, ERYL
instil, lentil, nil, nostril, pencil, Salsa- EVIL
bil, slatepencil, stencil, sweetbasil, ten- ILE**
dril, tonsil, tumbril, uncivil, until, ILL
utensil, vigil, Virgil, Vril, weevil ILLE
UIL
*ed-*ILD*

Jubilant, sibilant, vigilant **ILANT**
see
ANT*

Dissimilar, similar **ILAR**
see
AR*

Annihilate, dilate, jubilate, mutilate, **ILATE**
ventilate *see*
ATE

Filch, milch

ILCH
see

Brunhild, gild, regild

ILD*
see
IL-*ed*
UILD

Child, godchild, grandchild, mild, wild

ILD**
see
ILE*-*d*

Bewilder, builder, guilder

ILDER
see
ER

Anile, awhile, camomile, compile, crocodile, defile, erstwhile, exile, file, Gentile, juvenile, meanwhile, mile, Nile, pile, profile, reconcile, red-tile, reptile, revile, scissile, seldomwhile, senile, single-file, smile, statute mile, stile, tile, turnstile, vile, while, wile, woodpile

ILE*
see
ISLE
UILE
YLE
ed-ILD****

Anglophile, automobile, bastile, bibliophile, bissextile, Castile, cortile, docile, domicile, ductile, facile, febrile, fertile, flexile, fluviatile, fragile, futile, hostile, imbecile, immobile, mercantile, missile, mobile, pensile, prehensile, projectile, puerile, servile, sextile, sterile, subtile, tactile, tensile, textile, virile, versatile, volatile

ILE**
see
EAL*
EEL
IL

Campanile, facsimile, primummobile, simile

ILE***
see
E*

Compiler, tiler

ILER
see
ER

Merciless, penniless, pitiless

ILESS
see
ESS

Availeth, bewaileth, broileth, faileth, soileth

ILETH
see
ETH

Bilge

ILGE
see

Pavilion, postilion, vermilion

ILION
see
ION

Ability, anility, applicability, compatability, capability, civility, culpability, debility, dependability, disability, dividibility, durability, eligibility, facility, fallibility, fertility, flexibility, fraility, gentility, gullibility, immutability, impenetrability, inability, incivility, incompatibility, indefatigability, indefectibility, indelibility, inevitability, infallibility, instability, invisibility, liability, mutability, negligibility, nobility, notability, plausibility, possibility, probability, responsibility, senility, servility, stability, susceptibility, tangibility, tensibility, utility, virility, visibility, volubility, vulnerability

ILITY
see
E*

Asses' milk, bilk, buttermilk, ilk, **ILK**
milk, rawsilk, silk, skim milk   *see*

Ant-hill, bill, Bunker Hill, cambric-   **ILL**
frill, chill, cranes-bill, dill, distill, door-   *see*
sill, drill, duckbill, dunghill, fill, fire-   IL
drill, foothill, frill, fulfill, gill, goodwill,   UILL
frill, gristmill, handbill, hill, hornbill,   *ed*-ILD*
ill, ill-will, kill, mandrill, mill, mole-   *y*-ILLY
hill, pill, playbill, powder-mill, refill,
rill, sandhill, sawmill, shrill, sill, skill,
spill, spoonbill, standstill, still, stock-
still, swill, thill, thrill, till, treadmill,
trill, twill, uphill, whippoorwill, will,
windmill, window-sill, Yggdrasill

Camilla, cedilla, chinchilla, Cinder-   **ILLA**
illa, flotilla, gorilla, guerilla, mantilla,   *see*
Myrtilla, Priscilla, pulsatilla, sapodilla,   A**
sarsaparilla, scintilla, vanilla, villa

Bastille, chenille, dishabille, esca-   **ILLE**
drille, grille, Hotel de Ville, quadrille,   *see*
Seville, soyez tranquille, vaudeville   ILE**

Filler, miller, shriller, stiller, tiller,   **ILLER**
thriller   *see*
                                                   ER

Billion, cotillion, million, pillion,   **ILLION**
trillion, vermillion   *see*
                                                   ION

Armadillo, Murillo, negrillo, pecca-   **ILLO**
dillo   *see*
                                                   O*

Billy, chilly, evilly, filly, hillbilly, hilly, Piccadilly, silly, stilly, willy nilly

ILLY
see
E**
ILL-*y*

Film, sound-film

ILM
see

Brickkiln, kiln, limekiln

ILN
see

Full-tilt, gilt, hilt, jilt, kilt, lilt, silt, spilt, stilt, tilt, wilt

ILT
see
UILT

Filth, spilth, tilth

ILTH
see

German silver, quicksilver, silver, solid silver

ILVER
see
ER

Bodily, busily, cannily, clammily, clumsily, craftily, daily, daintily, doily, dreamily, drearily, drowsily, easily, eerily, family, faultily, gaudily, gloomily, greedily, guiltily, homily, lazily, lily, luckily, lustily, merrily, mightily, moodily, pluckily, pondlily, primarily, scantily, shabbily, Sicily, speedily, spunkily, stealthily, temporarily, uncannily, unluckily, verily, voluntarily, waterlily, wily, wittily

ILY
see
E**
EE

Bedim, brim, broadbrim, cherubim, dim, Elohim, grim, him, interim, maxim, megrim, Mount Gerizim, passim, pilgrim, prim, Purim, rim,

IM
see
ATIM
ITHM

seraphim, skim, slim, swim, teraphim, **IM**
Thummim, trim, Urim, victim, whim ONYM
YMN
YTHM

Bellissima, Cloaca Maxima, Fatima, **IMA**
lacrima, Lima, quadragesima, septua- *see*
gesima, sexagesima, Yima A**

Animal, decimal, infinitesimal, max- **IMAL**
imal, millesimal, primal *see*
AL

Animate, antipenultimate, approxi- **IMATE**
mate, climate, decimate, estimate, in- *see*
animate, intimate, legitimate, over- ATE
estimate, penultimate, primate, proxi-
mate, reanimate, sublimate, ultimate

Limb **IMB***
see

Climb **IMB****
see

Limber, tall-timber, timber **IMBER**
see
ER

Nimble, thimble, wimble **IMBLE**
see
EL
LE

Aforetime, bedtime, begrime, be- **IME***
time, cherry-time, chime, classtime, *see*
clime, crime, dime, grime, lifetime, YME

lilac-time, lime, mealtime, meantime, **IME***
ofttime, overtime, pantomime, pas-
time, prime, quicklime, ragtime, rime,
seedtime, slime, sometime, sparetime,
springtime, sublime, summer-time,
swingtime, time, wartime

Intime, maritime, mime, régime   **IME****
                                   see
                                   EAM

Regimen, specimen   **IMEN**
                      see
                      EN

Accompaniment, aliment, compli-   **IMENT**
ment, condiment, crack regiment,   *see*
detriment, embodiment, experiment, ENT
habiliment, impediment, liniment,
merriment, nutriment, orpiment, pre-
sentiment, raiment, regiment, re-em-
bodiment, rudiment, sediment, sentiment

Dimity, equanimity, magnanimity,   **IMITY**
proximity, sublimity, unanimity   *see*
                                     E**
                                     ITY

Dimmer, glimmer, shimmer, simmer,   **IMMER**
slimmer   *see*
                                      ER

Centimo, duodecimo, Eskimo, for-   **IMO**
tissimo, generalissimo, Geronimo, pia- *see*
nissimo, prestissimo, primo, proximo,   o*
ultimo

Blimp, crimp, imp, limp, pimp, **IMP**
primp, scrimp, shrimp, simp, skimp *see*
UIMP

Dimple, pimple, simple, wimple **IMPLE**
see
EL
LE

Glimpse **IMPSE**
see

A-cluckin' adrenalin, a-grin, akin, **IN**
Aladdin, all in, antitoxin, assassin, *see*
a-throbbin', bareskin, basin, bearskin, AMIN
begin, belaying pin, bewitchin', bin, ATIN
bodkin, bowfin, Brahmin, break-in, ELIN
buckskin, built-in, bulletin, bumpkin, ERIN
buskin, cabin, calfskin, Capuchin, INN
catkin, chagrin, chin, chinquapin, OLIN
Chopin, clavecin, clothespin, cock- UIN
robin, coffin, cousin, creeping-in, cre- *al*-AL
tin, cruisin', cryin', cumin, Darwin, *ed*-IND**
dauphin, deerskin, din, doeskin, dol- *s*-INS
phin, Dublin, duckpin, dunlin, ex-
ceedin', Fagin, feelin', fetchin', fin,
firkin, fit-in, florin, gelatin, gherkin,
gin, goblin, griffin, grimalkin, grin,
herein, highfalutin, hin, hobgoblin, in,
insulin, interruptin', Jacobin, jasmin,
jerkin, kaolin, khamsin, kin, king-pin,
Kremlin, lambskin, linchpin, listen-in,
logcabin, Lohengrin, lupin, mandarin,
mannikin, margin, martin, matin,
maudlin, Mazarin, mechlin, Merlin,
metheglin, moccasin, moleskin, muez-
zin, muffin, muslin, napkin, nine-pin,
nothin', nubbin, Odin, oilskin, origin,

paladin, paraffin, Pekin, Pepin, pepsin,   **IN**
pidgin, pigskin, pin, pippin, poplin,
prevailin', protein, puffin, pumpkin,
push-in, rabbin, ragamuffin, raisin,
ramekin, Redskin, replevin, resin,
rolling-pin, round robin, running-in,
Ruskin, saccharin, safety-pin, Saladin,
Sanhedrin, scarf-pin, sculpin, sealskin,
sea-urchin, sheepskin, shin, sin, skin,
sloe gin, spadassin, spavin, spillikin,
spin, St. Swithin, tailspin, tannin, tar-
paulin, tellin', terrapin, therein, There-
min, thin, thole-pin, Tientsin, tiffin,
tocsin, toxin, tune-in, twin, underpin,
urchin, vermin, virgin, wanderin',
washbasin, welkin, wherein, win, within, Yin

Ægina, Agrippina, ballerina, Caro-   **INA**
lina, Catalina, cavatina, China, Cochin   *see*
China, concertina, czarina, lamina,   A**
Maria Farina, Medina, Messalina,
ocarina, Proserpina, regina, retina,
saltina, Salva Regina, stamina, vina

Aboriginal, cardinal, criminal, final,   **INAL**
germinal, latitudinal, libidinal, longi-   *see*
tudinal, marginal, matutinal, nominal,   AL
original, paginal, Quirinal, subliminal,   IN-*al*
terminal, virginal

Culinary, extraordinary, imaginary,   **INARY**
luminary, ordinary, preliminary, san-   *see*
guinary, seminary, veterinary   ARY

Assassinate, culminate, determinate,   **INATE**
disseminate, dominate, eliminate, ex-   *see*
terminate, fascinate, fulminate, germi-   ATE

nate, hallucinate, illuminate, incrimi- **INATE**
nate, indeterminate, insubordinate,
nominate, obstinate, originate, pere-
grinate, predominate, procrastinate,
recriminate, ruminate, subordinate,
terminate, vaccinate

Zinc **INC**
see
INK

Black Prince, convince, evince, **INCE**
mince, prince, province, quince, since, *see*
wince INT-*s*

Bullfinch, chaffinch, cinch, clinch, **INCH**
finch, flinch, goldfinch, inch, pinch, *see*
winch YNCH

Distinct, extinct, indistinct, pre- **INCT**
cinct, succinct *see*
INK-*ed*

Behind, bind, blind, colorblind, **IND***
grind, humankind, kind, mankind, *see*
master mind, mind, never-mind, pur- IGN-*ed*
blind, remind, rind, unkind, unwind, INE*-*d*
wind, window-blind

Etesian wind, night-wind, rescind, **IND****
second wind, tamarind, trade-wind, *see*
west-wind, whirlwind, wind IN-*ed*

Binder, blinder, cinder, cylinder, **INDER**
grinder, hinder, path-finder, reminder, *see*
stem-winder ER

Brindle, dwindle, kindle, rekindle, spindle, swindle

INDLE
see
EL
LE

Airline, alkaline, Alpine, aniline, Apennine, aquiline, asinine, balloon vine, bovine, Brandywine, bread line, brine, canine, chalk-line, clothesline, coalmine, columbine, combine, concubine, confine, crystalline, decline, define, dine, disincline, divine, eglantine, enshrine, entwine, feline, fine, fishline, gadding vine, goldmine, grapevine, greedy-swine, headline, incline, intertwine, iodine, kine, leonine, line, lordly pine, lupine, mine, monkeyshine, moonshine, nine, opine, outline, Palatine, Palestine, pine, pitch-pine, plumbline, porcupine, port wine, quinine, ratline, recline, redwine, refine, repine, Rhine, rush line, saltmine, seabrine, sea-line, serpentine, shine, shoreline, shrine, side-line, sine, skyline, spine, streamline, strychnine, superfine, supine, swine, tapeline, thine, tine, trellised-vine, turbine, twine, undermine, valentine, vine, vulpine, water-line, whine, white wine, wine, woodbine

INE*
see
IGN
YNE
ed-IND*
s-INES

Adamantine, adrenaline, alexandrine, amaranthine, aquamarine, Argentine, atropine, Aventine, bandoline, Benedictine, benzine, brigantine, caprine, carmine, chlorine, clandestine, Constantine, crinoline, cuisine, destine,

INE**
see
AZINE
EAN
EEN
ENE

determine, discipline, doctrine, elephantine, engine, ermine, Euxine, Evangeline, famine, feminine, figurine, fluorine, gaberdine, gamine, gasoline, Ghibelline, grenadine, guillotine, heroine, horse marine, hyaline, illumine, imagine, incarnadine, intestine, jessamine, latrine, leporine, levantine, libertine, limousine, machine, margarine, marine, masculine, mazarine, medicine, mezzanine, muscadine, nectarine, opaline, ovine, palatine, paraffine, pelerine, peregrine, Philippine, Philistine, phocine, pilot-machine, porcine, praline, predestine, pristine, quarantine, rapine, ravine, routine, Sabine, saccharine, saline, Sibylline, Sistine, slot-machine, submarine, tambourine, tangerine, tourmaline, transpontine, ultramarine, undine, ursine, vaccine, vaseline, vitamine

INE**
ERINE
IENE
UIN
UINE

Continent, eminent, imminent, impertinent, incontinent, pertinent, preeminent, prominent

INENT
see
ENT

Ancient Mariner, diner, finer, forty-niner, liner, mariner, milliner, miner, moonshiner, ocean-liner, refiner, shiner, shriner

INER
see
ER

Bulkiness, business, cloudiness, coziness, dinginess, dowdiness, emptiness, fussiness, fustiness, ghastliness, giddiness, guiltiness, happiness, haughtiness, headiness, holiness, loneliness, loveliness, mightiness, mistiness, petti-

INESS
see
ES**
ESS

ness, readiness, silliness, steadiness, **INESS**
sultriness, surliness, tidiness, uneasi-
ness, weariness, wordiness, worthiness

Bassinet, bobbinet, cabinet, clarinet, **INET**
martinet, spinet *see*
ET

Absorbing, according, a-Maying, **ING**
amazing, ambling, amusing, angling, *see*
anything, apronstring, a-wing, awning, ARING
baffling, bee-keeping, beetling, befit- ATING
ting, begrudging, belting, bing, bless- EING
ing, bloodcurdling, blueing, bombing, OMING
boring, bowling, bowstring, boxing, ER-*ing*
bring, Browning, building, bungling, *ly*-E**
bunting, bustling, carding, carting, S-INGS
casing, ceiling, central-heating, chafing,
charming, chattering, cling, clinging,
closing, cod-fishing, coming, cotton-
batting, crystal-gazing, cruising, cun-
ning, curdling, damning, dancing, dar-
ling, dazzling, directing, dismantling,
diverting, do-nothing, drawing, dress-
ing, drifting, duckling, dumpling, dur-
ing, dwelling, dying, easy-going, en-
circling, ending, Erl-king, etching,
everlasting, face-lifting, far-reaching,
far-seeing, farthing, fawning, feeling,
flapping, fledgling, fleeting, flinching,
fling, flouting, flowing, foregoing, foun-
dling, fringing, frisking, gangling, glis-
tening, glowing, going, goodbreeding,
gosling, grilling, gurgling, gushing,
hamstring, harrowing, hasty pudding,
hazel-sapling, heat-lightning, heckling,
hedging, herring, Highland fling, hik-

ing, hireling, hobnobbing, hooting, **ING**
howling, huddling, hustling, hymning,
ill-feeling, imposing, incoming, in-
dwelling, ingrowing, inkling, jarring,
jolting, jostling, juggling, key-ring,
kidding, kindling, king, Kipling, kneel-
ing, knitting, landscaping, lapwing,
lashing, lasting, latchstring, law-abid-
ing, leave-taking, libelling, lightning,
liking, lining, lodging, log-rolling, long-
ing, long-standing, longsuffering, lung-
ing, luring, lurking, lutestring, lying,
mainspring, marshaling, mass meeting,
matting, maying, mellowing, merry-
making, mining, moiling, mooring,
morning, motoring, mumbling, Nan-
king, necking, nestling, never-ending,
nothing, notwithstanding, nursling,
obliging, offing, offspring, oncoming,
opening, out-building, outlying, out-
pouring, outstanding, overlooking,
padding, painstaking, painting, paling,
parting, Peiping, pervading, pettifog-
ging, petting, piffling, playing, poor-
thing, prevailing, priming, princeling,
prize-ring, prompting, prying, pudding,
purling, ranking, rattling, reckoning,
redwing, rigging, ring, rising, ruching,
rustling, sacking, sapling, scantling,
screaming, sea-faring, sea-going, sea-
king, seal-ring, seasoning, seedling,
seething, self-denying, sewing, sham-
bling, shelving, shepherd-king, shock-
ing, shoestring, shortening, shrouding,
sidesplitting, sightseeing, signet-ring,
shilling, simpling, sing, singing, skulk-
ing, sling, smattering, snarling, sooth-

ing, spooning, spraying, spring, star-   **ING**
gazing, starling, startling, sterling,
stilling, sting, stocking, string, strut-
ting, sucking, suckling, swaddling,
swelling, swing, swirling, swooping,
tantalizing, Tao-Teh-King, tap-danc-
ing, teeming, teething, thanksgiving,
thing, thorough-going, thronging, time-
serving, tingling, town-meeting, trek-
king, twinkling, ugly-duckling, under-
ling, underpinning, undying, unending,
unfeeling, unflinching, unknowing, un-
tiring, unveiling, upbuilding, uplifting,
upstanding, upswing, upyearning,
using, vanishing, varnishing, Viking,
wainscoting, waning, warning, waxing,
webbing, wedding, well-being, wend-
ing, whaling, whirling, whiting, wing,
winning, witling, worldling, wring,
writing, yawning, yearling, yearning

Astringe, binge, constringe, cringe,   **INGE**
fringe, hinge, impinge, infringe, inter-   *see*
tinge, singe, syringe, tinge, twinge,
unhinge

Finger, ginger, harbinger, lady-   **INGER**
finger, linger, minnesinger, porringer,   *see*
singer, slinger, wringer   ER

Commingle, ingle, intermingle, jin-   **INGLE**
gle, Kris Kringle, mingle, shingle,   *see*
single, surcingle, tingle   EL
    LE

Bingo, dingo, flamingo, gringo, jingo,   **INGO**
lingo, San Domingo   *see*
    O*

Apronstrings, armorial bearings, blessings, dwellings, innings, invisible wings, playthings, shillings, stockings, strings, things, wings

INGS
see
ING-*s*

Meringue

INGUE
see
ANG

Anno Domini, Benvenuto Cellini, contadini, Gemini, martini, Mussolini, Paganini, Puccini, Rimini, Rossini

INI
see
I**

Actinic, clinic

INIC
see
IC

Dominion, minion, opinion, pinion

INION
see
ION

Consanguinity, femininity, infinity, trinity, vicinity, virginity

INITY
see
E**
ITY

Bethink, blink, bobolink, brink, chewink, chink, clink, clovepink, drink, hoodwink, India-ink, interlink, jink, kink, link, mink, pen-and-ink, pink, prink, rink, rinky-dink, river-brink, shell pink, shrink, sink, slink, stink, think, wink

INK
see
INC
ed-INCT
s-INKS
INX
YNX

Blinker, diesinker, drinker, pinker, stinker, thinker, tinker

INKER
see
ER

Crinkle, periwinkle, Rip van Winkle, sprinkle, twinkle, wrinkle

INKLE
see
EL
LE

Cuff-links, golf-links, methinks

INKS
see
INK-*s*

Dinky, inky, kinky, pinky

INKY
see
E**

Inn, jinn, Tabard Inn, Wayside Inn

INN
see
IN

Dinner, inner, sinner, spinner, thinner, tinner, winner

INNER
see
ER

Finny, hinny, ninny, picaninny, shinny, tinny, whinny

INNY
see
E**

Albino, bambino, casino, domino, Filipino, maraschino, merino, Solferino

INO
see
O*

Bituminous, heinous, libidinous, luminous, mucilaginous, multitudinous, mutinous, ominous, platitudinous, resinous, ruinous, villainous, voluminous

INOUS
see
OUS

Asvins, fins, gherkins, ins, muggins, ninepins, nubbins, Redskins, shins, sins, skins, step-ins, Tom Collins, water-skins, wins

INS
see
IN-*s*

Rinse

INSE
see
INCE

Blueprint, cuckoopint, dint, finger-print, flint, footprint, glint, hint, hoof-print, imprint, lint, mezzotint, mint, peppermint, print, reprint, Septaugint, skinflint, sodamint, spearmint, splint, sprint, squint, stint, tint, varmint

INT
see
s-INCE

Inter, printer, splinter, sprinter, winter

INTER
see
ER

Absinth, Corinth, hyacinth, jacinth, labyrinth, plinth, terebinth

INTH
see

Faintly, quaintly, saintly

INTLY
see
E**

Chintz

INTZ
see
INT-s

Linus, minus, Ninus, Plotinus, Quirinus, sinus, Tarquinus, terminus

INUS
see
US

Jinx, minx, sphinx, Syrinx

INX
see
INK-s
YNX

Briny, destiny, hominy, ignominy, mutiny, Pliny, scrutiny, shiny, tiny

INY
see
E**

Adagio, addio, agio, arpeggio, Bellagio, Boccaccio, braggadocio, cheerio, Clio, Correggio, curio, ex-officio, finochio, Horatio, imbroglio, intaglio, internuncio, Io, nuncio, oratorio, patio, pistachio, Ponte Vecchio, presidio, punctilio, radio, ratio, Rio, Scipio, Scorpio, seraglio, solfeggio, studio, tertio, Tokio, trio

IO
see
ARIO
O*
OLIO

Hesiod, period

IOD
see
OD

Viol, vitriol

IOL
see
OL

Axiom, idiom

IOM
see
OM

Abjection, abortion, absorption, accordion, action, adhesion, adjunction, affection, air condition, Albion, Amphion, anthelion, ant lion, ascension, assertion, assumption, attention, battalion, benefaction, bisection, boon companion, bullion, carrion, caution, centurion, champion, circumscription, circumspection, coercion, Coeur de Lion, collection, collodion, companion, compulsion, conception, concoction, concretion, concussion, confection, congestion, conjunction, connection, contagion, contortion, contraction, contraption, convention, conversion,

ION
see
ASION
ATION
EGION
EON
ESSION
IATION
ICTION
ILION
ILLION
INION
ISION
ISSION
ITION

correction, corruption, counteraction, criterion, crucifixion, cushion, dandelion, deception, decoction, defection, dejection, description, Deucalion, dimension, discretion, discussion, disruption, distention, distortion, diversion, election, emotion, emulsion, enchiridion, Endymion, erection, exception, excursion, expansion, extension, extortion, extroversion, faction, fashion, film-version, fourth dimension, function, gammadion, ganglion, gumption, high tension, Hyperion, Ilion, inaction, inattention, incorruption, incursion, indigestion, indiscretion, induction, infraction, inhesion, injunction, inquisition, insertion, insurrection, intention, interjection, interruption, intervention, introspection, introversion, invention, inversion, Ion, irruption, Ixion, junction, lesion, lion, maladaption, mansion, Marmion, medallion, mention, mullion, objection, oblivion, old-fashion, onion, oppression, option, orchestrion, Orion, passion, pension, perception, percussion, perfection, perihelion, perversion, petrifaction, pincushion, portion, precaution, predilection, prelection, presumption, prevention, proportion, proscription, protection, putrefaction, Pygmalion, quaternion, question, rapscallion, reaction, recollection, redaction, redemption, reflection, reflexion, refraction, rejection, religion, repercussion, resumption, resurrection, revulsion, sanction, scion, scorpion, scul-

ION

ON
OSION
OTION
UCTION
UN
UNION
USION
UTION
al-AL
　IONAL

lion, section, selection, stallion, stan- **ION**
chion, subjection, subscription, sugges-
tion, suspension, suspicion, tension,
traction, transaction, transfixion, unc-
tion, version, vivisection

Confessional, conventional, dimen- **IONAL**
sional, emotional, exceptional, frac- *see*
tional, functional, intentional, inter- AL
national, irrational, national, notional,
occasional, optional, precessional, pro-
fessional, proportional, rational, recessional, sectional, sensational, traditional, transitional, vocational

Anterior, behavior, excelsior, exte- **IOR**
rior, inferior, interior, junior, Melchior, *see*
mother-superior, posterior, prior, sen- OR
ior, superior, ulterior, warrior ORE

A fortiori, a posteriori, a priori **IORI**
                              see
                              I**

Adios, Helios **IOS**
                              see
                              OS

Grandiose, otiose **IOSE**
                              see
                              OSE

Chariot, cheviot, compatriot, idiot, **IOT**
Judas Iscariot, patriot, riot *see*
                              OT

Abstemious, acrimonious, adsciti-
tious, adventitious, amphibious, anx-
ious, atrocious, auspicious, bilious,
bumptious, calumnious, capricious,
captious, cautious, ceremonious, com-
modious, compendious, conscientious,
conscious, contagious, contentious, co-
pious, curious, delicious, delirious,
disputatious, dubious, egregious, en-
vious, expeditious, fastidious, feloni-
ous, ferocious, fictitious, flagitious,
furious, glorious, gregarious, harmoni-
ous, hilarious, ignominious, impecuni-
ous, imperious, impervious, impious,
inauspicious, industrious, infectious,
ingenious, inglorious, inharmonious,
injudicious, injurious, insidious, invidi-
ous, irreligious, judicious, laborious,
licentious, lugubrious, luscious, luxuri-
ous, malicious, melodious, meretricious,
meritorious, multifarious, mysterious,
nefarious, notorious, noxious, nutri-
tious, oblivious, obnoxious, obsequious,
obvious, odious, officious, opprobrious,
ostentatious, overcurious, parsimoni-
ous, penurious, perfidious, pernicious,
pious, pluvious, precarious, precious,
precocious, pretentious, previous, pro-
digious, propitious, punctilious, rebel-
lious, religious, sacrilegious, salubrious,
sanctimonious, scrumptious, seditious,
self-conscious, serious, specious, spuri-
ous, studious, subconscious, supercili-
ous, superstitious, surreptitious, suspi-
cious, tedious, unceremonious, uncon-
scious, uxorious, vainglorious, various,
vexatious, vicarious, vicious, victorious

IOUS
see
ACIOUS
AMUS
EUS*
OUS
UOUS
US
ly-E**
   OUSLY

Adeptship, apostleship, battleship, buggy-whip, catnip, celery-tip, censorship, championship, chip, clip, clubship, companionship, cork-tip, courtship, cowslip, dictatorship, dip, drip, equip, fellowship, finger-tip, flip, gossip, grip, guardianship, hare-lip, hardship, hero-worship, hip, horsewhip, kinship, ladyship, lightship, leadership, lip, lordship, marksmanship, midship, nip, outstrip, ownership, parsnip, partnership, penmanship, phantom-ship, pillowslip, pleasure-trip, potato-chip, quip, round trip, ruby-lip, sailingship, scholarship, scrip, ship, showmanship, sip, skip, slip, snip, strip, tallowdip, tree-worship, trip, troop-ship, tulip, turnip, warship, whaleship, whip, worship, zip

IP
see
ed-IPT
YPT
s-IPSE

Assurbanipal, municipal, principal

IPAL
see
AL

Anticipate, dissipate, emancipate, participate

IPATE
see
ATE

Bagpipe, blowpipe, briar-pipe, cobpipe, gripe, guttersnipe, hornpipe, organpipe, over-ripe, pipe, pitchpipe, rareripe, reedpipe, ripe, sideswipe, snipe, stovepipe, stripe, swipe, tomahawk-pipe, tripe, unripe, windpipe, wipe

IPE
see
YPE

Juniper, pen-wiper, Pied Piper, piper, sandpiper, sniper, swiper, viper

IPER
see
ER

Caliph

IPH
see
IFF

Disciple, multiple, participle, principle, triple

IPLE
see
EL
LE

Big Dipper, clipper, dipper, flipper, gallinipper, lady's-slipper, ripper, shipper, skipper, slipper, tripper, worshipper, zipper

IPPER
see
ER

Cripple, nipple, ripple, stipple, tipple

IPPLE
see
EL
LE

Eclipse, ellipse

IPSE
see
IP-*S*

Gipsy, tipsy

IPSY
see
E**

Conscript, manuscript, nipt, nondescript, postscript, script, transcript

IPT
see
IP-*ed*
YPT
S-IPSE

Antique, bezique, cacique, clique, critique, lyrique, Mozambique, oblique, perique, physique, pique, pneumatique, pratique, technique, unique

IQUE
see
EAK*
EEK

Astir, bestir, decemvir, elixir, Elze-
vir, emir, fakir, fir, Guadalquivir,
kaffir, Kashmir, Mimir, nadir, Ophir,
sir, souvenir, stir, tapir, triumvir,
Vladimir, Ymir

IR
see
ARTYR
ERE**
IRR
UR
YRRH

Ça ira, Hegira, lira, Sapphira,
Sephira

IRA
see
A**

Conspiracy, piracy

IRACY
see
ACY
E**

Irate, pirate, triumvirate

IRATE
see
ATE

Besmirch, birch, smirch

IRCH
see
URCH

Arctic Circle, circle, encircle, semi-
circle, sewing-circle

IRCLE
see
EL
LE

Bird, blackbird, catbird, gird, jail-
bird, jaybird, lovebird, mockingbird,
night-bird, railbird, reedbird, secretary bird, third

IRD
see
ORD**
IR-*ed*
IRE-*d*

Admire, afire, aspire, attire, Ayrshire, **IRE**
back-fire, barb-wire, bonfire, campfire, *see*
conspire, cross-fire, crosswire, desire, ER
Devonshire, dire, empire, expire, fire, IAR
for-hire, grandsire, gunfire, haywire, IER***
hire, inspire, ire, live wire, mire, mis- OIR*
fire, perspire, pismire, quagmire, re- UIRE
spire, retire, samphire, sapphire, satire, YRE
shire, spare-tire, spitfire, suspire, tire, *ed*-EARD*
transpire, umpire, vampire, watch-fire, *s*-IRES
wildfire, wire

Dirge   **IRGE**
                                        see
                                        OURGE

Dirk, irk, kirk, quirk, shirk, smirk   **IRK**
                                        see
                                        ERK
                                        ORK

Flower-girl, girl, old-girl, skirl, swirl, **IRL**
twirl, whirl   *see*
                                        EARL
                                        URL
                                        ed-ORLD

Affirm, confirm, firm, infirm, squirm   **IRM**
                                        see
                                        ORM**

Andiron, castiron, Chiron, curling-   **IRON**
iron, environ, flatiron, grappling-iron, *see*
gridiron, iron, midiron, pig-iron, sad- ON
iron, wrought-iron

Whirr

IRR
see
IR

First, thirst

IRST
see
ORST
URST

Begirt, black shirt, dirt, flirt, girt, hobble-skirt, hoopskirt, outskirt, red shirt, seagirt, shirt, skirt, steel-girt, stuffed-shirt, undershirt

IRT
see
UIRT
URT

Birth, firth, girth, mirth, rebirth

IRTH
see
ORTH**

Inquiry, miry, spiry, wiry

IRY
see
E**

Aegis, amaryllis, analepsis, analysis, Annus Mirabilis, Anubis, aphis, Apis, Artemis, Atlantis, Attis, axis, Bubastis, caddis, Chablis, Charybdis, Clovis, Colchis, crisis, De Profundis, Dis, Eblis, Eleusis, ephemeris, epidermis, Fenris, finis, hamamelis, Harmachis, houris, ibis, Iblis, ichthyornis, iris, Isis, Lake Moeris, laryngitis, mantis, marquis, Memphis, morris, myosotis, non compos mentis, Nunc Dimittis, ora pro nobis, orris, Osiris, parvis, pelvis, Phyllis, portcullis, proboscis, prognosis, Propontis, psycho-analysis, rara avis, sacred-ibis, Salamis, Salmacis, salpiglossis, Sardis, Semiramis,

IS*
see
AIS
ALIS
ARIS
ASIS
ATIS
ESIS
ICE**
ISE****
ISS
OLIS
ONIS
OPSIS
OSIS
UCE**

semper fidelis, Serapis, Sesostris, Smer-   **IS***
dis, stephanotis, tennis, Thamyris,
Themis, thesis, Thetis, this, Tiflis,
Tigris, trellis, Tunis, Walpurgis

   Chassis, his, is, 'tis, this-is   **IS****
                    see
                    IZ
                    ACE-*s*
                    EACH-*s*

   Ambergris, verdigris   **IS*****
                    see
                    EESE**

   Artisan, Nisan, non-partisan, parti-   **ISAN**
san   *see*
                    AN*

   Disc   **ISC**
                    see
                    ISK

   Advise, anywise, apprise, arise, cate- **ISE***
chise, chastise, circumcise, coastwise,   *see*
comprise, compromise, contrariwise,   IZE
corner-wise, crosswise, demise, despise,   EYE-*s*
devise, edgewise, enterprise, exercise,   IE**-*s*
exorcise, franchise, improvise, incise,   IES*
leastwise, lengthwise, likewise, mer-
chandise, moonrise, mortal-wise, no-
wise, otherwise, penny-wise, revise,
rise, slant-wise, suchwise, sunrise, su-
pervise, surmise, surprise, thuswise,
unwise, weatherwise, wise

Concise, Paradise, precise

ISE**
see
ICE*

Cerise, chemise, Heloise, marquise, valise

ISE***
see
EASE**
EESE**
ESE

Anise, mortise, practise, premise, promise, treatise

ISE****
see
ISS

Appetiser, despiser, Kaiser, miser, wiser

ISER
see
ER

Accomplish, admonish, apish, astonish, backshish, banish, blemish, bluefish, bookish, boorish, boyish, brackish, brandish, British, brutish, bulldoggish, burnish, butterdish, cat-fish, cattish, chafing-dish, churlish, cloddish, clownish, coltish, Cornish, crawfish, dervish, devilish, disrelish, elfish, embellish, English, establish, famish, fetish, finish, fish, Flemish, flourish, foolish, freakish, furbish, furnish, garish, garnish, girlish, goldfish, grayish, greenish, hashish, heathenish, hellish, hoggish, horseradish, hoydenish, impish, Irish, jelly-fish, Jewish, knavish, lavish, loutish, mannish, mawkish, minish, modish, monkish, Moorish, mulish, oafish, offish, ogreish, outlandish, paganish, parish, peevish, pilot-fish, pound-fool-

ISH
see
EESH
ERISH
OLISH
UISH
ly-E**

ish, priggish, prudish, publish, punish, **ISH**
radish, rakish, ravish, reddish, relish,
replenish, rubbish, sawfish, selfish,
sheepish, shellfish, shrewish, skirmish,
skittish, slavish, sluggish, snobbish,
Spanish, squeamish, starfish, stiffish,
sunfish, swish, swordfish, tarnish, Tar-
shish, ticklish, undiminish, vanish,
varnish, waggish, waspish, whirling
dervish, whitish, wish, womanish, Yid-
dish

Fisher, garnisher, kingfisher, pub- **ISHER**
lisher, well-wisher *see*
ER

Decision, derision, division, elision, **ISION**
envision, incision, indecision, precision, *see*
prevision, provision, revision, super- ION
vision, television, vision

Asterisk, basilisk, bisk, brisk, disk, **ISK**
frisk, obelisk, risk, tamarisk, whisk *see*
ISQUE

Frisky, risky, whisky **ISKY**
see
E**

Aisle, blessed-isle, Carlisle, Emerald **ISLE**
Isle, fairy-isle, lisle, safety-isle, sea- *see*
swept-isle ILE*

Actinism, altruism, analogism, an- **ISM**
thropomorphism, aphorism, asterism, *see*
atavism, baptism, barbarism, Bolshe- AISM
vism, Brahmanism, Buddhism, cate- ALISM
chism, chauvinism, chrism, collecti- ICISM
vism, conservatism, despotism, dyna- ONISM

mism, egoism, egotism, empiricism, **ISM**
epicurism, exorcism, Fascism, galvan- UISM
ism, gormandism, henotheism, heroism, YSM
hyperbolism, incendiarism, Islamism,
magnetism, mannerism, mechanism,
mesmerism, metabolism, micro-orga-
nism, modernism, monotheism, Nazism,
nepotism, nihilism, occultism, Ophism,
optimism, organism, ostracism, paci-
fism, paganism, pantheism, pedagog-
ism, pessimism, phallicism, polytheism,
prism, proletarianism, propagandism,
pugilism, purism, quietism, recidivism,
red-tapism, republicanism, rheuma-
tism, rowdyism, Sabæanism, sabba-
tism, Sadism, savagism, schism, Shiism,
sinapism, skepticism, solecism, som-
nambulism, sophism, Sufism, surreal-
ism, sybaritism, syllogism, symbolism,
theism, totemism, vandalism, voodoo-
ism, witticism

Benison, bison, caparison, compari- **ISON**
son, garrison, imprison, jettison, Kyrie *see*
eleison, liaison, orison, poison, prison, ON
unison, venison

Crisp, lisp, will-o'-the-wisp, wisp **ISP**
see

Bisque, odalisque **ISQUE**
see
ISK

Amiss, bliss, cumiss, dismiss, hiss, **ISS**
kiss, miss, Swiss, remiss *see*
IS*
YSS
ed-IST

Admission, emission, intermission, mission, omission, permission, remission, submission, transmission

ISSION
see
ION

Fissue, issue, tissue

ISSUE
see
UE

Alarmist, alchemist, apiculturist, artist, atheist, atomist, atwist, autoist, balladist, banjoist, Baptist, bicyclist, bigamist, Bonapartist, caricaturist, cartoonist, chemist, cist, colonist, columnist, Communist, computist, conformist, consist, copyist, cubist, cyclist, deist, dentist, desist, druggist, egoist, egotist, equilibrist, enlist, eucharist, evangelist, exist, exorcist, fabulist, Fascist, fatalist, feminist, fist, florist, futurist, gist, glossarist, grist, herbalist, hist, hobbyist, homilist, humorist, insist, journalist, jurist, leftist, list, lobbyist, loyalist, Methodist, miniaturist, mist, moralist, motorist, naturalist, nihilist, non conformist, novelist, nudist, obscurantist, occultist, Oliver Twist, opportunist, optimist, optometrist, organist, orientalist, pacifist, palmist, parodist, Paulist, persist, pessimist, pharmaceutist, pharmacist, philatelist, physicist, physiognomist, physiologist, pianist, plagiarist, polytheist, propagandist, psalmist, psychist, pugilist, purist, pyramidologist, Quietist, realist, resist, revivalist, rhapsodist, rightist, ritualist, Romanist, royalist, Sadist, satirist, scientist, Scotch-mist,

IST*
see
OGIST
ONIST
UIST
YST*
ICE**-*ed*

shortist, soloist, somnambulist, sophist, **IST***
specialist, strategist, stylist, subsist,
surrealist, taxlist, thaumaturgist, the-
ist, theurgist, tourist, Trappist, twist,
violinist, vocalist, whist, wrist, wist

Christ **IST****
see

Ballista, genista, vista **ISTA**
see
A**

Artiste, batiste, modiste **ISTE**
see
EAST*
YST**

Administer, barrister, blister, can- **ISTER**
ister, minister, mister, register, sinister, *see*
sister **ER**

Altruistic, anachronistic, animistic, **ISTIC**
anomalistic, artistic, cabalistic, Cal- *see*
vinistic, casuistic, characteristic, chre- **IC**
mastistic, deistic, egoistic, egotistic,
Elohistic, euphuistic, fatalistic, inar-
tistic, Jehovistic, linguistic, militaris-
tic, modernistic, optimistic, panthe-
istic, pessimistic, phlogistic, realistic,
ritualistic, sadistic, spiritistic, statistic

Bristle, epistle, gristle, peanut whis- **ISTLE**
tle, thistle, whistle *see*
EL
LE

Artistry, chemistry, ministry, palm-
istry, papistry, registry, sophistry

ISTRY
see
E**

Accredit, adit, admit, affidavit,
audit, bandit, befit, benefit, bit, bottomless pit, bowsprit, chit, coalpit,
cock-pit, comfit, commit, cubit, cul-
prit, davit, debit, decline-it, decrepit,
deposit, digit, discomfit, dispirit, emi-
gravit, emit, exit, explicit, fit, flit, grit,
habit, half-wit, hermit, hit, Holy Writ,
howbeit, illicit, inhabit, intermit, ipse-
dixit, it, jack-in-the-pulpit, kit, knit,
lamplit, licit, lickety-split, limit, lit,
make-up kit, manumit, misfit, moonlit,
nimble-wit, nit, nit-wit, no-hit, obit,
omit, orbit, outfit, outwit, permit, pit,
plaudit, posit, profit, prohibit, prosit,
pulpit, pundit, rabbit, refit, remit, re-
visit, Sanskrit, sit, skit, slit, so-be-it,
spirit, spit, split, sprit, starlit, stonepit,
submit, summit, Tashmit, tidbit, tit,
to wit, transit, twit, unfit, unit, visit,
vomit, welsh-rabbit, whit, wit, writ

IT
see
EDIT
EIT**
ERIT
IBIT
ICIT
ITE**
UIT*
ed-ED
s-ITS

Amrita, per capita, Sita

ITA
see
A**

Charitable, habitable, hospitable,
illimitable, indubitable, inevitable, in-
hospitable, inimitable, profitable, suitable, veritable

ITABLE
see
ABLE

Capital, hospital, marital, non-com-
mital, orbital, recital, requital, vital

ITAL
see
AL

Cosmopolitan, metropolitan, Neapolitan, puritan, Samaritan

ITAN
see
AN*

Annuitant, concomitant, exorbitant, habitant, inhabitant, irritant, militant, visitant

ITANT
see
ANT*

Agitate, cogitate, felicitate, gravitate, gurgitate, hesitate, imitate, incapacitate, irritate, meditate, necessitate, precipitate, premeditate, regurgitate, rehabilitate, solicitate

ITATE
see
ATE
ed-ED

Auction pitch, backstitch, bewitch, bitch, czarevitch, ditch, featherstitch, flitch, hemstitch, hitch, itch, lockstitch, low pitch, pitch, stitch, switch, twitch, whipstitch, witch

ITCH
see
ICH

Aconite, Adamite, aerolite, Amalekite, Ammonite, anchorite, anthracite, Aphrodite, appetite, apposite, Areopapagite, ashy-white, backbite, bite, blatherskite, bobwhite, box-kite, Canaanite, Carmelite, cenobite, cite, contrite, cyanite, despite, dolomite, dynamite, ebonite, Edomite, eremite, erudite, excite, expedite, finite, frostbite, Gilroy's kite, graphite, Hepplewhite, hermaphrodite, hoplite, hyposulphite, incite, incondite, indite, invite, Israelite, Jacobite, kite, labradorite, lazulite, lignite, lyddite, malachite, meteorite, midshipmite, milkwhite, mite, Muscovite, Nazarite, niccolite, parasite, phosphite, plebiscite, polite, poor white,

ITE*
see
EIGHT**
IGHT
YTE

quite, recite, recondite, requite, rite, **ITE***
satellite, Semite, Sethite, Shiite, Shu-
nammite, site, smite, socialite, spite,
sprite, stalactite, stalagmite, subur-
banite, sulphite, Sybarite, termite, thal-
mite, theodolite, trite, underwrite,
unite, vulcanite, white, widow's mite,
write

Definite, exquisite, favorite, granite, **ITE****
indefinite, infinite,. marguerite, oppo- *see*
site, perquisite, preterite, requisite IT

Arbiter, ghost writer, Jupiter, liter, **ITER**
miter, niter, scimiter, typewriter, writer *see*
ER

Aerolith, blacksmith, crith, forth- **ITH**
with, frith, goldsmith, Judith, kith, *see*
Lilith, locksmith, megalith, Meredith, YTH
monolith, Neith, neolith, pith, silver-
smith, smith, Tanith, with, zenith

Blithe, lithe, tithe, writhe **ITHE**
see
YTHE

Dither, nowhither, slither, thither, **ITHER**
whither, wither, zither *see*
ER

Logarithm **ITHM**
see
YTHM

Haiti, prakriti, Tahiti, wapiti **ITI**
see
I**

Critic, mephitic, parasitic, politic **ITIC**
see
IC

Abolition, admonition, air-condition, **ITION**
ambition, apparition, apposition, attri- *see*
tion, audition, coalition, coition, com- ION
petition, composition, condition, con-
trition, decomposition, disposition,
ebullition, edition, exhibition, expedi-
tion, exposition, extradition, fruition,
ignition, imposition, inhibition, Inquisition, intuition, juxtaposition, muni-
tion, nutrition, opposition, partition,
perdition, petition, position, predispo-
sition, premonition, prohibition, recog-
nition, recondition, rendition, repeti-
tion, requisition, sedition, special edition, superstition, supposition, tradi-
tion, tuition, volition

Auditive, competitive, fugitive, gen- **ITIVE**
itive, infinitive, inquisitive, partitive, *see*
primitive, prohibitive, punitive, sensi- IVE**
tive, transitive, volitive

Gitche Manito, incognito, mosquito, **ITO**
Quito *see*
O*

Auditor, city-editor, competitor, **ITOR**
creditor, depositor, inquisitor, janitor, *see*
monitor, progenitor, servitor, solicitor, OR
suitor, traitor, visitor

Calamitous, circuitous, felicitous, **ITOUS**
gratuitous, iniquitous, solicitous, ubiq- *see*
uitous OUS
US

Bitter, flitter, fritter, glitter, jitter, litter, outfitter, quitter, sitter, titter, transmitter, twitter

ITTER
see
ER

Belittle, brittle, lickspittle, little, spittle, tittle, vittle, whittle

ITTLE
see
EL
LE

Ditty, gritty, kitty, witty

ITTY
see
E**

Altitude, amplitude, aptitude, attitude, beatitude, certitude, decreptitude, exactitude, fortitude, gratitude, habitude, inaptitude, incertitude, ineptitude, infinitude, ingratitude, lassitude, latitude, longitude, magnitude, multitude, nigritude, platitude, plenitude, promptitude, rectitude, servitude, similitude, solicitude, solitude, turpitude, vicissitude, virisimilitude

ITUDE
see
UDE

Ad libitum, infinitum

ITUM
see
UM

Discomfiture, expenditure, forfeiture, furniture, garniture, geniture, investiture, portraiture, primogeniture

ITURE
see
URE

Emeritus, Hermaphroditus, St. Vitus, Tacitus, Theocritus, Titus, Unigenitus

ITUS
see
US

Constitute, destitute, institute, prostitute, substitute

ITUTE
see
UTE
ed-ED

Absurdity, alacrity, amity, anonymity, benignity, caducity, calamity, cavity, celebrity, chastity, city, comity, complexity, concavity, conformity, corporeity, credulity, deformity, density, depravity, dignity, enmity, enormity, entity, eternity, fatality, fecundity, fidelity, fraternity, frivolity, gravity, heredity, identity, immensity, indemnity, indignity, infidelity, infirmity, integrity, intensity, jollity, laity, laxity, maternity, necessity, nonconformity, nonentity, nudity, nullity, obesity, oddity, paucity, perplexity, perversity, pity, polity, probity, profundity, prolixity, propensity, quantity, Radio City, rotundity, salubrity, sanctity, sanity, scarcity, self-pity, solemnity, spontaneity, suavity, taciturnity, tensity, uniformity, university, varsity, velocity

ITY
see
ACITY
ALITY
ANITY
ARITY
E**
EITY
ENITY
ERITY
EVITY
ICITY
IDITY
ILITY
IMITY
INITY
IVITY
OCITY
ORITY
OSITY
UITY
UNITY
URITY

Fritz, seidlitz, sitz

ITZ
see

Howitzer, kibitzer

ITZER
see
ER

Alluvium, aquarium, atrium, bdellium, Belgium, Byzantium, calcium, chromium, compendium, cranium, decennium, delirium, delphinium, diluvium, effluvium, elysium, encomium, eulogium, euphorbium, exordium, geranium, gymnasium, harmonium, helium, herbarium, iridium, magnesium, medium, megatherium, millennium, nasturtium, odium, opium, opprobrium, osmium, palladium, pandemonium, peculium, pericranium, planetarium, polonium, potassium, premium, principium, proscenium, protevangelium, radium, rose-geranium, scholium, selenium, sodium, stadium, stramonium, symposium, tedium, trifolium, trillium, trivium, uranium

IUM
see
EUM
OM*
OME*
ORIUM
UM
UMN

Æsculapius, Apuleius, Aquarius, Athanasius, Boëthius, Cassius, Confucius, Dionysius, Erichthonius, expurgatorius, genius, Helvetius, Lucretius, Marcus Aurelius, Mencius, nisi prius, Pluvius, Polonius, Procopius, radius, Sagittarius, Sirius, Stradivarius, Suetonius, Tiberius, Titus Livius, Vesuvius

IUS
see
US

Arrival, carnival, festival, outrival, revival, rival, survival

IVAL
see
AL

Activate, cultivate, motivate, private, recidivate, titivate

IVATE
see
ATE

Alive, archive, arrive, beehive, chive, connive, contrive, deprive, dive, five, hive, revive, scared-alive, strive, survive, thrive

IVE*
see
YVE
S-IFE-S
IVES

Active, adhesive, aggressive, attentive, captive, cohesive, collective, compressive, consumptive, convective, convictive, cursive, decisive, defective, descriptive, destructive, detective, diminutive, directive, elective, endive, eruptive, executive, exhaustive, expansive, expensive, expressive, extensive, festive, forgive, furtive, give, housewive, impassive, inactive, incentive, inexpensive, inoffensive, instinctive, intensive, invective, inventive, irrespective, Khedive, live, massive, misgive, missive, objective, obstructive, offensive, ogive, olive, oppressive, outlive, passive, pendentive, pensive, perceptive, perspective, persuasive, pervasive, perversive, plaintive, presumptive, progressive, projective, prospective, qui vive, radioactive, receptive, reflective, respective, restive, retentive, retrogressive, secretive, selective, skive, sportive, suasive, subjective, submissive, substantive, subversive, suggestive, susceptive, vindictive, votive, wive

IVE**
see
ATIVE
IEVE**
ITIVE
OSIVE
OTIVE
USIVE

Drivel, shrivel, snivel, swivel

IVEL
see
EL
LE

Deliver, diver, driver, giver, law-giver, liver, purling-river, quiver, receiver, river, screw driver, slave-driver, shiver, sliver, waiver

IVER
see
ER

Delivery, livery

IVERY
see
E**

Archives, hives, housewives, pocket-knives

IVES
see
IVE*-*s*

Civet, privet, rivet, trivet

IVET
see
ET

Acclivity, activity, captivity, declivity, festivity, inactivity, nativity, objectivity, passivity, proclivity, receptivity, relativity, selectivity

IVITY
see
E**
ITY

Administratrix, affix, Aix, appendix, betwixt, calix, cicatrix, crucifix, felix, fix, infelix, intermix, janitrix, matrix, mix, nix, Phoenix, prefix, prolix, radix, semper felix, six, spadix, suffix, testatrix, transfix, Vercingetorix

IX
see
YX
IC-*s*
ICK-*s*
ed-IXT

Betwixt, 'twixt

IXT
see
IX-*ed*

Agassiz, biz, Cadiz, friz, Hafiz, phiz, rheumatiz, viz , whiz

IZ
see
IES**
IS**
IZZ
UIZ

Advertize, affinitize, anathematize, anglicize, apologize, apotheosize, assize, atomize, attitudinize, authorize, baptize, barbarize, botanize, capsize, cauterize, centralize, civilize, criticize, crystallize, demobilize, demoralize, deodorize, emphasize, energize, epitomize, eulogize, evangelize, extemporize, familiarize, fertilize, foreignize, fossilize, fraternize, galvanize, gormandize, headsize, hybridize, idolize, itemize, jeopardize, latinize, lionize, memorize, mercerize, mesmerize, minimize, mobilize, modernize, monopolize, neutralize, Nobel prize, organize, ostracize, overemphasize, oxidize, particularize, plagiarize, polarize, popularize, `prize, proselytize, pulverize, rhapsodize, recognize, satirize, scandalize, scrutinize, sensitize, size, solemnize, soliloquize, stabilize, sterilize, stigmatize, syllogize, sympathize, synchronize, temporize, terrorize, theorize, tranquilize, undersize, utilize, vaporize, victimize

IZE
see
ALIZE
ONIZE
EYE-*s*
IES*
ISE*
UISE*

Bedizen, citizen, denizen, wizen

IZEN
see
EN

Appetizer, atomizer, criticizer, fertilizer, organizer, vocalizer

IZER
see
ER

Fizz, gin fizz

IZZ
see
IZ

Drizzle, fizzle, frizzle, sizzle, swizzle **IZZLE**
see
EL
LE

O SOUNDS

Accelerando, akimbo, Alamo, Aleppo, alfresco, allegro, ambo, antipasto, Apollo, Aquilo, Ariosto, arroyo, auto, autogyro, banjo, Banquo, basso, basso-profundo, basso relievo, bayamo, bilbo, bravo, broncho, burro, Cairo, Cagliostro, calabozo, Callisto, Calypso, certo, chiaroscuro, chromo, Co., Colombo, concerto, Consuelo, conto, corso, cui bono, de facto, Dido, ditto, dodo, Draco, dynamo, echo, ego, embryo, ergo, fiasco, Figaro, forego, fresco, fro, gaucho, gazebo, ginkgo, go, Gran Chaco, Guido, gusto, hidalgo, H_2O, Hoang-Ho, hobo, indigo, inferno, in toto, ipso facto, Jericho, Jethro, jocko, junco, Juno, kilo, kimono, lasso, let-go, libido, Lido, limbo, lo, Lorenzo, maestro, major-domo, Manchukuo, manifesto, mestizo, Michael Angelo, Monaco, Monte Carlo, Monte Cristo, Morocco, mulatto, Mumbo-Jumbo, Navajo, negro, no, octavo, oho, Orinoco, Palermo, papagayo, papyro, perfecto, Pernambuco, peso, photo, pico, Pizarro, placebo, Pluto, Po, poncho, pro, Prosilipo, proviso, pueblo, quarto, Quasimodo, rancho, recto, re-echo, righto, rococo, Salerno, salvo, San Diego, San Francisco, Sappho, Sargasso, secundo,

O*

see

ADO
AGO
ALO
ANGO
ANO
ANTO
AO
ARGO
ATO
EAU
EDO
EGO
ELLO
ENDO
ENTO
EO
ERO
ESTO
ETO
ETTO
ICO
ILLO
IMO
INGO
INO
IO
ITO
OE**

shako, Shinto, silo, sirocco, so, so and so, so-ho, so-so, status quo, St. Elmo, stucco, tabasco, tally-ho, tardo, taro, Tasso, tempo, Terra del Fuego, testudo, theorbo, to and fro, tobacco, torso, tufo, tyro, undergo, Valparaiso, verso, veto, Virgo, Yao, yo-ho, Zeno

O*
OLO
OSO
OTTO
OUGH*
OW*
OWE
S-OSE*
OWS

Ado, came-to, do, heave-to, hitherto, how-d'ye-do, lean-to, outdo, overdo, that-will-do, thereunto, to, to-do, two, underdo, undo, unto, well-to-do, we-two, who

O**
see
AGUE***
EW
IEW
OE*
OO
OU*
OUGH****
OUX
U
UE*

Balboa, boa, cocoa, Genoa, goa, proa, protozoa, Samoa, whoa

OA
see
A**

Accroach, approach, broach, coach, cockroach, encroach, poach, reproach, roach, slow coach, stage coach

OACH
see
OCHE

Abroad, broad, carload, corduroy-road, crossroad, goad, highroad, horned-toad, inroad, load, overload, railroad, road, shipload, toad, tree toad, unload, woad

OAD
see
ODE
OW*-*ed*

Loaf, oaf

OAF
see
OPHE**

Bathcloak, Charter Oak, cloak, croak, holm-oak, live-oak, oak, scrub-oak, soak, uncloak, white-oak

OAK
see
OKE
S-OAX

Cannel coal, charcoal, coal, foal, goal, shoal

OAL
see
OL
OUL**

Foam, gloam, loam, roam, Siloam, sea-foam

OAM
see
OMB**
OME**

Bemoan, Darby and Joan, groan, loan, moan, roan

OAN
see
ONE*

Soap

OAP
see
OPE

Bezoar, boar, dripping-oar, hoar, muffled-oar, roar, soar, torrent's-roar, uproar, wild-boar

OAR
see
OOR*
ed-OARD
S-OR-S

Aboard, above board, all aboard, billboard, blackboard, board, bristol board, buckboard, cardboard, chequerboard, chess board, clapboard, cupboard, dashboard, hoard, inboard,

OARD
see
ORD*
OAR-*ed*
OR-*ed*

keyboard, lapboard, larboard, mop- **OARD**
board, mortarboard, ouija-board, out-
board, overboard, pasteboard, running-
board, school-board, shipboard, shuffle-
board, sideboard, signboard, sounding-
board, starboard, switch-board

Boast, cinnamon toast, coast, corn- **OAST**
roast, dry-toast, milktoast, pot-roast, *see*
roast, toast OST**
ed-ED

Afloat, bloat, blue-coat, boat, bum- **OAT**
boat, canal boat, coat, cut-throat, *see*
ferryboat, float, fur-coat, gloat, goat, OTE
great-coat, gunboat, jolly-boat, life *s*-OATS
boat, moat, motorboat, nanny-goat,
oat, overcoat, packet-boat, petticoat,
police boat, red coat, rowboat, sailboat,
scapegoat, shoat, speedboat, steam-
boat, surcoat, throat, topcoat, torpedo
boat, turncoat, U-boat, waistcoat,
whaleboat

Inchoate **OATE**
see
ATE

Loath, oath **OATH**
see
OTH*

Wild-oats **OATS**
see
OAT-*s*

Blob, bob, cob, corncob, fob, gob, heart-throb, hob, hobnob, Jacob, job, knob, lob, mob, nabob, rob, slob, snob, sob, soft job, thingumbob, throb

OB*
see
AB**
UAB

Job

OB**
see
OBE

Approbate, probate, reprobate

OBATE
see
ATE

Dobber, jobber, robber, slobber

OBBER
see
ER

Cobble, gobble, hobble, wobble

OBBLE
see
EL
LE

Blobby, bobby, hobby, knobby, lobby

OBBY
see
E**

Disrobe, globe, lap-robe, lobe, microbe, nightrobe, probe, robe, wardrobe

OBE
see
OB**

October, sober

OBER
see
ER

Ennoble, ignoble, noble

OBLE
see
EL
LE

En bloc, havoc, langue d'Oc, Medoc, opodeldoc, roc, Tlaloc

OC
see
OCH

Bifocal, equivocal, focal, local, reciprocal, vocal

OCAL
see
AL

Allocate, dislocate, equivocate, invocate, locate, reciprocate, suffocate

OCATE
see
ATE

Antioch, Enoch, epoch, loch, Moloch, pibroch

OCH
see
OC
OCK

Troche

OCHE
see
OACH

Ochre

OCHRE
see
ER

Atrocity, ferocity, precocity, reciprocity, velocity

OCITY
see
E**
ITY

Alpenstock, bedrock, block, bock, bullock, burdock, buttock, cassock, chock-a-block, chopping-block, clock, cock, crock, deadlock, dock, fetlock, firelock, flintlock, flock, forelock, frock, game-cock, grandfather's clock, haddock, hammock, hassock, haycock,

OCK
see
OC
OCH
ed-OCT
s-OX

hemlock, hillock, hock, hollyhock, **OCK**
hummock, interlock, jabberwock,
joint-stock, knock, laughing-stock,
livestock, lock, lovelock, mattock,
minster-clock, mock, moss-grown-
rock, oarlock, o'clock, overstock, pad-
dock, padlock, peacock, pock, pollock,
poppy-cock, Plymouth Rock, Rappa-
hannock, rowlock, shaddock, sham-
rock, shell-shock, shock, shuttlecock,
Shylock, smock, sock, stock, stopcock,
stumbling-block, Tarpeian Rock, tick-
tock, town-clock, traprock, tussock,
unfrock, unlock, warlock, weathercock,
wedlock, white rock, woodcock

Knickerbocker, knocker, locker, **OCKER**
rocker, shilling shocker *see*
ER

Crocket, docket, locket, pickpocket, **OCKET**
pocket, rocket, sky-rocket, socket, *see*
sprocket ET

Mediocre **OCRE**
see
ER

Concoct, decoct **OCT**
see
OCK-*ed*

Crocus, focus, hocus-pocus, locus **OCUS**
see
US

Aaron's rod, Cape Cod, clod, coal-hod, cod, decapod, demigod, divining-rod, downtrod, dryshod, ephod, gas-tropod, God, goldenrod, Herod, hexa-pod, hod, land-o-Nod, lightning-rod, megapod, method, Nimrod, nod, Nov-gorod, od, pea-pod, platypod, plod, pod, prod, ramrod, rod, roughshod, sea-god, shod, slipshod, sod, sun-god, synod, tripod, trod, unshod, well-shod

OD
see
IOD
ODD
UAD

Bi-carbonate of soda, coda, pagoda, sal soda

ODA
see
A**

Odd

ODD
see
OD

Abode, à la mode, anode, bestrode, bode, cathode, code, commode, cor-rode, decode, discommode, episode, epode, erode, explode, forebode, in-commode, lode, mode, monopode, node, ode, outmode, rode, strode

ODE
see
OAD
OW*-*ed*

Dislodge, dodge, hodge-podge, lodge

ODGE
see

Anodic, episodic, melodic, odic, par-odic, periodic, prosodic, spasmodic

ODIC
see
IC

Coryphodon, glyptodon, mastodon

ODON
see
ON

Heterodox, orthodox

ODOX
see
OX

Anybody, body, chiropody, custody, disembody, embody, everybody, melody, monody, nobody, parody, prosody, psalmody, rhapsody, somebody, threnody, torpedo body

ODY
see
E**

Canoe, horseshoe, overshoe, shoe, snowshoe, Tippecanoe

OE*
see
O**
S-USE*

Aloe, Arapahoe, Crusoe, Defoe, doe, floe, foe, John Doe, mistletoe, oboe, pekoe, roe, shadroe, sloe, throe, tip-toe, toe, woe

OE**
see
O*
OW*
ed-OAD
   OW*-*ed*
S-OSE

Poem, proem

OEM
see
EM

Boer, church-goer, doer, evil-doer, good-doer, o'er, shoer

OER
see
ER

Of, unheard of, thereof, whereof

OF
see
OVE**

Cast-off, cut-off, doff, far-off, kick-off, off, palm-off, ring-off, Romanoff, scoff, send-off, show-off, stand-off, take-off, tee-off, toff

OFF
see
OUGHT*****
ed-OFT

Coffer, offer, proffer, scoffer **OFFER**
see
ER

Aloft, cockloft, croft, hayloft, how- **OFT**
oft, loft, Lowestoft, oft, soft *see*
OFF-*ed*

Agog, backlog, befog, bog, bullfrog, **OG**
clog, cog, cranberry bog, dog, egg-nog, *see*
firedog, flog, fog, frog, Gog, golliwog, OGUE*
grog, ground-hog, hedgehog, hog, hot
dog, house-dog, incog., jog, knotty-log,
lapdog, leapfrog, log, Magog, megafog,
peat-bog, polly-wog, prairie-dog, river-
hog, roadhog, sand-hog, sea-dog, sea-
hog, spitz-dog, sundog, under-dog,
watch-dog

Saratoga, toga, yoga **OGA**
see
A**

Abrogate, arrogate, interrogate, sur- **OGATE**
rogate *see*
ATE

Doge, horologe, gamboge **OGE**
see

Cyanogen, hydrogen, nitrogen, oxy- **OGEN**
hydrogen *see*
EN

Boggle, goggle, horn-swoggle, joggle, **OGGLE**
woggle *see*
EL
LE

Boggy, doggy, foggy, groggy, soggy   **OGGY**
see
E**

Geologic, logic, pedagogic, philologic   **OGIC**
see
IC

Anthologist, apologist, bacteriol-   **OGIST**
ogist, biologist, craniologist, entomol-   *see*
ogist, etymologist, fossilologist, geol-   IST
ogist, graphologist, neurologist, ontol-
ogist, ornothologist, philologist, phre-
nologist, physiologist, psychologist,
sinologist, teratologist

Bologne, Bourgogne, eau de Cologne   **OGNE**
see
ONE*

Ideogram, kilogram, monogram,   **OGRAM**
parallelogram, program, radiogram,   *see*
seismogram   AM

Ogre   **OGRE**
see
ER

Analogue, apologue, catalogue, Dec-   **OGUE***
alogue, demagogue, dialogue, duo-   *see*
logue, eclogue, epilogue, monologue,   OG
mystagogue, pedagogue, prologue, pro-
rogue, sinologue, theologue, travelogue

Brogue, rogue, vogue   **OGUE****
see

Amphilogy, analogy, eulogy, fogy,   **OGY**
genealogy, logy, mineralogy, pedagogy,   *see*
stogy, tetralogy, trilogy   E**
OLOGY

Oh, Pharaoh, Shiloh

OH
see
O*

Kohl

OHL
see
OL

Demi-john, Prester John

OHN
see
ON

Hoi polloi, Borzoi, Tolstoi

OI
see
OY

Choice, invoice, joice, rejoice, voice

OICE
see
ed-OIST
S-EZ

Alkaloid, aneroid, anthropoid, aster-
oid, avoid, celluloid, deltoid, devoid,
ichthyoid, mattoid, negroid, ornithoid,
planetoid, rhomboid, spheroid, tab-
loid, thyroid, typhoid, void

OID
see
OY-*ed*

Coif

OIF
see
OFF

Coign

OIGN
see
OIN

Boil, broil, cinquefoil, coil, despoil,
embroil, foil, free-soil, fusel oil, hard-
boil, midnight-oil, oil, panbroil, par-

OIL
see
OYLE

boil, quatrefoil, recoil, roil, salad-oil, **OIL**
soil, spark coil, spoil, subsoil, tinfoil,
toil, trefoil, turmoil, uncoil

Benzoin, coin, disjoin, enjoin, groin, **OIN**
heroin, join, loin, purloin, rejoin, sir-   *see*
loin, subjoin, tenderloin   OIGN

Heroine, Macedoine   **OINE**
see
INE

Anoint, appoint, dewpoint, disap-   **OINT**
point, fingerpoint, joint, needlepoint,   *see*
point, spear-point, standpoint, start-   *ed-ED*
ing-point, vanishing-point, viewpoint,
vowel point, West Point

Choir   **OIR***
see
IRE

Boudoir, memoir, peignoir, recevoir, **OIR****
rouge et noir   *see*
AR*

Armoire, bête noire, Directoire, es-   **OIRE**
critoire, Grimoire, pourboire, reper-   *see*
toire   OIR**

Avoirdupois, chamois, Marguerite **OIS**
de Valois, patois   *see*

Counterpoise, equipoise, noise, poise, **OISE**
porpoise, tortoise, turquoise   *see*
OY-*s*

Foist, hoist, joist, moist

OIST
see
OICE-*d*

Adroit, exploit, maladroit, quoit

OIT
see

Amok, O.K., Ragnarok, Zadok

OK
see
OCK

Artichoke, awoke, bespoke, bloke, broke, choke, coke, convoke, downstroke, evoke, fog-smoke, invoke, joke, moke, poke, provoke, revoke, Roanoke, smoke, spoke, stoke, stroke, sunstroke, upstroke, woke, yoke

OKE
see
OAK
OLK
OQUE
en-OKEN
s-OAX

Bespoken, betoken, broken, Hoboken, outspoken, plainspoken, spoken, token, unspoken

OKEN
see
EN

Broker, choker, croker, joker, pawnbroker, poker, soker, stockbroker, stoker

OKER
see
ER

Alcohol, Bath kol, carol, consol, control, entresol, extol, fal-de-rol, frijol, gambol, horse-pistol, idol,· lysol, menthol, old Sol, parasol, patrol, petrol, pistol, protocol, Sebastopol, self-control, symbol, systol, Tyrol

OL
see
IOL
OLE
ULL**
ed-OLD

Cupola, dongola, gondola, gorgonzola, Loyola, parabola, pergola, pianola, Pico della Mirandola, Romola, Savonarola, victrola, viola, Zola

OLA
see
A**

Chocolate, desolate, disconsolate, etiolate, inviolate, isolate, percolate, violate

OLATE
see
ATE

Age-old, behold, blindfold, bold, Childe Harold, Cloth of Gold, cold, cuckold, enfold, finegold, fold, foothold, foretold, fourfold, gold, hold, household, hundredfold, kobold, manifold, marigold, marsh marigold, mold, molten-gold, ninefold, old, scaffold, scold, sevenfold, sheepfold, sold, stonecold, stranglehold, stronghold, tenfold, thousandfold, threefold, threshold, told, unfold, untold, uphold, withhold, wold

OLD
see
OULD*
OL-*ed*
OLE-*d*
y-E**

Bolder, cigarette-holder, colder, folder, holder, landholder, older, shareholder, smolder

OLDER
see
ER

Air-hole, aureole, barberpole, barcarole, blowhole, bunghole, cajole, camisole, casserole, cigarette-hole, cole, condole, console, Creole, cubby-hole, dole, drole, girandole, glory-hole, groundmole, hole, keyhole, loophole, manhole, mole, North Pole, Old King Cole, oriole, parole, peephole, pigeonhole, pin-hole, pistole, pole, port-hole, ridge-pole, rigmarole, role, Seminole, sole, South Pole, tadpole, tent-pole, thole, totem-pole, whole

OLE*
see
OAL
OL
OLL*
OUL**
ed-OL-*ed*
OLD

Hyperbole, frijole

OLE**
see
E**

Indolent, insolent, malevolent, redolent, somnolent, violent

OLENT
see
ENT

Golf, werewolf, wolf

OLF
see

Argoli, broccoli, Gallipoli, Rivoli, tivoli

OLI
see
I**

Anatolia, magnolia, melancholia, Mongolia

OLIA
see
IA

Alcoholic, bucolic, carbolic, catholic, colic, diabolic, frolic, non-alcoholic, parabolic, symbolic

OLIC
see
IC

Semi-solid, solid, stolid

OLID
see
ID

Etiolin, lanolin, mandolin, violin

OLIN
see
IN

Folio, olio, portfolio

OLIO
see
IO

Acropolis, Annapolis, anolis, Heliopolis, metropolis, necropolis, Persepolis

OLIS
see
IS*

Abolish, coolish, demolish, foolish, polish

OLISH
see
ISH

Country-folk, fisher-folk, folk, gen-   **OLK**
tle-folk, kinsfolk, yolk   *see*
                                 OQUE
                                 S-OAX

Boll, breakfast-roll, droll, enroll,   **OLL***
knoll, mossy-knoll, muster-roll, pay-   *see*
roll, roll, scroll, stroll, toll, troll, unroll   OLE
                                 OUL**

Doll, loll, moll, poll   **OLL****
                                 see

Collar, dollar, trade dollar   **OLLAR**
                                 see
                                 AR

Dolly, folly, holly, jolly, polly, sea   **OLLY**
holly   *see*
                                 E**

Coco-bolo, Fra Diavolo, gigolo,   **OLO**
Marco Polo, piccolo, polo, solo, trem-   *see*
olo, water polo   O*

Anthology, apology, archæology,   **OLOGY**
astro-theology, biology, bryology,   *see*
Christology, chronology, cryptology,   OGY
dactylology, demonology, dermatol-
ogy, doxology, Egyptology, eschatol-
ogy, ethnology, etymology, geology,
glossology, graphology, hagiology, ho-
mology, horology, ichthyology, ideol-
ogy, lexicology, martyrology, meteor-
ology, metrology, morphology, myth-
ology, neology, nephology, nostology,
numerology, odontology, ontology,

oölogy, ornithology, orthology, osteology, pathology, penology, philology, photology, phraseology, phrenology, physiology, psychology, pyramidology, seismology, sinology, tautology, technology, teleology, teratology, terminology, theology, toxicology, zoölogy **OLOGY**

Ben Bolt, bolt, colt, dolt, iron-bolt, jolt, king-bolt, micro-volt, molt, revolt, thunderbolt, volt **OLT** *see*

Absolute, dissolute, irresolute, resolute, volute **OLUTE** *see* UTE

Absolve, devolve, dissolve, evolve, involve, resolve, revolve, solve **OLVE** *see*

Absolver, dissolver, resolver, revolver **OLVER** *see* ER

Holy, melancholy, moly, monopoly, roly-poly, unholy **OLY** *see* E**

Accustom, besom, blossom, boredom, bosom, bottom, buxom, cardamom, carom, Christendom, Chrysostom, cockneydom, custom, Edom, embosom, envenom, Epsom, fathom, freedom, from, hansom, heathendom, kingdom, lissom, maelstrom, martyrdom, officialdom, Om, Peeping Tom, phantom, Pithom, pogrom, random, ransom, rock bottom, rush-bottom, serfdom, **OM*** *see* EUM IUM OME* OSM UM

Sodom, stardom, symptom, thralldom, **OM***
tomtom, unbosom, venom, whilom,
wisdom

Whom   **OM****
                                                see
                                                OOM

Aroma, coma, diploma, La Paloma,   **OMA**
Oklahoma, pleroma, Point Loma, soma   *see*
                                                A**

Dragoman, Ottoman, toman, woman,   **OMAN**
yeoman   *see*
                                                AN*

Aplomb, bomb, rhomb   **OMB***
                                                see

Catacomb, comb, coxcomb, curry-   **OMB****
comb, hecatomb, honey-comb, tomb,   *see*
uncomb, womb   UMB

Become, blithesome, burdensome,   **OME***
come, cumbersome, fearsome, four-   *see*
some, frolicsome, gladsome, gruesome,   IUM
handsome, income, irksome, lissome,   OM*
loathsome, lonesome, meddlesome,   UM
mettlesome, noisome, outcome, over-   UMN
come, quarrelsome, rollicksome, some,
tiresome, toilsome, toothsome, trouble-
some, venturesome, wearisome, well-
come, wholesome, winsome

Chrome, dome, gnome, hippodrome,   **OME****
home, metronome, monochrome, palin-   *see*
drome, polychrome, Rome, St. Jerome,   OAM
tome, vela-drome, Vendome

Abdomen, cognomen, omen, women **OMEN**
see
EN

Astronomer, customer, Homer, in-**OMER**
comer, misnomer, newcomer, omer *see*
ER

Comet, Mahomet **OMET**
see
ET

Atomic, comic, economic, gastro-**OMIC**
nomic, gnomic, serio-comic *see*
IC

Blossoming, coming, homing, in-**OMING**
coming, on-coming, spring-blossoming, *see*
Wyoming ING

Chromo, Como, Ecce Homo, major-**OMO**
domo *see*
O*

Pomp, romp **OMP**
see
AMP**

Prompt **OMPT**
see

Anatomy, antinomy, economy, phle-**OMY**
botomy, physiognomy, zoötomy *see*
E**

Abandon, æon, Agamemnon, Ajalon, **ON**
Anglo-Saxon, anon, antiphon, apron, *see*
Armageddon, Ascalon, Audubon, au-AGON
tomaton, Avalon, Avignon, Babylon, ÀN**

backgammon, bacon, barbiton, baron, beckon, be-ribbon, blue-ribbon, bonbon, bon-ton, bouillon, Bourbon, boustrophedon, caisson, call-upon, cannon, canon, canton, capon, carbon, carillon, carry on, cauldron, cedar of Lebanon, Celadon, Ceylon, chanson, Charon, chevron, chiffon, chiton, cinnamon, citron, colon, common, cordon, corydon, cotillon, cotton, coupon, crimson, crouton, damson, Demogorgon, Devon, dodecahedron, don, donjon, egg-on, eidolon, electron, emblazon, Emerson, epsilon, falcon, fanfaron, gallon, gibbon, gnomon, goings-on, gonfalon, Gorgon, grandson, griffon, gryphon, guerdon, guncotton, hanger-on, head-on, Hebron, horizon, Huron, jargon, Jupiter Ammon, klaxon, Kwannon, Lacedæmon, Laocöon, Lisbon, London, Mammon, marathon, matron, Memnon, mescal button, mignon, Milton, Mme. de Maintenon, Mormon, moron, Mother Shipton, myrmidon, neuron, Nippon, non, Oberon, on, pardon, parson, patron, pennon, person, phaëton, phenomenon, Phlegethon, piston, plastron, pompon, Poseidon, Princeton, pro and con, prolegomenon, python, rayon, reckon, rhododendron, ribbon, Rimmon, sabbaton, saffron, salmon, salon, Samson, Sanchoniathon, Sandalphon, Sargon, Saxon, semi-colon, sermon, sexton, Sheraton, Sidon, Simple Simon, simpleton, siphon, Solomon, Solon, son, soupçon, squadron, Stevenson, summon, talon, tampon, tarpon,

ON

ASON
AZON
EACON
EASON
ELON
EMON
EON
ERON
ETON
ICON
ION
IRON
ISON
ODON
OHN
ONE***
OPHON
UAN
UN
UTTON
YLON
YON
ed-UND

tendon, Tennyson, tetragrammaton, thereupon, torchon, Trianon, trilithon, triton, trogon, Typhon, uncommon, upon, wagon, wanton, Washington, weapon, welsh-mutton, whereon, yon, Yukon, zircon

ON

Arizona, Barcelona, Bellona, chincona, corona, Cremona, Crotona, Desdemona, Dodona, Latona, madrona, Pomona, Verona

ONA
see
A**

Ammonal, conditional, confessional, congressional, coronal, denominational, devotional, diagonal, dimensional, emotional, fourth dimensional, functional, gravitational, hexagonal, impersonal, international, meridional, national, notional, occasional, octagonal, optional, precessional, processional, prohibitional, rational, recessional, regional, seasonal, septentrional, sulphonal, traditional, unconditional, vegetational, veronal, visional

ONAL
see
AL

Dictionary, legionary, missionary, pulmonary, reactionary, revolutionary, stationary, visionary

ONARY
see
ARY

Donate, detonate, impersonate, intonate, passionate, pulmonate

ONATE
see
ATE

Once

ONCE*
see
UNCE

Ensconce, nonce, sconce

ONCE**
see
ONSE

Conch

ONCH
see
ONK

Abscond, almond, baby bond, be-
yond, blond, bond, correspond, despond, diamond, fond, frond, Phara-
mond, pond, reedy-pond, respond,
Richmond, second, Slough of Despond,
split-second, Trebizond, vagabond

OND
see
AND**

Anaconda, Gioconda, Golconda

ONDA
see
A**

Fonder, ponder, wonder, yonder

ONDER
see
ER

Alcyone, alone, anti-cyclone, atone,
backbone, baritone, barkstone, blood-
stone, bone, breast-bone, brimstone,
brownstone, canzone, capstone, chap-
erone, cheekbone, cicerone, cobble-
stone, condone, cone, cornerstone,
crone, crossbone, curbstone, cyclone,
dethrone, dictaphone, doorstone,
drone, fir-cone, fishbone, foundation-
stone, freestone, frozen zone, funny-
bone, gramophone, graphophone,
gravestone, grindstone, half-tone,
headstone, hearthstone, herringbone,
holystone, hone, intone, jackstone,

ONE*
see
OWN*

jawbone, keystone, knucklebone, Ladrone, limestone, megaphone, memorial-stone, microphone, milestone, millstone, monotone, moonstone, neurone, oilstone, outshone, overtone, ozone, ozytone, padrone, paroxytone, philosopher's stone, phone, postpone, prone, rawbone, rolling-stone, Rosetta stone, sandstone, saxophone, scone, semitone, shin-bone, shone, soapstone, steppingstone, stone, throne, tombstone, tone, torrid-zone, tottering-throne, trombone, undertone, whalebone, whetstone, xylophone, Yellowstone, zone

ONE*

Agone, begone, bygone, gone, woebegone

ONE* *
see
AWN

Done, none, one, outdone, overdone, someone, underdone, undone, welldone

ONE* **
see
UN

Component, exponent, opponent

ONENT
see
ENT

Almoner, executioner, falconer, practitioner, wagoner

ONER
see
ER

Nones, sawbones

ONES
see
ONE-*s*

Baronet, bayonet, canzonet, clarionet, coronet

ONET
see
ET

Honey, money, papermoney, pin-money
ONEY
see
EY

Age-long, along, among, belong, cradle-song, ding-dong, erelong, even-song, folksong, furlong, gong, head-long, headstrong, Hong Kong, livelong, long, mah-jong, oblong, oolong, ping-pong, prolong, prong, sarong, sidelong, singsong, siren's song, so-long, song, strong, swan song, thong, throng, tong, warsong, wrong
ONG
see
ONGUE
UNG

Sponge
ONGE
see
UNGE

Mother-tongue, ox-tongue, sacred tongue, silver tongue, tongue
ONGUE
see
ONG
UGN

Macaroni, Marconi, Zanoni, yoni
ONI
see
I**

Ammonia, begonia, Caledonia, Fran-conia, Harmonia, Macedonia, Pata-gonia, pneumonia
ONIA
see
IA

Bubonic, chronic, cyclonic, demonic, diatonic, electronic, harmonic, histri-onic, iconic, Ionic, ironic, laconic, mnemonic, moronic, Platonic, phil-harmonic, polyphonic, sardonic, Sla-vonic, symphonic, telephonic, Teu-tonic, tonic
ONIC
see
IC

Adonis, Coronis, Draconis

ONIS
see
IS*

Anachronism, antagonism, exhibitionism, hedonism, reactionism, synchronism, unionism

ONISM
see
ISM

Abolitionist, antagonist, cartoonist, hedonist, impressionist, protagonist

ONIST
see
IST

Agonize, canonize, carbonize, colonize, harmonize, lionize, patronize

ONIZE
see
IZE

Honk, monk

ONK
see
UNK

Commonly, matronly, only, wantonly

ONLY
see
E**

Belladonna, Madonna, primadonna, Vittoria Colonna

ONNA
see
A**

Carcassonne, Sorbonne

ONNE
see
ON

Absonous, anachronous, autochthonous, cacophonous, gluttonous, poisonous, synchronous

ONOUS
see
OUS

Blazonry, falconry, freemasonry, masonry, solid masonry

ONRY
see
E**

Response

ONSE
see
ONCE

Confront, dont, font, front, Hellespont, shirtfront, water-front, wont

ONT
see
ANT**
UNT

Billionth, millionth, month, trillionth, twelfth-month

ONTH
see

Acrimony, agony, agrimony, alimony, antimony, antiphony, balcony, betony, bony, bryony, cacophony, ceremony, chalcedony, colony, crony, disharmony, ebony, euphony, felony, gluttony, harmony, hegemony, inharmony, irony, Mark Anthony, monotony, nudist colony, parsimony, patrimony, peony, phony, pony, scammony, Shetland pony, testimony, theogony

ONY
see
E**

Anonym, caconym, pseudonym, synonym

ONYM
see
IM

Bonze, bronze

ONZE
see

Ballyhoo, bamboo, bazoo, boo, boohoo, Bronx-Zoo, cockatoo, coo-coo, cuckoo, goo-goo, halloo, hoodoo, hullaballoo, igloo, kangaroo, karoo, moo,

OO
see
ABOO
O**

shampoo, shoo, skidoo, tattoo, tick-
tack-too, too, toodle-oo, voodoo, Wa-
terloo, Whangpoo, woo, yoo-hoo, zoo

OO
OUGH****
U

Boob

OOB
see
UBE

Brooch, hooch, mooch, scooch

OOCH
see

Basswood, blueblood, boxwood,
briarwood, brushwood, camphorwood,
candlewood, childhood, cottonwood,
cypress wood, deadwood, dogwood,
driftwood, firewood, good, gopher
wood, greenwood, hardihood, holy-
rood, hood, ironwood, kindling-wood,
knighthood, likelihood, livelihood, log-
wood, matchwood, misunderstood,
monkhood, motherhood, neighborhood,
no good, priesthood, Red Riding Hood,
redwood, Robin Hood, rosewood, san-
dal-wood, satinwood, selfhood, stood,
teakwood, understood, Wedgwood,
wildwood, withstood, wood

OOD*
see
OULD

Blood, blueblood, cold blood, flood

OOD**
see
UD

Brood, food, mood, rood, snood,
solid food

OOD***
see
UDE

Broody, goody, moody, woody

OODY
see
E**

Aloof, bombproof, bulletproof, dis-
proof, fireproof, foolproof, galley-proof,
gas-proof, high-proof, hoof, proof, rain-
proof, reproof, roof, shadoof, spoof,
waterproof, woof

OOF
see

Scrooge, stooge

OOGE
see
UGE

Pooh-pooh

OOH
see
OO

Betook, book, brook, buttonhook,
cook, crook, doomsday book, fishhook,
forsook, guide-book, hook, Holy Book,
ingle-nook, log-book, look, minnowy-
brook, mistook, murmuring-brook,
nook, nuthook, outlook, overlook,
pocketbook, pothook, prayerbook,
psalm-book, Sandy Hook, school book,
scrapbook, shepherd's crook, shook,
sketch book, story-book, tenterhook,
textbook, took, undertook, unhook,
visitor's book

OOK*
see

Nansook, spook

OOK**
see
UKE

Gadzooks

OOKS
see

April-fool, campstool, cool, cotton-
wool, drool, ducking-stool, faldstool,
finishing-school, fool, footstool, Liver-
pool, millpool, mineral wool, pool, rock

OOL
see
OUL***
ULE

wool, school, spool, stool, Sunday school, swimming-pool, toadstool, tool, whirlpool, wool

OOL

Ante-room, bloom, book room, boom, bridegroom, broadloom, broom, club room, doom, elbow-room, foredoom, gloom, greenroom, grillroom, groom, guest-room, heirloom, jib-boom, keeping-room, loom, messroom, mushroom, show-room, smoke-room, spare-room, stateroom, store-room, taproom, waiting-room, zoom

OOM
 see
 OM**
 OMB***
 UME

Bloomer, roomer

OOMER
 see
 ER

Afternoon, anæmic-moon, aswoon, baboon, balloon, bassoon, boon, buffoon, cartoon, cocoon, coon, croon, curved-moon, doubloon, dragoon, eftsoon, festoon, forenoon, galloon, half-moon, harpoon, harvest moon, honeymoon, hunter's moon, lagoon, lampoon, loon, macaroon, maroon, monsoon, moon, mushroon, new moon, noon, octoroon, pale-moon, Pantaloon, picaroon, platoon, poltroon, pontoon, quadroon, raccoon, Rangoon, rigadoon, saloon, sandal-shoon, shalloon, shoon, silverspoon, simoon, soon, spittoon, spoon, swoon, teaspoon, typhoon, woodenspoon, zoon

OON
 see
 EWN
 UNE

Crooner, honeymooner, schooner, spooner

OONER
 see
 ER

Coop, droop, goop, hen-coop, hoop, loop, nincompoop, poop, scoop, scroop, sloop, snoop, stoop, swoop, troop, war-hoop, whoop

OOP
see
OUP
OUPE**
UPE

Barndoor, door, floor, indoor, next-door, stage-door, threshing-floor, trap-door, waxed-floor

OOR*
see
OR

Blackamoor, boor, Kohinoor, land-poor, moor, poor, spoor

OOR**
see
URE

Burnoose, caboose, calaboose, choose, goose, loose, mongoose, moose, Mother Goose, noose, papoose, unloose, va-moose

OOSE
see
UCE*
USE*

Tarboosh

OOSH
see

Boost, roost

OOST
see

Afoot, alumroot, arrowroot, bandi-coot, barefoot, bitter-root, bloodroot, boot, cahoot, calamus-root, cheroot, coot, crowfoot, cube root, eryngo root, flagroot, flatfoot, forefoot, hoot, hot-foot, lightfoot, loot, moot, offshoot, overshoot, presser foot, pussyfoot, root, scoot, shoot, snakeroot, snoot, soot, splayfoot, square root, taproot, tenderfoot, toot, underfoot, uproot, webfoot

OOT
see
UIT**
UT*
ed-ED

Booth, buck-tooth, eye-tooth, for-
sooth, smooth, sooth, tooth, walrus-
tooth

OOTH
see
OUTH*

Booty, snooty, sooty

OOTY
see
E**

Behoove, groove

OOVE
see
OVE***

Booze, ooze, snooze

OOZE
see
USE*

Æsop, archbishop, bishop, bucket-
shop, chimney-top, chop, cop, crop,
Cyclop, develop, dewdrop, drop, ear-
drop, eavesdrop, flop, forest-top, gal-
lop, grogshop, gumdrop, hop, house-
top, hyssop, lollypop, lop, milksop,
mop, Mrs. Malaprop, non-stop, organ-
stop, orlop, overdevelop, overtop,
pawnshop, pegtop, plop, pop, pork-
chop, prop, raindrop, scallop, shallop,
shop, shortstop, slip slop, slop, snow-
drop, stop, strop, sweatshop, sweetsop,
swop, teardrop, tip-top, top, tree-top,
trollop, wallop, whop, wild-hyssop,
workshop

OP
see
AP**
UP
ed-OPT
s-OPS

Copal, episcopal, opal

OPAL
see
AL

Allopath, homeopath, neuropath, **OPATH**
osteopath *see* ATH

Antelope, bellrope, Cape of Good **OPE***
Hope, chromoscope, cope, cymoscope, *see*
dope, electroscope, elope, envelope, OAP
grope, guyrope, heliotrope, hope, horo-
scope, interlope, kaleidoscope, kineto-
scope, microscope, mirrorscope, misan-
thrope, mope, moviescope, myope, ope,
periscope, pope, pyrope, rope, scope,
slope, stanhope, spectroscope, syncope,
telescope, tight-rope, trope, wire-rope

Calliope, Merope, Parthenope, Pe- **OPE****
nelope *see*
E*

Catastrophe **OPHE***
see
E*

Antistrophe, strophe **OPHE****
see
OAF

Gopher, philosopher, St. Christopher **OPHER**
see
ER

Bellerophon, colophon, Zenophon **OPHON**
see
ON

Anthroposophy, atrophy, philoso- **OPHY**
phy, theosophy, trophy *see*
E**

Cornucopia, Ethiopia, Utopia   **OPIA**
see
IA

Canopic, Ethiopic, kaleidoscopic, **OPIC**
microscopic, myopic, philanthropic, *see*
telescopic, topic, tropic   IC

Chopper, clodhopper, copper, corn- **OPPER**
popper, cropper, grasshopper, hopper, *see*
topper, whopper, woodchopper   ER

Choppy, floppy, poppy, sloppy, **OPPY**
soppy   *see*
E**

Cecrops, Cheops, cyclops, Ops, Pe- **OPS**
lops   *see*
OP-*s*

Copse   **OPSE**
see
OPE-*s*

Ampelopsis, calliopsis, coreopsis, **OPSIS**
synopsis, thanatopsis   *see*
IS*

Adopt, coöpt, Copt, epopt, opt   **OPT**
see
OP-*ed*

Canopus, magnum opus, octopus, **OPUS**
opus, Rhodopus   *see*
US

Baroque, toque

OQUE
see
OKE

Colloquy, obloquy, soliloquy

OQUY
see
E**

Abettor, abhor, ancestor, anchor, antecessor, arbor, armor, Asia Minor, author, bachelor, boa-constrictor, camphor, candor, cantor, captor, carburetor, Castor, censor, chancellor, clangor, color, condor, conductor, confessor, councilor, counselor, conveyor, demeanor, discolor, doctor, done for, donor, dor, endeavor, Endor, ephor, error, father-confessor, favor, fervor, flavor, for, governor, Hathor, honor, horror, humor, ichor, impostor, instructor, inventor, labor, languor, liquor, lor', louis d'or, Luxor, major, manor, mayor, mentor, metaphor, meteor, milor, minor, mirror, misdemeanor, motor, Mount Tabor, neighbor, Nestor, non-conductor, nor, odor, off-color, oppressor, or, pallor, parlor, pastor, phosphor, preceptor, predecessor, presentor, proctor, professor, proprietor, protestor, purveyor, rancor, razor, rector, reflector, rigor, rumor, sailor, savor, sculptor, sector, señor, sheet anchor, social error, splendor, sponsor, squalor, straw-color, stupor, successor, succor, suitor, supervisor, surveyor, survivor, technicolor, tenor, terror, Thor, tor, tormentor, tremor, tricolor,

OR
see
ACTOR
ADOR
AMOR
ATOR
AUR
ECTOR
IDOR
IOR
ITOR
OAR
OOR*
ORE
OUR**
UTOR
ed-OARD
ORD*
s-ORES
ORS

Tudor, unlooked-for, Ursa Major, **OR**
Ursa Minor, valor, vapor, vendor, vic-
tor, vigor, visor, watercolor, Windsor

Agora, amphora, angora, aurora, **ORA**
carnivora, Cora, Diaspora, fedora, flora, *see*
Leonora, mandragora, Marmora, Pan- A**
dora, plethora, signora, sora

Anchorage, borage, forage, harbor- **ORAGE**
age, storage   *see*
   AGE

Balmoral, caporal, chloral, choral, **ORAL**
coral, corporal, floral, immoral, littoral, *see*
moral, oral, pastoral, pectoral, tem- AL
poral

Anaxagoras, Pythagoras **ORAS**
   see
   AS

Ameliorate, commemorate, corpo- **ORATE**
rate, corroborate, deteriorate, directo- *see*
rate, elaborate, evaporate, expectorate, ATE
incorporate, invigorate, meliorate, pas-
torate, perforate, perorate, protecto-
rate, reinvigorate

Absorb, orb, resorb, sorb **ORB**
   see

Divorce, enforce, force, perforce, re- **ORCE**
inforce, tour de force   *see*
   ORSE*

Blowtorch, porch, scorch, torch **ORCH**
   see

Accord, afford, broadsword, chord, clavichord, concord, cord, discord, ford, harpsichord, Hartford, hexachord, lord, monochord, Norwegian fiord, overlord, Oxford, record, sword, war-lord, whip-cord

ORD*
see
OARD
ORDE
ORE-*d*
ed-ED

By-word, catchword, crossword, foreword, one-word, password, watch-word, word

ORD**
see
EARD*
ERD
IRD
URD

Horde

ORDE
see
ORD

Border, corder, disorder, order, re-corder

ORDER
see
ER

Adore, afore, alongshore, ashore, battledore, before, bore, chain-store, chore, coldsore, commodore, core, de-plore, drug-store, encore, evermore, explore, folk-lore, fore, foreshore, four-score, furore, furthermore, galore, gore, hellebore, heretofore, ignore, implore, inshore, lore, more, nevermore, off-shore, ore, pebbled-shore, pinafore, pore, restore, score, semaphore, shore, Singapore, snore, sophomore, sore, spore, stevedore, store, sycamore, Ta-gore, Terpsichore, therefore, threescore, tore, underscore, wherefore, whore, wore, yore

ORE
see
IOR
OAR
OOR*
OR
OUR**
ed-OARD
ORD*
s-ORES

Ad valorem, theorem **OREM**
see
EM

Swedenborg **ORG**
see

Disgorge, drop-forge, St. George, **ORGE**
gorge *see*

Morgue **ORGUE**
see

Gloria, noria, phantasmagoria, Vic- **ORIA**
toria *see*
IA

Armorial, consistorial, dictatorial, **ORIAL**
editorial, gladiatorial, gubernatorial, *see*
immemorial, inspectorial, memorial, IAL
phantasmagorial, pictorial, piscatorial,
purgatorial, sartorial, senatorial, sen-
sorial, territorial, tonsorial

Dorian, gregorian, historian, saluta- **ORIAN**
torian, stentorian, valedictorian *see*
IAN

Allegoric, Amoric, amphoric, boric, **ORIC**
caloric, Doric, historic, paregoric, ple- *see*
thoric, prehistoric, rhetoric, toric IC

Anteriority, authority, inferiority, **ORITY**
majority, minority, priority, sonority, *see*
sorority, superiority E**
ITY

Auditorium, emporium, moratorium, sanatorium, scriptorium

ORIUM
see
IUM

Cork, fork, New York, pitchfork, pork, stork, tuning fork, York

ORK*
see

All-work, basketwork, brickwork, butcher-work, clock-work, earthwork, fancywork, field-work, framework, fretwork, frostwork, groundwork, guesswork, handiwork, hard work, needlework, network, open-work, overwork, schoolwork, scrollwork, stonework, trellis-work, trestlework, waxwork, welfare work, wickerwork, work

ORK**
see
ERK

Schorl, whorl

ORL
see
URL

Netherworld, underworld, upperworld, world

ORLD
see
IRL-*ed*
URL-*ed*

Barnstorm, chloroform, conform, deform, dust-storm, form, inform, iodoform, misinform, norm, perform, platform, reform, sandstorm, sea-storm, snowstorm, thought-form, thunderstorm, transform

ORM
see
ARM**
IFORM

Angleworm, armyworm, bookworm, earthworm, glow-worm, grubworm, inchworm, silkworm

ORM**
see
ERM
IRM

Formal, informal, normal, sub-
normal, supernormal

ORMAL
see
AL

Acorn, adorn, barleycorn, baseborn,
bicorn, bighorn, blackthorn, born,
broomcorn, buckthorn, bugle-horn,
Cape Horn, Capricorn, careworn, corn,
drinking-horn, earthborn, firstborn,
foghorn, footworn, forsworn, freeborn,
goat's horn, greenhorn, hartshorn,
hawthorn, horn, inborn, Leghorn, long-
horn, lorn, manor born, morn, new-
born, Norn, outworn, overworn, pop-
corn, powder horn, pronghorn, ram's
horn, saxhorn, scorn, seaborn, shoe-
horn, shopworn, shorn, shorthorn,
staghorn, stubborn, suborn, sweetcorn,
sworn, thorn, twice-born, unborn, uni-
corn, unshorn, water-born, war-torn,
wayworn, worn

ORN
see
ARN**
OURN

Amorous, carnivorous, dolorous,
glamorous, humorous, languorous,
malodorous, odorous, omnivorous,
phosphorous, porous, rancorous, rigorous, sonorous, stertorous, vigorous

OROUS
see
OUS

Dorp, thorp

ORP
see
ARP**

Corpse

ORPSE
see
ORP-s

Lorry, sorry, worry

ORRY
see
E**

Scissors

ORS
see
OR-*s*

Clotheshorse, cockhorse, gorse, hobby-horse, horse, indorse, Norse, race-horse, remorse, rockinghorse, sawhorse, seahorse, stalking-horse, studhorse, worse

ORSE
see
ORCE
OURCE

Worst

ORST
see
ERST
URST

Abort, assort, bellwort, cavort, cohort, colewort, comfort, comport, consort, contort, davenport, deport, discomfort, disport, distort, effort, escort, exhort, export, extort, field-sport, figwort, fort, gipsywort, import, liverwort, mugwort, passport, port, purport, report, resort, retort, ribwort, seaport, short, snort, sort, spiderwort, sport, support, transport, what sort

ORT
see
ART**
OURT
UART
ed-ED

Immortal, mortal, portal

ORTAL
see
AL

Ottoman Porte, Sublime Porte

ORTE
see
ORT

Exporter, importer, porter, reporter, shorter, sorter, supporter

ORTER
see
ER

Forth, go-forth, henceforth, Kenil-
worth, north, thenceforth, Words-
worth, worth

ORTH
see
ARTH
OURTH

Decorum, forum, pons asinorum,
quorum, Roman Forum, sanctum
sanctorum

ORUM
see
UM

Apollodorus, Bosphorus, chorus, hel-
leborus, Horus, phosphorus

ORUS
see
US

Accessory, allegory, armory, audi-
tory, category, chicory, compulsory,
cursory, desultory, directory, dormi-
tory, dory, evocatory, factory, fish-
story, ghost-story, glory, gory, hickory,
history, illusory, introductory, inven-
tory, invocatory, ivory, lory, memory,
morning-glory, non-compulsory, offer-
tory, Old Glory, olfactory, peremp-
tory, perfunctory, pillory, porphory,
pre-inventory, priory, promissory,
promontory, rectory, refectory, refrac-
tory, repository, satisfactory, savory,
sensory, short-story, story, succory,
territory, theory, tory, transitory,
vainglory, valedictory, vapory, victory

ORY
see
ATORY
E**

Abydos, Anteros, Argos, asbestos,
Atropos, Barbados, bathos, Bucepha-
los, caballeros, chaos, Chronos, cosmos,
dithyrambos, Encelados, Eos, epos,
Eros, Galapagos, Hyksos, Hypnos,
Lemnos, Lesbos, logos, Minos, Mount
Athos, naos, Ninon de l'Enclos, Om-

OS
see
IOS
OSS

phalos, os, Parthenos, pathos, Patmos,   **OS**
Patroclos, Pergamos, pharos, Psycho-
pompos, pueblos, reredos, rhinoceros,
Samos, S.O.S., Tantalos, Tenedos,
thanatos, thermos, Triptolemos

Amorosa, Formosa, Mater Dolorosa,   **OSA**
mimosa, scabiosa, sub rosa, via dolorosa   *see*
    A**

Adipose, albuminose, appose, aquose,   **OSE***
arose, bellicose, bottlenose, cellulose,   *see*
chose, close, comatose, compose, crys-   IOSE
talose, damask rose, decompose, de-   O*-*es*
pose, disclose, dispose, dose, equipose,   OE**-*s*
expose, frostnipt-nose, foreclose, glu-   OTHE-*s*
cose, hooknose, hose, impose, inclose,   OW*-*s*
interpose, jocose, juxtapose, lachry-   OWS
mose, metamorphose, morose, Nivose,   OZE
nose, oppose, overdose, overexpose,
plumose, Pluviose, pope's nose, pose,
predispose, presuppose, primrose, pro-
pose, prose, pruinose, purpose, repose,
Roman nose, rose, scapose, 'spose,
suppose, tea-rose, those, transpose,
tuberose, unclose, Ventose, verbose,
wildrose

Lose, whose   **OSE****
    see
    USE

Closet, marmoset   **OSET**
    see
    ET

Bosh, cohosh, galosh, gosh, josh, kibosh, mackintosh, Oshkosh, slosh

OSH
see
ASH**
UASH

Corrosion, erosion, explosion

OSION
see
ION

Apodosis, apotheosis, diagnosis, hypnosis, kenosis, metamorphosis, metempsychosis, necrosis, prognosis, psychoneurosis, psychosis, sorosis, tuberculosis

OSIS
see
IS*

Anfractuosity, aquosity, curiosity, generosity, gibbosity, impetuosity, jocosity, luminosity, monstrosity, nebulosity, pomposity, ponderosity, sabulosity, sinuosity, tortuosity, verbosity, virtuosity

OSITY
see
ITY

Corrosive, erosive, explosive

OSIVE
see
IVE

Bosk, kiosk

OSK
see
OSQUE

Macrocosm, microcosm

OSM
see
OM*

Amoroso, capriccioso, gracioso, Orlando Furioso, so-so, virtuoso, whoso

OSO
see
O*

Kiosque, mosque

OSQUE
see
OSK

Across, albatross, boss, bugloss, Charing-Cross, criss-cross, cross, double-cross, dross, emboss, engross, Florida moss, floss, gloss, golden-cross, gross, hoss, iron cross, joss, loss, moss, peat-moss, Red Cross, Southern Cross, toss

OSS
see
AUCE
OS
OSSE

Fosse, lacrosse, posse

OSSE
see
OSS

Bossy, flossy, glossy, mossy

OSSY
see
E**

Accost, Bifrost, cost, defrost, embost, frost, hoarfrost, Jack Frost, longlost, lost, Pentecost

OST*
see
AUST
ed-ED

Almost, easternmost, foremost, ghost, hindermost, host, impost, inmost, innermost, middlemost, milepost, most, nethermost, northernmost, outpost, parcel post, post, provost, signpost, southernmost, topmost, uppermost, utmost, westernmost, whipping-post

OST**
see
OAST

Apostle, jostle, throstle

OSTLE
see
EL
LE

Closure, composure, disclosure, enclosure, exposure, foreclosure, inclosure, overexposure, underexposure

OSURE
see
URE

Argosy, nosy, posy, prosy, rosy

OSY
see
E**

Euphrosyne, Mnemosyne

OSYNE
see
E*

All-hot, allot, apricot, ballot, begot, bergamot, bloodshot, blot, bowknot, bowshot, buckshot, Camelot, carrot, coffee-pot, co-pilot, cot, despot, diglot, divot, dot, dryrot, earshot, ergot, fagot, fairy-grot, fleshpot, flowerpot, forget-me-not, forgot, foxtrot, gallipot, Gordian-knot, got, grapeshot, grot, harlot, helot, hot, hotspot, Hottentot, ingot, jackpot, jogtrot, jot, knot, lot, loveknot, maggot, marmot, marplot, mascot, monoglot, not, paletot, parrot, pilot, piping hot, pivot, plot, polyglot, pot, redhot, reef-knot, rot, ryot, sabot, Scot, shot, slingshot, slipknot, slot, snapshot, sot, spot, teapot, tender spot, tommyrot, topknot, tot, touch-me-not, trot, turbot, turkeytrot, try-pot, unguent-pot, upshot, wainscot, wateringpot, whatnot, wildcarrot, wot, zealot

OT*
see
ACHT
AT**
ATT
IGOT
IOT
OTT
OTTE

Argot, bon mot, depot, Huguenot, jabot, matelot, Pierrot, robot, tarot

OT**
see
O*

Dakota, iota, Minnesota, quota, rota

OTA
see
A**

Dotage, flotage, sabotage

OTAGE
see
AGE

Annotate, connotate, rotate

OTATE
see
ATE

Blotch, botch, crotch, hopscotch, hot-Scotch, notch, Scotch, splotch, top-notch

OTCH
see
ATCH**

Anecdote, antidote, banknote, capote, chorus-note, connote, cote, coyote, creosote, demote, denote, devote, dote, dovecote, footnote, keynote, misquote, mote, note, quote, promote, redingote, remote, rote, sheepcote, smote, straw vote, table d'hote, tote, treasury note, vote, wrote

OTE
see
OAT
S-OATS

Both, quoth, Sabbaoth, sloth, Succoth

OTH*
see
OATH
OWTH

Ashtaroth, azoth, behemoth, beroth, betroth, broadcloth, broth, cheesecloth, cloth, fishbroth, froth, Goth, mammoth, moth, neckcloth, oilcloth, sackcloth, Sephiroth, Thoth, troth, Visigoth, wroth

OTH**
see

Clothe   **OTHE**
see
OATH

Another, bother, brother, foster-mother, grandmother, half-brother, mother, other, pother, smother, step-mother, tother   **OTHER**
see
ER

Chaotic, demotic, despotic, epizoötic, exotic, hypnotic, idiotic, narcotic, neurotic, patriotic, quixotic   **OTIC**
see
IC

Commotion, devotion, emotion, locomotion, lotion, love potion, motion, notion, perpetual motion, potion, promotion, slow-motion   **OTION**
see
ION

Automotive, locomotive, motive, promotive   **OTIVE**
see
IVE

Boycott, Scott   **OTT**
see
OT
OTTE

Calotte, charlotte, cocotte, gavotte, sans culotte, Wyandotte   **OTTE**
see
OT
OTT

Bluebottle, bottle, mottle, throttle, smelling-bottle   **OTTLE**
see
EL
LE

Blotto, Giotto, grotto, lotto, motto, **OTTO**
Otto, risotto, sotto · · · · · · · · · · · · · *see*
o*

Anjou, bayou, bijou, caribou, frou- **OU***
frou, loup garou, marabou, sou, you · · *see*
UE*

Thou · **OU****
see
OUGH
OW**

Doubt, misdoubt, redoubt · · · · · · · · · **OUBT**
see
OUT

Caoutchouc · **OUC**
see
OOK*

Avouch, bridal-couch, couch, crouch, **OUCH***
game-pouch, grouch, ouch, pouch, · · *see*
slouch, vouch

Retouch, touch · · · · · · · · · · · · · · · · · · **OUCH****
see
UCH*

Barouche, cartouche, douche, Scara- **OUCHE**
mouche · *see*

Aloud, becloud, cloud, enshroud, **OUD**
loud, overcloud, overloud, proud, · · *see*
purse-proud, shroud, stroud, thunder- OWD
cloud ow**-*ed*

Rouge	**OUGE** *see*
Although, borough, dough, furlough, though, thorough	**OUGH*** *see* o*
Acacia-bough, apple-bough, bough, Golden Bough, plough, slough, sough	**OUGH**** *see* ow** s-ouse**
Enough, rough, slough, tough	**OUGH***** *see* uff
Through	**OUGH****** *see* u
Cough, hiccough, trough	**OUGH******* *see* off
Afterthought, besought, bethought, bought, brought, drought, forethought, fought, inwrought, methought, nought, ought, sought, take thought, thought, unsought, well-fought, wrought	**OUGHT** *see* aught* aut*
Bedouin	**OUIN** *see* uin
Saint Louis	**OUIS** *see* e**

Afoul, befoul, foul

OUL*
see
OWL

Over-soul, soul

OUL**
see
OL

Ghoul, Stamboul

OUL***
see
ULE

Mould

OULD*
see
OLD

Could, should, would

OULD**
see
OOD

Boulder, shoulder

OULDER
see
ER

Noun, pronoun

OUN
see
OWN**

Announce, bounce, cherrybounce, denounce, flounce, jounce, ounce, pounce, pronounce, renounce, trounce

OUNCE
see

Abound, aground, around, astound, background, blood-hound, bound, camping-ground, compound, dumbfound, expound, found, greyhound, harehound, hidebound, homeward-

OUND
see
OWN**-*ed*
ed-ED

bound, horehound, hound, impound, **OUND**
ironbound, merry-go-round, mound,
musclebound, outward bound, play-
ground, pound, profound, propound,
rebound, redound, resound, round,
sleuth-hound, snowbound, sound, spell-
bound, staghound, stamping-ground,
surround, underground, vantage-
ground, whimpering-hound, wound

Bounder, flounder, founder, ground- **OUNDER**
er, rounder *see*
ER

Coffee-grounds, fish pounds, zounds **OUNDS**
see
OUND-*s*

Young **OUNG**
see
UNG

Lounge **OUNGE**
see

Account, amount, catamount, count, **OUNT**
discount, dismount, fount, miscount, *see*
mount, paramount, recount, surmount,
tantamount, viscount

Bounty, county, mounty **OUNTY**
see
E**

Croup, group, pea-soup, recoup, **OUP***
thick soup, soup, troup *see*
OOP
OUPE**
UPE

Coup **OUP****
see
OU
UE

Cantaloupe **OUPE***
see
OPE

Troupe **OUPE****
see
OUP
UPE

Amour, armour, belabour, colour, **OUR**
détour, devour, dour, downpour, fa- see
vour, flavour, flour, four, giaour, glam- EUR
our, half-hour, honour, hour, ill-favour, OAR
labour, our, outpour, paramour, par- OR
lour, Pompadour, pour, rumour, sav- OWER
iour, scour, sour, splendour, succour, URE
tambour, tour, troubadour, vigour,
your

Resource, source **OURCE**
see
OURSE

Gourd **OURD**
see
URD

Scourge **OURGE**
see
ERGE
IRGE
URGE

Adjourn, bourn, sojourn

OURN*
see
URN

Mourn

OURN**
see
ORN

All fours, hours, ours, velours, yours

OURS
see
OUR-*s*

Bourse, concourse, course, discourse, intercourse, of-course, race-course, re-course, water-course

OURSE
see
ORSE
OURCE

Court, divorce court, police court, Supreme Court

OURT
see
ORT

Fourth

OURTH
see
ORTH

Ambidextrous, analogous, andro-gynous, anepigraphous, anonymous, barbarous, bibulous, blasphemous, bulbous, callous, chivalrous, cumbrous, declivous, desirous, diaphanous, dis-astrous, enormous, famous, frivolous, gibbous, gluttonous, hazardous, homol-ogous, idolatrous, infamous, joyous, lithophagous, ludicrous, magnanimous, mischievous, molluscous, momentous, monstrous, multifidous, murmurous, nervous, nitrous, nubilous, ominous,

OUS*
see
ALOUS
EOUS
EROUS
INOUS
IOUS
ITOUS
ONOUS
OROUS
ULOUS
UOUS

parlous, pendulous, perilous, pompous, portentous, posthumous, prognathous, pusillanimous, rapturous, raucous, ravenous, rigorous, riotous, scurrilous, stupendous, sulphurous, synonymous, torturous, tremendous, troublous, tyrannous, unanimous, venomous, venous, venturous, viscous, wondrous

OUS*
US
ly-E**
  OUSLY

Entre nous, rendevous

OUS**
see
U

Almshouse, blue-titmouse, bughouse, chapterhouse, chophouse, coach-house, custom-house, dormouse, douse, farmhouse, flitter-mouse, full-house, greenhouse, grouse, hot house, house, lighthouse, log-house, louse, meeting-house, mouse, penthouse, playhouse, poorhouse, power-house, rough-house, roundhouse, schoolhouse, shrew-mouse, souse, state house, storehouse, summerhouse, titmouse, wheel-house, White House, workhouse

OUSE*
see

Arouse, blouse, carouse, espouse, rouse, spouse

OUSE**
see
OUGH**-*s*
OWSE

Assiduously, continuously, copiously, curiously, furiously, instantaneously, joyously, previously, simultaneously, viciously

OUSLY
see
E**
IOUS-*ly*
OUS-*ly*

Joust, oust, roust **OUST**
see

About, blow-out, bout, boyscout, **OUT***
clout, cut-out, devout, dugout, eke out, *see*
fingerling trout, flatten-out, flout, gad- AUT**
about, gout, hereabout, in and out, OUBT
knockout, knout, layout, long-drawn-
out, lookout, lout, out, out and out,
pig's-snout, pout, right-about, root-
out, roundabout, rout, salmon trout,
scout, set-out, shout, snout, spout,
sprout, stout, thereabout, throughout,
tout, trout, try-out, turn-out, walkout,
wash-out, waterspout, whereabout,
without, worn-out

Mahout, marabout, surtout **OUT****
see
OOT**

Passe partout, ragout **OUT*****
see
OU*

Route **OUTE**
see
OUT*

Couth, Plymouth, uncouth, ver- **OUTH***
mouth, Yarmouth, youth *see*
UTH

Drouth, mouth, south **OUTH****
see

Billet-doux, Sioux **OUX**
see
O**

Approval, disapproval, oval, removal **OVAL**
see
AL

Innovate, ovate, renovate **OVATE**
see
ATE

Alcove, clove, cove, drove, grove, **OVE***
hove, interwove, Jove, mangrove, rove, *see*
shrove, stove, strove, throve, treasure AUVE
trove, trove, wove

Above, belove, boxing-glove, dove, **OVE****
foxglove, glove, kid-glove, ringdove, *see*
self-love, shove, turtledove, unglove OF

Approve, disapprove, disprove, im- **OVE*****
prove, move, prove, remove, reprove *see*
OOVE

Grovel, hovel, novel, shovel **OVEL**
see
EL
LE

Beethoven, cloven, disproven, inter- **OVEN**
woven, oven, proven, sloven, woven *see*
EN

Clover, cover, discover, four-leaved **OVER**
clover, hang-over, Hanover, hover, *see*
lover, moreover, over, Passover, plover, ER

popover, recover, rover, runover, stop-over, turnover, uncover, undercover **OVER**

After-glow, aglow, backflow, barge-tow, bellow, below, bestow, billow, blow, borrow, bungalow, burrow, cross-bow, crow, dormer-window, elbow, fan window, fiddlebow, flow, follow, fore-shadow, furbelow, Glasgow, glow, goodmorrow, grass-widow, hedge-row, inflow, Jim Crow, know, low, meadow, minnow, morrow, mow, outgrow, over-flow, overshadow, overthrow, peach-blow, peepshow, pillow, plow, pussy-willow, rainbow, roadshow, rose-win-dow, row, rum-row, saddlebow, scare-crow, shadow, show, show window, slow, snow, sorrow, stone's-throw, stow, throw, tomorrow, tow, undertow, widow, willow, window, winnow

OW*
see
ALLOW
ARROW
EAU
ELLOW
OE**
OUGH*
OWE
URROW
ed-OAD
ODE
er-ER
OUR*
ly-E**
OWLY
s-OSE*
OZE

Allow, anyhow, avow, bow, bow-wow, brow, Chinese-chow, chowchow, cow, dhow, disavow, endow, enow, ere now, eyebrow, for-now, Hankow, high-brow, how, kowtow, Moscow, Nankow, now, plow, pow-wow, row, scow, snow-plow, somehow, sow, trow, vow, wow

OW**
see
AU***
OU**
OUGH**
ed-OUD
OWD
s-OUSE**

Crowd, overcrowd

OWD
see
OUD

Chowder, gunpowder, powder

OWDER
see
ER

Crowdy, dowdy, howdy, rowdy **OWDY**
see
E**

Owe **OWE**
see
O*

Bowel, dowel, paper-towel, roller- **OWEL**
towel, towel, trowel, vowel *see*
EL

Borrower, bower, candlepower, cauli- **OWER**
flower, cornflower, cower, dower, em- *see*
bower, empower, flower, gilliflower, ER
glower, horsepower, Leaning Tower, OUR*
left-bower, lotus-flower, lower, may- ow*-*er*
flower, Mouse Tower, overpower, ower,
passion flower, power, right-bower,
shower, sunflower, tower, wallflower,
watchtower, widower, wood-flower

Bowery, flowery, lowery **OWERY**
see
ERY

Bowl, finger-bowl, pipe-bowl, wassail **OWL***
bowl *see*
OUL**

Cowl, fowl, growl, howl, jowl, night- **OWL****
owl, prowl, river-fowl, scowl, screech- *see*
owl, sea-fowl, water-fowl, yowl OUL*

Lowly, narrowly, slowly **OWLY**
see
E**

Blown, disown, flown, fullblown, fullgrown, grown, highflown, known, mown, new-mown, outgrown, overblown, overthrown, own, self-sown, shown, sown, strown, thrown, unblown, unknown, unsown, well-known

OWN*
see
OAN
ONE*

A-down, brown, Cape Town, Chinatown, clown, comedown, crown, down, downtown, dressing-gown, drown, frown, gown, knock-down, let-down, low-down, marked-down, nightgown, plank down, renown, shakedown, showdown, shutdown, sit-down, Southdown, sun-down, swan's-down, thistledown, thrown-down, touch-down, town, tumbledown, uncrown, upsidedown, uptown

OWN**
see
OUN
ed-OUND

Bellows, gallows, overgrows, whoknows

OWS
see
OSE*
OW*-*s*

Browse, drowse

OWSE
see
OUSE**
OW**-*s*

Growth, overgrowth, undergrowth

OWTH
see
OATH
OTH*

Billowy, shadowy, willowy

OWY
see
E**

Ballot-box, bandbox, box, chatter-box, cowpox, deposit box, ditty-box, equinox, fox, letterbox, musicbox, muskox, Nox, ox, paddlebox, Pandora's box, paradox, pepperbox, phlox, pillbox, prowling-fox, rosewood box, saltbox, shooting-box, smallpox, snuffbox, soapbox, spitbox, strongbox, tinderbox

OX
see
OCK-*s*
ODOX

Doxy, foxy, heterodoxy, orthodoxy, proxy

OXY
see
E**

Ahoy, alloy, altar boy, annoy, baby-boy, boy, bus boy, cabin-boy, charpoy, cloy, convoy, corduroy, coy, decoy, destroy, employ, enjoy, envoy, errand-boy, hautboy, Helen of Troy, highboy, joy, killjoy, lowboy, newsboy, old boy, overjoy, playboy, Rob Roy, savoy, sepoy, ship-ahoy, teapoy, tomboy, toy, viceroy

OY
see
UOY
*ed-*OID
*s-*OISE

Loyal, pennyroyal, royal, unloyal

OYAL
see
AL

Lloyd, sloyd

OYD
see
OID

Gargoyle, Hoyle

OYLE
see
OIL

Bulldoze, doze, froze **OZE**
see
OSE*
OW*-*s*

U SOUNDS

Babu, Bantu, bhikshu, Danu, emu, fichu, gnu, Hindu, Honolulu, impromptu, I.O.U., Jehu, ju-jitsu, juju, Khosru, Khufu, menu, Meru, Mu, Nu, ormolu, pari passu, parvenu, perdu, Peru, poilu, Shu, Timbuktu, Vishnu, zebu, Zulu

U
see
AGUE**
EW
IEU
IEW
INUE
O**
OO
OU
OUGH****
UE*
URU
UT**
S-EW-S
  OOSE**
  OOZE
  OSE**
  OUS**
  UISE**
  USE*

Aqua, Chatauqua, Gargantua, Joshua, Nicaragua, Padua, Papua

UA
see
A**

Equable, invaluable, valuable

UABLE
see
ABLE

Quad, squad
UAD
see
OD

Dissuade, overpersuade, persuade
UADE
see
ADE*
EDE**

Quaff
UAFF
see
AFE**

Agglutinative language, assuage, language
UAGE
see
AGE*

Actual, annual, bi-annual, bilingual, casual, co-equal, contextual, continual, conventual, dual, effectual, eventual, gradual, habitual, homo-sexual, individual, ineffectual, intellectual, lingual, manual, mutual, perpetual, punctual, residual, ritual, sensual, sexual, spiritual, unusual, usual, victual, virtual, visual
UAL
see
AL
ly-UALLY

Casually, eventually, habitually, mutually, perpetually, punctually, spiritually, unusually, usually, virtually
UALLY
see
ALLY
E**

Qualm
UALM
see
ALM

Assuan, Don Juan, gargantuan, San Juan
UAN
see
AN**

Nuance, piquance, pursuance

UANCE
see
ANCE

Piquant, pursuant, truant

UANT
see
ANT

Blackguard, bodyguard, coastguard, guard, lifeguard, mud-guard, safeguard, vanguard

UARD
see
ARD

Quarry

UARRY
see
ORY

Mary Stuart, quart

UART
see
ART**
ORT

Quartz

UARTZ
see
ORT-*s*

Actuary, antiquary, electuary, estuary, February, January, mortuary, obituary, ossuary, reliquary, residuary, sanctuary, statuary, voluptuary

UARY
see
AIRY
ARY
E**

Crookneck-squash, quash, musquash, squash

UASH
see
ASH**

Kumquat

UAT
see
AT**

Accentuate, actuate, adequate, anti-
quate, attenuate, devaluate, evacuate,
evaluate, extenuate, fluctuate, gradu-
ate, inadequate, individuate, infatuate,
insinuate, perpetuate, postgraduate,
punctuate, sinuate, situate, superannu-
ate, undergraduate

UATE
see
ATE

Suave, Zouave

UAVE
see

Cawquaw, musquaw, squaw

UAW
see
AW

Paraguay, quay, Uruguay

UAY
see
AY

Bathtub, Beelzebub, club, cub, dub,
grub, hubbub, Indian club, pub, rub,
rub-a-dub, scrub, shrub, sillabub, slub,
snub, strawberry shrub, stub, sub, tub,
yacht club

UB
see

Blubber, India-rubber, landlubber,
rubber, snubber

UBBER
see
ER

Chubby, fubby, grubby, hubby,
nubby, scrubby, snubby, tubby

UBBY
see
E**

Cube, inner-tube, jujube, rube,
speaking-tube, tube

UBE
see

Dissoluble, double, insoluble, re-
double, resoluble, rouble, soluble, trouble, voluble

UBLE
see
EL
LE

Adduce, Bruce, conduce, deuce,
educe, induce, introduce, lettuce, pro-
duce, puce, reduce, reproduce, seduce,
spruce, superinduce, traduce, truce

UCE
see
EUS
OOSE*
UICE

Forasmuch, inasmuch, much, non-
such, overmuch, such

UCH*
see
OUCH**
UTCH

Eunuch, Pentateuch

UCH**
see
UKE

Ruche

UCHE
see

Amuck, awestruck, bestruck, buck,
Calmuck, Canuck, chuck, cluck, duck,
Friar Tuck, goodluck, horror-struck,
luck, moonstruck, muck, muscovy
duck, pluck, pot-luck, Puck, roebuck,
sawbuck, shuck, struck, stuck, suck,
tuck, truck, woodchuck

UCK
see
OK

Buckle, chuckle, honeysuckle,
knuckle, muckle, shoebuckle, suckle

UCKLE
see
EL
LE

Lucre **UCRE**
see
ER

Abduct, conduct, construct, duct, **UCT**
induct, instruct, misconduct, obstruct, *see*
product, reconstruct, safe conduct, via- EDUCT
duct

Auction, deduction, destruction, in- **UCTION**
struction, obstruction, overproduction, *see*
production, reduction, reproduction, ION
ruction, seduction, suction

Bestud, bud, collar-stud, cud, dud, **UD**
mud, rosebud, scud, spud, stud, Tal- *see*
mud, thud OOD**

Rudder, shudder, udder **UDDER**
see
ER

Befuddle, fuddle, huddle, muddle, **UDDLE**
puddle *see*
EL
LE

Allude, collude, conclude, crude, **UDE**
delude, desuetude, dude, elude, etude, *see*
exclude, exude, include, inquietude, EUD
interlude, intrude, mansuetude, nude, ITUDE
obtrude, preclude, prelude, protrude, OOD***
prude, quietude, rude, seclude IEW-*ed*
UE*-*ed*
S-UDES

Begrudge, budge, drudge, fudge,
grudge, judge, misjudge, nudge, sludge,
smudge, trudge

UDGE
see

Soapsuds

UDS
see
UD-*S*

Accrue, argue, avenue, barbecue,
blue, clue, construe, continue, cue,
curlycue, due, ensue, flue, glue, hue,
imbue, ingenue, marble-statue, mis-
construe, out-argue, overdue, pursue,
queue, rescue, retinue, revenue, revue,
ring-true, robin's egg blue, rue, sky-
blue, slue, statue, subdue, sue, true,
true-blue, undervalue, undue, untrue,
value, vendue, virtue

UE*
see
AGUE***
ISSUE
U
ed-EWD
UDE
S-EW-*S*
UISE**
USE

Fatigue, intrigue, overfatigue

UE**
see
AGUE**

Cruel, duel, fuel, gruel, Pantagruel,
Samuel, sequel

UEL
see
EL

Guelph

UELPH
see

Affluence, congruence, consequence,
effluence, eloquence, sequence

UENCE
see
ENCE

Minuend

UEND
see
END

Abluent, affluent, confluent, constit-
uent, delinquent, effluent, eloquent,
fluent, frequent, grandiloquent, incon-
sequent, influent, infrequent, refluent,
sequent, subsequent, unguent

UENT
see
ENT

Beleaguer, chequer, exchequer, lac-
quer, pursuer

UER
see
ER

Quern

UERN
see
ERN

Bequest, conquest, follow-guest,
guest, inquest, quest, request

UEST
see
EAST**

Banquet, bluet, cruet, duet, minuet,
paroquet, piquet

UET*
see
ET

Croquet, parquet, sobriquet, tourni-
quet

UET**
see
A*

Bluff, buff, cuff, dandruff, duff, fisti-
cuff, fluff, gruff, guff, handcuff, herbal
snuff, huff, luff, Macduff, muff, plum-
duff, puff, rebuff, ruff, scruff, scuff,
snuff, sob-stuff, stuff

UFF
see
OUGH**
ed-UFT

Candytuft, puft, tuft

UFT
see
UFF-*ed*

Bug, chug-chug, drug, dug, firebug,
fire-plug, hearth-rug, hug, humbug,

UG
see

jug, lady-bug, lightning-bug, lug,   **UG**
mealy-bug, mug, plug, potato-bug,
pug, rug, shrug, slug, smug, snug,
spark-plug, thug, tug, vinegar jug,
wicker-jug

Kali Yuga, Satya Yuga   **UGA**
see
A**

Centrifugal, frugal, fugal, Portugal   **UGAL**
see
AL

Deluge, huge, refuge, subterfuge   **UGE**
see

Drugget, nugget   **UGGET**
see
ET

Juggle, smuggle, snuggle, struggle   **UGGLE**
see
EL
LE

Buggy, muggy, puggy, sluggy   **UGGY**
see
E**

Impugn, oppugn   **UGN**
see
UNG

Alleluia   **UIA**
see
IA

Squib **UIB**
see
IB

Juice, fruitjuice, grapejuice, sluice, **UICE**
tomato-juice *see*
USE**

Druid, fluid, languid, liquid, quid, **UID**
squid, tertian quid *see*
ID

Guide, misguide **UIDE**
see
IDE

Guayaquil, jonquil, tranquil **UIL**
see
IL

Build, guild, upbuild **UILD**
see
ILD*
ILL-*ed*

Beguile, guile **UILE**
see
ILE*

Goose-quill, quill, squill **UILL**
see
ILL

Bedquilt, built, clipper-built, guilt, **UILT**
quilt *see*
ILT
ed-ED

Guimp **UIMP**
see
IMP

Algonquin, Bedouin, beguin, bruin, **UIN**
harlequin, lambrequin, mannequin, *see*
palanquin, penguin, ruin, sequin, Tar- IN
quin UINE

Equine, genuine, sanguine **UINE**
see
INE**

Acquire, esquire, inquire, quire, re- **UIRE**
quire, squire *see*
IRE

Quirt, squirt **UIRT**
see
IRT
URT

Disguise, guise **UISE***
see
IZE

Bruise, cruise **UISE****
see
USE

Anguish, bluish, cliquish, distin- **UISH**
guish, extinguish, languish, relinquish, *see*
roguish ISH

Altruism, truism, ventriloquism **UISM**
see
ISM

Altruist, casuist, linguist, ventrilo- **UIST**
quist *see*
IST

Acquit, biscuit, circuit, conduit, **UIT***
Jesuit, pilot-biscuit, quit, short-circuit *see*
IT

Breadfruit, bruit, dress-suit, follow **UIT****
suit, fruit, grapefruit, lawsuit, pursuit, *see*
recruit, suit, unionsuit UTE

Mesquite, suite, tout de suite **UITE***
see
EAT*

Quite, requite **UITE****
see
ITE*

Ambiguity, annuity, antiquity, con- **UITY**
gruity, equity, gratuity, incongruity, *see*
inequity, ingenuity, iniquity, longin- E**
quity, obliquity, perpetuity, perspicu- ITY
ity, propinquity, superfluity, tenuity,
ubiquity

Quiz **UIZ**
see
IZ

Habakkuk, Kalmuk, Marduk, Sa- **UK**
rouk, Volapuk *see*
UCH**
UKE

Archduke, cuke, duke, fluke, Luke, **UKE**
Mameluke, peruke, rebuke   *see*
    OOK**
    UK

Annul, artful, awful, baleful, bane- **UL**
ful, bashful, brimful, bulbul, caracul,   *see*
careful, cheerful, consul, cupful, de-   IFUL
lightful, distrustful, doleful, doubtful,   ULL*
Elul, eyeful, faithful, fateful, fitful, for-
getful, fretful, graceful, grateful, harm-
ful, heartful, heedful, hurtful, ireful,
lawful, lustful, masterful, mindful,
mirthful, Mogul, mournful, mouthful,
needful, pailful, painful, plateful, play-
ful, powerful, prayerful, proconsul,
purposeful, regretful, remorseful, re-
proachful, resentful, restful, revenge-
ful, rueful, shameful, shovelful, sloth-
ful, sorrowful, tearful, thankful, thim-
bleful, thoughtful, tuneful, unfaithful,
ungrateful, unmirthful, useful, venge-
ful, wakeful, watchful, wilful, wishful,
wistful, woeful, wonderful, worshipful,
wrathful, wrongful, youthful

Calendula, Caligula, campanula, co- **ULA**
matula, copula, fibula, formula, Gula,   *see*
hula-hula, incunabula, nebula, penin-   A**
sula, scapula, spatula, spicula, St. Ur-
sula, tarantula

Angular, binocular, cellular, circular, **ULAR**
corpuscular, funicular, granular, glob-   *see*
ular, insular, irregular, jocular, jugu-   AR
lar, lenticular, lobular, lunular, molec-
ular, monocular, muscular, nebular,

oracular, orbicular, particular, penin-   **ULAR**
sular, perpendicular, popular, rectan-
gular, regular, secular, semi-circular,
singular, spectacular, triangular, tubu-
lar, unpopular, valvular, vascular, ve-
hicular, vernacular

Articulate, calculate, circulate, co-   **ULATE**
agulate, confabulate, congratulate,   *see*
consulate, ejaculate, emulate, expostu-   ATE
late, formulate, granulate, immaculate,
inarticulate, inoculate, insulate, jacu-
late, manipulate, matriculate, miscal-
culate, modulate, osculate, peculate,
perambulate, populate, postulate, recapitulate, regulate, simulate, specu-
late, stimulate, stipulate, strangulate,
tabulate, ululate, undulate

Bulb, electric-light bulb, gladiola   **ULB**
bulb, rubber-bulb   *see*

Mulch   **ULCH**
                                             see

Animacule, capsule, cellule, corpus-   **ULE**
cule, crepuscule, ferrule, footrule, glob-   *see*
ule, golden-rule, granule, lobule, mi-   OOL
nuscule, misrule, module, molecule,   OUL***
mule, nodule, over-rule, plumbrule,
pule, pustule, reticule, ridicule, rule,
schedule, sumpter-mule, tule, vesti-
bule, yule

Corpulent, fraudulent, opulent, suc-   **ULENT**
culent, truculent, turbulent, virulent   *see*
                                             ENT

Amulet, Capulet, epaulet, rivulet   **ULET**
see
ET

Engulf, gulf   **ULF**
see

Bulgar, vulgar   **ULGAR**
see
AR

Bulge, divulge, effulge, indulge, pro- **ULGE**
mulge   *see*

Fulgent, effulgent, indulgent, over- **ULGENT**
indulgent   *see*
ENT

Bulk, hulk, skulk, sulk   **ULK**
see

Bulky, sulky   **ULKY**
see
E**

Armfull, bull, chestfull, chock-full,   **ULL**
cull, dull, full, gull, hull, jaw-full, jig- *see*
full, lull, mull, null numskull, pull,   OL
scull, sea-gull, skull, you'll   UL

Tulle   **ULLE**
see
ULE

Bully, carefully, dully, fully, gully,   **ULLY**
ruefully, spitefully, sully, truthfully,   *see*
untruthfully, wilfully   E**

Credulous, cumulous, fabulous, garrulous, homunculous, incredulous, meticulous, miraculous, nebulous, pendulous, populous, querulous, ridiculous, scrupulous, tremulous, tumulous, unscrupulous

ULOUS
see
OUS
US

Gulp, pulp

ULP
see

Pulse, impulse, repulse

ULSE
see
ULT-*s*

Adult, antepenult, catapult, consult, cult, difficult, exult, insult, occult, penult, result, semi-occult, tumult

ULT
see
ed-ED
S-ULSE

Difficulty, faculty, faulty

ULTY
see
E**

Calculus, convolvulus, ranunculus, Romulus, stimulus, tumulus

ULUS
see
US

Duly, patchouly, truly, unruly

ULY*
see
E**

July

ULY**
see
I*
Y

Addendum, adytum, alarum, album, alburnum, alum, annum, antidotum, arboretum, asylum, bay rum, begum, bum, bunkum, candelabrum, capsicum, cerebrum, chewing-gum, chrysanthemum, chum, colchicum, conundrum, corrigendum, curriculum, date-plum, doldrum, drum, E pluribus unum, ergastulum, factotum, Fatum, fe-fi-fo-fum, fulcrum, glum, gum, gypsum, harum-scarum, hokum, hoodlum, horrendum, hum, humdrum, index rerum, interregnum, kettledrum, Khartum, labarum, laburnum, lignum, magnum, maximum, memorandum, minimum, modicum, momentum, mum, nostrum, oakum, opossum, pabulum, panjandrum, pax vobiscum, pendulum, peplum, per-annum, platinum, plectrum, plum, quantum, referendum, regnum, rostrum, rum, sanctum, scrum, scum, scutum, sedum, serum, simulacrum, sistrum, slum, sorghum, spectrum, strum, sugar-plum, sum, summum bonum, sweet alyssum, tantrum, Targum, thrum, tintinnabulum, Tum, unguentum, unum, vade-mecum, vellum, viaticum, wampum, yum-yum

UM
see
ANUM
ATUM
AUM
EUM
ITUM
IUM
OM*
OME*
ORUM
OMB
UUM

Montezuma, Numa, puma, Satsuma, Uma

UMA
see
A**

Hanuman, human, inhuman, superhuman

UMAN
see
AN*

Benumb, crumb, dumb, numb, plumb, succumb, thumb, Tom Thumb

UMB
see
OMB**

Cucumber, cumber, encumber, lumber, number, slumber, outnumber

UMBER
see
ER

Bumble, crumble, fumble, grumble, humble, jumble, mumble, rumble, stumble, tumble

UMBLE
see
EL
LE

Gumbo, jumbo, Mumbo Jumbo

UMBO
see
O*

Penumbra, umbra

UMBRA
see
A**

Assume, brume, consume, costume, exhume, flume, fume, illume, legume, nom de plume, perfume, plume, presume, resume, quivering-plume, subsume, volume

UME
see
OOM

Acumen, albumen, bitumen, catechumen

UMEN
see
EN

Argument, document, emolument, instrument, integument, monument, wind-instrument

UMENT
see
ENT

Humid, tumid

UMID
see
ID

Drummer, hummer, Indian-summer, midsummer, mummer

UMMER
see
ER

Chummy, dummy, gummy, mummy, thingummy, tummy

UMMY
see
E**

Autumn, column, fluted column

UMN
see
UM

Air-pump, bump, chump, clump, dump, frump, hump, jump, lump, mugwump, plump, pump, rump, slump, stump, thump, trump

UMP
see
S-UMPS

Crumpet, trumpet, strumpet

UMPET
see
ET

Galumph, humph, triumph

UMPH
see

Dumps, mumps

UMPS
see
UMP-*s*

Air-gun, begun, Bull Run, bun, dun, fun, gun, homespun, hot-cross-bun, Hun, injun, machine gun, Maxim-gun, nun, out-run, over-run, popgun, pun, rising-sun, run, shotgun, spun, sun, tun

UN
see
ION
ON
ONE**

Arjuna, Fortuna, lacuna, luna, tuna, una, Varuna, vicuna

UNA
see
A**

Quidnunc | **UNC**
see
UNK

Dunce | **UNCE**
see
ONCE*

Bunch, crunch, hunch, lunch, munch, Planter's punch, punch, quick-lunch, scrunch | **UNCH**
see

Adjunct, defunct | **UNCT**
see

Bund, fecund, fund, furibund, gerund, jocund, moribund, orotund, refund, rotund, sinking-fund, Sigismund | **UND**
see

Asunder, blunder, sunder, thunder, under | **UNDER**
see
ER

Foundry, laundry, sundry | **UNDRY**
see
E**

Bay of Fundy, Burgundy, maundy, Mrs. Grundy | **UNDY**
see
E**

Commune, demilune, dune, fortune, good-fortune, immune, importune, jejune, June, misfortune, Neptune, opportune, picayune, prune, rune, sandy-dune, triune, tune | **UNE**
see
EWN
OON

Bung, clung, dung, far-flung, flag-
strung, flung, high-strung, hung, lung,
moss-hung, rung, slung, sprung, strung,
stung, sung, swung, underhung, un-
hung, unstrung, unsung, wide-flung,
wrung

UNG
see
ONG**

Expunge, lunge, plunge

UNGE
see
ONGE

Bunion, communion, non-union, re-
union, union

UNION
see
ION

Community, immunity, impunity,
opportunity, unity

UNITY
see
E**
ITY

Bunk, chipmunk, chunk, drunk,
dunk, flunk, funk, hunk, junk, plunk,
punk, Saratoga trunk, shrunk, skunk,
slunk, spunk, stunk, sunk, tree-trunk,
trunk

UNK
see

Funnel, runnel, tunnel

UNNEL
see
EL

Bunny, funny, gunny, sunny

UNNY
see
E**

Blunt, brunt, hunt, punt, runt,
shunt, stunt

UNT
see
ONT*

Cluny, luny, puny

UNY
see
E**

Ambiguous, anfractuous, arduous, congruous, conspicuous, contemptuous, contiguous, continuous, deciduous, fatuous, flexuous, impetuous, incestuous, incongruous, inconspicuous, indeciduous, ingenuous, insinuous, mellifluous, presumptuous, promiscuous, sensuous, sinuous, strenuous, sumptuous, superfluous, supersensuous, tempestuous, tumultuous, tenuous, tortuous, unctuous, vacuous, virtuous, voluptuous

UOUS
see
OUS
US

Breeches-buoy, buoy, life-buoy

UOY
see
OY

Acorn-cup, buttercup, check-up, chirrup, clean-up, close-up, cup, dried-up, drinkingcup, flare-up, frame-up, get-up, gold-cup, grown-up, hang-up, het-up, hiccup, holdup, hook-up, ketchup, keyed-up, kick-up, larrup, let-up, line-up, lockup, loving-cup, make-up, painted-cup, pent-up, pick-me-up, pickup, puffed-up, pup, round-up, scup, set-up, seven-up, shake-up, shut up, smash-up, speed-up, standing-up, step-up, stirrup, stirrup-cup, stuck-up, sup, syrup, teacup, toss-up, up, up and up, well-brought-up, wind-up

UP
see
OP

Dupe, Guadalupe

UPE
see
OOP

Cupid, stupid

UPID
see
ID

Abrupt, bankrupt, corrupt, disrupt, erupt, interrupt

UPT
see

Ashur, augur, Baldur, concur, Côte d'Azur, cur, demur, fur, incur, King Arthur, larkspur, lemur, murmur, Nippur, Nishapur, non sequitur, occur, recur, slur, spur, sulphur, Ur, Vidur, Yom Kippur

UR
see
ERE***
EUR
URE
URR
ed-URD
s-URS

Angostura, Asura, aura, camera-obscura, coloratura, datura, Estremadura

URA
see
A**

Augural, conjectural, guttural, inaugural, intramural, mural, natural, plural, preternatural, rural, scriptural, structural, subnatural, supernatural, unnatural, Ural

URAL
see
AL

Accurate, commensurate, curate, inaccurate, inaugurate, incommensurate, obdurate, saturate, triturate

URATE
see
ATE

Blurb, curb, disturb, perturb, suburb, uncurb

URB
see
ERB

Church, lurch **URCH**
see
EARCH
ERCH
IRCH

Absurd, curd, Kurd, surd **URD**
see
EARD*
ERD
URE-*d*

Curdle, hurdle **URDLE**
see
EL
LE

Hurdy-gurdy, sturdy **URDY**
see
E**

Abjure, adventure, agriculture, al- **URE**
lure, aperture, assure, azure, brochure, see
capture, censure, cincture, cocksure, ASURE
coiffure, conjure, culture, cure, deben- ATURE
ture, demure, departure, disfigure, em- EUR
bouchure, embrasure, endure, enrap- ICURE
ture, ensure, failure, faith-cure, figure, ITURE
fissure, fixture, floriculture, gesture, OOR**
gravure, high-pressure, horticulture, OSURE
imposture, impure, indenture, injure, OUR**
insecure, insure, inure, jointure, junc- *ed*-ERD
ture, lay figure, lecture, leisure, low- IRD
pressure, lure, manufacture, manure, ORD**
mind cure, misadventure, mixture, URD
moisture, mure, nurture, obscure, over-
ture, pasture, pelure, peradventure,

perjure, photogravure, picture, por-   **URE**
traiture, posture, prefecture, prefigure,
premature, pressure, procedure, pro-
cure, puncture, pure, quadrature, rap-
ture, reassure, reinsure, Scripture, se-
cure, seizure, sepulture, sinecure, struc-
ture, sure, suture, tenure, texture,
tincture, tonsure, torture, transfigure,
venture, verdure, vesture, vulture, wax
figure, you're

Treasurer, usurer   **URER**
see
ER

Surf, turf   **URF**
see
ERF

Gettysburg, Strasburg, Vicksburg   **URG**
see
ERG

Demi-urge, inner urge, Panurge,   **URGE**
purge, scourge, splurge, spurge, surge,   *see*
thaumaturge, urge   **ERGE**
IRGE

Dramaturgy, liturgy, metallurgy,   **URGY**
thaumaturgy, theurgy   *see*
E**

Futurity, impurity, insecurity, ma-   **URITY**
turity, obscurity, purity, security, semi-   *see*
obscurity   **E****
ITY

Lurk, murk, Turk **URK**
see
ERK
IRK

Churl, curl, furl, hurl, purl, unfurl **URL**
see
EARL
IRL
ORL
ed-ORLD

Curly, burly, hurly-burly, surly **URLY**
see
E**

Auburn, burn, churn, lectern, mor- **URN**
tuary-urn, nocturn, overturn, return, see
Saturn, spurn, sunburn, taciturn, turn, EARN
Tyburn, upturn, urn OURN*

Diurnal, journal, nocturnal **URNAL**
see
AL

Burnt, sunburnt **URNT**
see

Usurp **URP**
see
ed-ERPT

Aaron Burr, blurr, burr, purr **URR**
see
UR

Burrow, furrow **URROW**
see
OW*

Curry, flurry, furry, hurry, scurry   **URRY**
see
E**

Accurse, curse, cut-purse, disburse, **URSE**
impurse, nurse, purse, reimburse, shep-   *see*
herd's-purse, wet-nurse   EARSE
ERCE
ed-ED

Accurst, burst, cloudburst, curst, **URST**
durst, nurst, outburst, sunburst   *see*
IRST
ed-ED

Blurt, curt, Frankfurt, hurt, spurt, **URT**
yurt   *see*
ERT
IRT
UIRT

Hurtle, mockturtle, snapping turtle, **URTLE**
turtle   *see*
EL
LE

Guru   **URU**
see
U

Arcturus, Epicurus, Eurus   **URUS**
see
AURUS
US

A-curve, curve, incurve   **URVE**
see
ERVE

Augury, bury, Canterbury, century,   **URY**
conjury, fury, injury, jury, luxury,   *see*
Mercury, penury, perjury, tilbury,   E**
treasury, usury

Abacus, Academus, acanthus, Æolus,   **US**
agnus, ailanthus, Albertus Magnus,   *see*
alumnus, amaranthus, angelus, animus,   AGUS
ankus, Antæus, arbutus, Augustus,   ALUS
Autolycus, Avernus, Bacchus, bacillus,   AMPUS
Belus, bogus, bolus, bonus, Brutus,   AMUS
bus, cactus, Cadmus, Catullus, Cau-   ATUS
casus, caucus, Celsus, census, cholera-   AURUS
morbus, cirrus, citrus, colossus, Co-   EOUS
lumbus, Comus, consensus, conspectus,   ERUS
Copernicus, Coriolanus, corpus, Crœ-   ETUS
sus, Cronus, cultus, cuniculus, cyprus,   EUS*
Cyrus, demiurgus, dianthus, Diodorus,   INOUS
discobolus, discus, Duns Scotus, En-   INUS
celadus, Ephesus, Erasmus, Erebus,   IOUS
eucalyptus, exodus, faunus, fungus,   ITOUS
habeas corpus, Halicarnassus, helian-   ITUS
thus, Hephæstus, Herodotus, hibiscus,   IUS
humus, Hyacinthus, Hymettus, Iam-   OCUS
blicus, Icarus, ictus, ignis-fatuus, im-   OPUS
petus, incubus, isthmus, Janus, Jesus,   ORUS
Josephus, Judas Maccabæus, litmus,   OUS
Leviticus, lotus, Lucullus, magnus,   ULOUS
maybush, Menelaus, mittimus, modus,   ULUS
Momus, mucus, narcissus, nautilus,   URUS
negus, Nicodemus, Nilus, nimbus,   USS
Ninus, nisus, nonplus, obolus, Oceanus,   YLUS
Œdipus, Olympus, omnibus, onus,   YRUS
opus, ornithorhynchus, Paracelsus, pa-
radus, Parnassus, Patroclus, Pegasus,
Peloponnesus, Pentelicus, Phœbus,
platypus, plexus, plus, polyanthus,

Polygnotus, Polyphemus, Pontus, Pri- **US**
apus, prospectus, pus, Pyrrhus, raucus,
rebus, Remus, Rhadamanthus, rhom-
bus, rumpus, sanctus, Silenus, Sil-
vanus, Sisyphus, solus, Somnus, status,
strophanthus, stylus, surplus, syllabus,
Tacitus, Tarsus, Tartarus, tetanus,
thaumaturgus, Theophrastus, thesaurus, thus, thyrsus, Trismegistus,
uræus, Uranus, Ursus, U.S., us, Venus,
versus, virus, walrus, Xanthus

    Anchusa. Arethusa, Medusa, Susa   **USA**
                              see
                              A**

    Carousal, causal, espousal, perusal,   **USAL**
refusal   *see*
                              AL

    Abstruse, abuse, accuse, amuse,   **USE**
bemuse, confuse, diffuse, disuse, Druse,   *see*
effuse, enthuse, excluse, excuse, fuse,   OOSE*
hypotenuse, infuse, interfuse, misuse,   OSE**
muse, obtuse, peruse, profuse, recluse,   UISE**
refuse, ruse, suffuse, transfuse, use,   EW-*s*
Vauclause   OE*-*s*
                              U-*s*
                              UE*-*s*

    Ambush, blush, brush, bulrush,   **USH**
bush, crush, flush, gush, hush, inrush,   *see*
lush, mush, onrush, plush, push, rush,
sagebrush, scrubbing-brush, shad-bush,
slush, spicebush, steeple-bush, thrush,
toothbrush, tush

Allusion, conclusion, confusion, delusion, disillusion, exclusion, fusion, illusion, inclusion, infusion, intrusion, obtrusion, profusion

USION
see
ION

Conclusive, delusive, elusive, exclusive, illusive, inclusive, intrusive, obtrusive, unobtrusive, preclusive

USIVE
see
IVE

Dusk, husk, mollusk, musk, rusk, tusk

USK
see
USQUE

Cusp

USP
see

Brusque

USQUE
see
USK

Blunderbuss, buss, cuss, discuss, fuss, muss, percuss, puss, sour puss, truss

USS
see
US

Adjust, anti-rust, august, brickdust, bust, combust, crust, disgust, distrust, dust, entrust, gold-dust, gust, incrust, intrust, just, locust, lust, mistrust, must, piecrust, portrait-bust, readjust, robust, rust, sawdust, star-dust, thrust, trust, unjust, wanderlust

UST
see

Adjuster, baluster, bluster, buster, cluster, duster, filibuster, fluster, luster, muster

USTER
see
ER

Bustle, hustle, rustle   **USTLE**
see
BL
LE

Crusty, dusty, fusty, gusty, lusty,   **USTY**
musty, rusty, trusty   *see*
E*
UST-*y*

Abut, betelnut, brazil-nut, brut,   **UT***
but, butternut, catgut, chestnut, chut,   *see*
clear-cut, cocoanut, Connecticut, cross-   OOT*
cut, cut, doughnut, gamut, halibut,
hut, jut, Lilliput, Mut, nut, output,
put, peanut, rebut, rut, sackbut, scut,
short-cut, shut, slut, smut, strut, tut,
uncut, walnut, woodcut

Début   **UT****
see
U

Brutal, refutal   **UTAL**
see
AL

Clutch, crutch, Dutch, hutch,   **UTCH**
smutch   *see*
UCH*

Acute, astute, brute, Canute, chute,   **UTE**
commute, compute, confute, cute,   *see*
deaf-mute, dilute, dispute, disrepute,
electrocute, execute, flute, hirsute,
jute, lute, minute, mute, parachute,
persecute, pollute, prosecute, refute,
repute, salute, transmute, tribute, Ute

Azimuth, bismuth, Ruth, truth, untruth, vermuth

UTH
see
EUTH
OOTH
OUTH*

Ablution, circumlocution, constitution, contribution, dissolution, distribution, elocution, evolution, involution, locution, persecution, pollution, prosecution, restitution. retribution, revolution, solution

UTION
see
ION

Contributor, distributor, executor, interlocutor, persecutor, prosecutor, tutor

UTOR
see
OR

Mutt, putt

UTT
see
UT*

Butter, clutter, cutter, flutter, gutter, mutter, peanut butter, putter, revenue cutter, shutter, sputter, stonecutter, stutter, utter

UTTER
see
ER

Button, glutton, mutton

UTTON
see
ON

Nutty, putty, smutty

UTTY
see
E**

Beauty, deputy, duty

UTY
see
E**

Meum et tuum, residuum, vacuum

UUM
see
UM

Chef d'œuvre, Louvre, manœuvre

UVRE
see
ER

Afflux, conflux, crux, efflux, fiat lux, flux, influx, Ku Klux, Pollux, reflux

UX
see
UCK-*s*
UCT-*s*

Buy, guy

UY
see
Y

Santa Cruz, St. Jean de Luz, Tammuz, Uz, Vera Cruz

UZ
see
OOZE

Guzzle, muzzle, nuzzle, puzzle

UZZLE
see
EL
LE

Y SOUNDS

Apply, awry, blackfly, blue-sky, **Y**
butterfly, by, by and by, cry, damsel *see*
fly, dragonfly, dry, espy, firefly, fly, EFY
fry, gad-fly, go-by, hereby, housefly, EYE
imply, lullaby, mayfly, mid-sky, mis- I*
apply, multiply, my, nearby, occupy, IFY
outcry, passerby, Paul Pry, ply, pre- IGH
occupy, pry, reply, satisfy, shoo-fly, ULY**
shy, sky, sly, small fry, spanish fly, UY
spry, spy, stand-by, sty, supply, YE*
thereby, thy, try, war-cry, whereby,
why, wry

Cherimoya, Libya, Maitreya, Surya **YA**
see
A**

Dryad, dyad, hamadryad **YAD**
see
AD

Triptych **YCH**
see
ECK

Bicycle, cycle, kilocycle, megacycle, **YCLE**
Metonic Cycle, motorcycle, tricycle *see*
EL
LE

Jamshyd   **YD**
see
EED

Clepsydra, hydra   **YDRA**
see
A**

Aye, bye, dye, eye, goodbye, lye, **YE***
rye, tye   *see*
I**
Y

Ye   **YE****
see
E*

Oxygen   **YGEN**
see
EN

Dyke, tyke, Vandyke   **YKE**
see
IKE

Beryl, dactyl, idyl, methyl, sibyl   **YL**
see
EL

Adactyle, hypostyle, peristyle, pro- **YLE**
style, style   *see*
ILE*

Babylon, pylon   **YLON**
see
ON

Sylph	**YLPH** *see*
Rhyme, thyme	**YME** *see* IME*
Hymn	**YMN** *see* IM
Lymph, nymph, woodnymph	**YMPH** *see*
Lynch	**YNCH** *see* INCH
Anodyne, auld lang syne, dyne, heterodyne	**YNE** *see* INE*
Larynx, lynx, pharynx	**YNX** *see* INX
Amphictyon, amphitryon, Apollyon, canyon, halcyon	**YON** *see* ON
Gyp, polyp	**YP** *see* IP
Archetype, daguerreotype, linotype, monotype, prototype, stereotype, tintype, type	**YPE** *see* IPE

Anaglyph, glyph, hieroglyph, tri-glyph

YPH
see
IF

Apocalypse

YPSE
see
IP-S

Crypt, Egypt

YPT
see
IPT

Martyr, satyr, zephyr

YR
see
AR*
ER

Byre, gyre, lyre, pyre, Tyre

YRE
see
IRE

Myrrh

YRRH
see
IR

Papyrus, zephyrus

YRUS
see
US

Abysm, cataclysm, paroxysm

YSM
see
ISM

Chlamys

YS
see
IS*

Abyss

YSS
see
IS*

Amethyst, analyst, catalyst, cyst, tryst

YST
see

Acolyte, neophyte, proselyte, troglodyte

YTE
see
IGHT
ITE*

Myth

YTH
see
ITH

Scythe

YTHE
see
ITHE

Rhythm

YTHM
see
IM

Gyve

YVE
see
IVE*

Onyx, oryx, Pnyx, pyx, sardonyx

YX
see
IX

OTHER BOOKS OF INTEREST